S0-ATT-174

COLORADO MOUNTAIN COLLEGE

I 83 0001268052

D 511 .A29 1990
Adams, Michael C. C., 1945-
The great adventure

DATE DUE

COLORADO

MOUNTAIN
COLLEGE

Alpine Campus
Learning Resource
Center
P.O. Box 774688
Steamboat Springs,
CO 80477

DEMCO

THE
GREAT
ADVENTURE

THE
GREAT
ADVENTURE

Male Desire and the
Coming of World War I

MICHAEL C. C. ADAMS

RECEIVED

OCT 2 4 1991

CMC ALPINE CAMPUS
LEARNING RESOURCE CENTER

Indiana University Press

BLOOMINGTON AND INDIANAPOLIS

© 1990 by Michael C. C. Adams

All rights reserved

No part of this book may be reproduced or utilized in any
form or by any means, electronic or mechanical, including
photocopying and recording, or by any information storage
and retrieval system, without permission in writing from the
publisher. The Association of American University Presses'
Resolution on Permissions constitutes the only exception to
this prohibition.

The paper used in this publication meets the minimum
requirements of American National standard for Information
Sciences—Permanence of Paper for Printed
Library Materials, ANSI Z39.48–1984.

⊗ ™

MANUFACTURED IN THE UNITED STATES OF AMERICA

Library of Congress Cataloguing-in-Publication Data

Adams, Michael C. C.
    The great adventure : male desire and the coming of World
War I / Michael C.C. Adams.
       p.   cm.
    ISBN 0–253–30136–X (alk. paper)
    1. World War, 1914–1918——Causes. 2. War—Attitudes.
  3. War—Psychological aspects. I. Title.
D511.A29 1990
940.3'11—dc20   89–46339
                                          CIP

1 2 3 4 5 94 93 92 91 90

For Susan

There is very little idealism in the world so far. So far, the only thing which really produces idealism is, unfortunately, war and the thing called patriotism. When a war breaks out, thousands of leisured young men, who have hitherto thought of little but of how to enjoy themselves, who have hitherto turned their backs on all that was unpleasant and all that provoked thought, suddenly discover that, though it was not "up to them" to live for their country in peace time, yet it is absolutely their duty to die for it in war time, and fling their lives away with heroism. It is, apparently, easier to fight for one's country than to devote one's leisure to social problems.

> Lieutenant Malcolm Graham White
> King's College Cambridge and
> The Rifle Brigade
> Killed in Action July 1, 1916
> Aged 29

No! There never was a thrill like the early days of August, 1914, in Paris, and although I grow to be a kind of pacifist as years pass, I wouldn't have missed it for all the money in the world—.

I felt the thrill of it—even I, a hard-boiled soldier of fortune—a man who was not supposed to have the slightest trace of nerves. I felt my throat tighten and several times the scene of the marching columns swam in oddly elliptical circles. By God, I was shedding tears.

> Bert Hall
> American Aviator

Now, God be thanked Who has matched us with His hour,
    And caught our youth, and wakened us from sleeping,
With hand made sure, clear eye, and sharpened power,
    To turn, as swimmers into cleanness leaping,
Glad from a world grown old and cold and weary,
    Leave the sick hearts that honour could not move,
And half-men, and their dirty songs and dreary,
    And all the little emptiness of love!

> Rupert Brooke
> "Peace," 1914

Military honour, when it teaches him [a man] to go to his own death with a smile, helps him to a little virtue. To die young is by no means an unmitigated misfortune; to die gaily in the unselfish pursuit of what you believe to be a righteous cause is an enviable and not a premature end.

As we survivors of the war pass into a sordid unheroic middle age, it is not pity that we feel for those who died on the field of honour. God grant that we may be as lucky in the occasion of our death, and may meet it with a soldier's gay courage.

Charles Carrington
British Great War Veteran

Peter was not quite like other boys; but he was afraid at last. A tremour ran through him, like a shudder passing over the sea; but on the sea one shudder follows another till there are hundreds of them, and Peter felt just the one. Next moment he was standing erect on the rock again, with that smile on his face and a drum beating within him. It was saying, "To die will be an awfully big adventure."

J. M. Barrie,
Peter Pan

Contents

ILLUSTRATIONS

PREFACE

When I was a small boy in Nottinghamshire, England, my parents would drive over regularly to see our grandparents, who lived in Hasland, Derbyshire. My grandfather was a severe man but, if we were good, we children might expect a treat. His special one was to walk us up to the park. Outside the gates stood a gaily painted cart from which a vendor sold slabs of ice cream between wafers. The pleasure was a little spoiled for me at first because of a stone war memorial which stood inside the park and could be seen through the railings. On the sides were the names of the men and women from Hasland who had fallen in Britain's twentieth-century wars. Atop the monument stood a soldier in the peaked cap and puttees of 1914. Initially the man frightened me because I thought that he was a real dead soldier, marbled over and made to stand there forever. I thought that he might sometime suddenly move or cry out.

When I got familiar with the soldier, I felt sad for him. This sadness has returned periodically during my adult life as I have struggled to comprehend the enormity of that first great twentieth-century debacle. The armed forces of the belligerent nations lost between ten and thirteen million lives. The horror did not end in 1918. The harsh peace of Versailles, the economic and moral dislocation of Europe, helped to bring about the rise of fascism and a second debilitating struggle (the name of my uncle, Charles Corringham Adams, RAF Fighter Command, killed in action 1944, is on one side of the monument). As a result of that war we live under the threat of nuclear annihilation. The holocaust led to the creation of Israel and a volatile political situation which could still precipitate the third global conflagration of the century. Quite a lot has evolved from the events of 1914.

As I have looked back at the faraway summer when Europe descended into slaughter, I have wanted to understand how such an enormity could occur in a world of seeming refinement and progress. We have isolated many reasons for the war. There were imperial and trade rivalries, backed up by an arms race, particularly between Britain and Germany. France sought revenge for humiliation in 1870. Russia thought a foreign war could draw domestic attention away from internal difficulties. The Austro-Hungarian empire blustered into war trying to preserve its crumbling hegemony over a potpourri of peoples. Overall hung the prideful assertiveness of modern nationalism, egging on competing peoples in the name of progress.

Yet there was something else, a current less obvious, less calculating than economic rivalries or diplomatic alliances. None of the conventional motives would inevitably lead to war and none would imply that wars, once begun, have to be fought to ghastly finishes. That requires further explanation. In part, it can be glimpsed in the cheering crowds who exuberantly welcomed the fighting and went on supporting the killing long after it made political sense. Far from seeing the conflict as a tragedy, many welcomed it as a healthy development for their society, a relief from peace. This is what F. Scott Fitzgerald had in mind when he wrote that the Great War took "years of plenty and tremendous sureties . . . You had to have a whole-souled sentimental equipment going back further than you could remember," including memories of Christmas "and going to the Derby and your grandfather's whiskers." The nineteenth and early twentieth centuries created a cultural milieu in which war could be seen as an intrinsically valuable human endeavor. It is this atmosphere that I want to explore; to recreate some of the intellectual trends that made war seem a natural and high expression of social values. Thus, this is not a book about the specific causes of World War I but a study of the mood in which it could take place.[1]

Feminist scholarship has pointed to the importance of gender as a determinant in human affairs. I have tried to stress that war is in many ways a gender-specific activity and I have concentrated on male thinking about the subject because men were most directly involved with fighting. Sandra M. Gilbert and Susan Gubar have suggested recently that women had their own reasons, often antithetical to those of men, for seeing positive benefits in the Great War. Not only gender but social class shapes lives and ideas. The men who most interest me came not from the lower orders or the rising wealthy but from the older established classes of gentlemen farmers, lawyers, professors, military officers. These people often had the most concern about the direction of modernity and were most vocal about war's salutary effects.[2]

My case is built from materials relating to Britain and the United States, because I live in these countries, I teach their cultures, and they illustrate as well as any could the points which I wish to make. This is not to say that Britain and the United States shared a common identity or synonymous experience during the period. The structure of society changed more radically in the United States. Older elites could not hold onto the influence which traditionally powerful groups in Britain retained through the exclusive public schools and the "old boy" system. The United States' experience of World War I was shorter and less pervasive than was Britain's. Nevertheless, there were sufficient shared trends to make a cross-cultural approach worthwhile. Many of the same intellectual currents could be found at play in Germany, France, or Italy.

I am indebted to my colleague W. Frank Steely for his observation that boredom is an underrated factor in history. For permission to quote from the J. F. C. Fuller, Basil Liddell Hart, and Frederick Maurice papers, I am grateful to the Trustees of the Liddell Hart Centre for Military

Archives, King's College London. The director of the Hove Public Library graciously gave me unrestricted access to the Garnet Wolseley collection. The faculty senate and academic administration of Northern Kentucky University provided grants of time and money. The interlibrary loan staff of the university cheerfully and efficiently located many volumes for me. Professor Patrick Brantlinger read the entire manuscript and made many first-rate suggestions. Susan S. Kissel was my able tutor in feminist criticism. To her this book is dedicated.

THE
GREAT
ADVENTURE

Responses to Change

"It was the best of times, it was the worst of times." With these famous lines Charles Dickens began *A Tale of Two Cities*. He continued: "It was the season of Light, it was the season of Darkness, it was the spring of hope, it was the winter of despair, we had everything before us, we had nothing before us, we were all going direct to Heaven, we were all going direct the other way—."

Ostensibly Dickens is describing humanity on the eve of the French Revolution but, as he mentions, he could easily have been depicting his own time, 1859. For the ambiance, the mingling of hope and fear, of excitement and dread, is quintessentially Victorian. The nineteenth century had to cope with great change and the threat of change, which affected not only the physical milieu but the political, social, and psychological environments also. In many ways change was stimulating and provoked optimism; people lived better than they ever had. Mass production brought manufactured goods within the range of ordinary folk, hence the Victorian obsession with bric-a-brac. The steamboat and railroad brought people closer and meant that they lived better. Henry David Thoreau noted that the train rushed fresh produce to the undernourished city dweller: "All the Indian huckleberry hills are stripped, all the cranberry meadows are raked into the city." But the noisy engine also shattered his physical and mental solitude at Walden Pond. "The whistle of the locomotive penetrates my woods summer and winter, sounding like the scream of a hawk sailing over some farmer's yard," he said. The telegraph too was an exciting invention but Thoreau wondered if its influence would ultimately be good or bad: "Our inventions are wont to be pretty toys, which distract our attention from serious things. They are but improved means to an unimproved end."[1]

The pace of change was fast and made people seem lost in their own times. William Makepeace Thackeray, bemoaning the end of the stagecoach, said that perhaps he should have disappeared too: "We who lived before railways are antediluvians—we must pass away. We are growing scarcer every day; and old—old—very old relics of the times when George was still fighting the Dragon." Psychology notes that change, even for the good, is stressful, and many in the nineteenth century were not convinced that everything happening around them was for the better. Skepticism was most acute among the older established leading classes, the aristocracy of Britain but more particularly the gentry and nonindustrial professionals of Britain and America: lawyers, doctors, clergy, gentleman farmers or planters, military officers. These people were not Luddites simply trying to destroy the progress which threatened them. They lived in their age and used its products but they were frequently ill at ease. They took advantage of the speed and convenience of the railroad but did not wish to get its grime on their clothes. They used the machine gun on natives but refused to recognize its import for the future of conventional warfare and the status of their class. It is with this group that we are primarily concerned.[2]

In politics, the roots of change went back a long way, in the English-speaking world at least to the Glorious Revolution of 1688 and the modern struggle for parliamentary liberties. Nearer at hand, the world had not been quite the same since American rebels had confronted His Majesty's forces at Lexington, April 19, 1775. Much as the American Revolution was a conservative event in many ways, inaugurating no radically new economic or social arrangement of society, it nevertheless struck a resounding philosophical blow for the equality of man. The cry was taken up in France where soldiers who had fought in America helped to overthrow monarchical power.

Throughout the eighteenth century there had been thinkers who argued for the greater dignity of humanity through the widening of the franchise, the lessening of the gap between the classes, the greater freedom of women. Unfortunately, revolutions are never without upheaval and bloodshed. France's revolution precipitated twenty-five years of Continental war and during this period both the French and radicalism in ideas lost the support of many British and American thinkers. Americans repudiated the far left in their own revolution, people like Samuel Adams and Thomas Paine. In Britain Edmund Burke was typical of those who underwent a revulsion of feeling against the French because, far from encouraging liberty, they appeared to be engaged in an orgy of anarchy, immorality, and butchery. This sense of events across the Channel was to stay with the British and to be reflected in Dickens's portrait of Madame Defarge and Baroness Orczy's scenes of Paris under the Terror. In *The Scarlet Pimpernel* we have the essence of Victorian British conservatism: Sir Percy, the cool, rather passionless English gentleman, full of taste and good breeding, versus Chauvelin, "the not very prepossessing little figure . . . with a curious foxlike expression" who represents upstart French democracy.[3]

The conservative reaction took place in morals as well as in politics. The revolutionary era became associated with laxness in sexual mores.

As a Britisher warns a Frenchman in *The Scarlet Pimpernel*, "Do not, I pray, bring your loose foreign ways into this most moral country." Political liberty, it seemed, induced social libertinism. The connection was not entirely incorrect. Eighteenth century thinkers in all western countries had questioned accepted sexual as well as political norms. The Marquis de Sade may have been a pornographer but his works also had political content: people are raped literally and symbolically by those with wealth and power. The *ancien régime* put Sade in the Bastille and the nineteenth century banned his works. One biographer notes: "Only at the time of the French Revolution and at the present day have his books been available to the general public."[4]

The eighteenth century had assumed that sex was a part of life and had got a candid enjoyment from it that was alien to the nineteenth century. One cannot imagine a Victorian novel in which Fielding's hero Tom Jones could have sex with his natural mother and get away with it. Nor is it easy to see an American diplomat enjoying both the intellectual and sexual adventure of Europe as Benjamin Franklin did. Victorian gentlemen did not talk of "rogering" their wives in the manner of William Byrd of Westover. By 1800 a moral counter-revolution was underway, headed by Evangelical ministers and their allies among the gentry and middle classes. Disgust with Romantics, including drug-taking Coleridge and sexually promiscuous Byron, speeded the determination to regulate sexuality and control it in society's interest. Propriety triumphed. John Buchan, a popular author, wrote after reading Byron's papers: "I waded through masses of ancient indecency . . . the thing nearly made me sick."[5]

In Britain and America education was made into a tool of conservatism and moral control. An Eton old boy, justifying the harsh discipline of Dr. John Keate as a master of the school, noted that he had come there in 1797 when revolutionary ideas had spread to the British fleet, causing mutinies at Spithead and the Nore: "Our good grandsires were forced to do honour to ferocity because of the Mutinies. The very time of Keate's beginning work as an Assistant is also the Mutiny time. . . ." Schoolmasters and shipmasters "had to be terrible when there were real dangers to the Commonwealth; and the squires who knew how hard it was to rule the peasants wished no doubt to have their beefy brats coerced sharply." Thomas Arnold of Rugby was a more famous educator who was to put his stamp on schools in the century. Lytton Strachey argues that "his liberalism was tempered by an 'abhorrence of the spirit of 1789, of the American War, of the French Economistes, and of the English Whigs of the latter part of the seventeenth century.' . . ." In America, growing rigidity was illustrated at Transylvania College in Lexington, Kentucky. Known as the "Athens of the West," with an internationally recognized faculty, the school appeared to have a boundless future.

But the president, Horace Holley, was a liberal in politics and religion. In 1827 the Board forced his resignation. The best faculty went with him and the school declined. Among Holley's offences were nude classical statues in his garden.[6]

Change could not be escaped, however. In the year following Holley's resignation Andrew Jackson of Tennessee, a bumptious self-made man, took the Presidency from the incumbent, John Quincy Adams, a New England gentleman, in a landslide. To many, a second American revolution was underway. For those moving up, change was thrilling. For those being elbowed aside, change was threatening. Gentlemen of property and standing, challenged by assertive Jacksonianism, lashed out with mob violence at all reformers and eccentrics. They feared, as the French writer Alexis de Tocqueville put it, a tyranny of the majority, a bullying of the refined few by the crude many. "I know of no country in which there is so little independence of mind and real freedom of discussion as in America," he wrote. Gentlemen protected their dignity and safety by withdrawing from politics. John MacGregor, a visiting British lawyer, found that "every gentlemen . . . abjures politics; and, in proportion to his sense, appears anxious to assure you he is not a politician." Gentlemen were left with deep insecurities which would help to bring on the Civil War.[7]

Across the Atlantic the established classes also faced challenges. France and Germany witnessed further revolutions. In Britain, partly encouraged by Jackson's election, a Parliamentary reform bill of 1832 extended the franchise to new elements of the middle class and redistricted constituencies to recognize the growth of modern industrial towns. This despite the opposition of such critics as Frances Trollope, who had observed Jacksonian democracy and warned her compatriots that "they will incur the fearful risk of breaking up their repose by introducing the jarring tumult and universal degradation which invariably follow the scheme of placing all the power of the state in the hands of the populace." Thank goodness for this "lady of sense and acuteness," said the *Quarterly Review*, "when so much trash and falsehood pass current respecting that 'terrestrial paradise of the west.' "[8]

The new men elbowing their way into power appeared to bring different values with them. The age seemed increasingly obsessed with the making of money and the consumption of things that money could buy. Even in the southern states of America, which prided themselves on being less materialistic than Yankeedom, speculation and get-rich-fever seemed rampant. Joseph G. Baldwin, a lawyer who practiced in Alabama and Mississippi during the boom times of the 1830s and 40s, wrote: "With the change of times and the imagination of wealth easily acquired came a change in the thoughts and habits of the people." Ethics were lost: "The old rules of business and the calculations of prudence were alike disregarded, and profligacy, in all the departments of the *crimen falsi*, held riotous carnival."[9]

The Midas disease appeared worst in the industrial sector. Of all the changes that the nineteenth century had to face, the most far-reaching and potentially traumatic was the industrial revolution. Beginning with Britain, spreading to France and the northeastern United States, modern business-industrial growth brought about huge changes in the landscape, with mushrooming cities and an urban proletariat, radical movements in patterns of consumption and material expectations, severe shifts in values. It appeared that industrial leaders were becoming corrupted by their success and tarnishing the fabric of society.

The most famous stricture on acquisitiveness is in the opening chapter of *Walden* where Thoreau envisages men dragging bundles of their possessions through life and homes crashing due to the weight of belongings and mortgages. "When I consider how our houses are built and paid for, or not paid for, and their internal economy managed and sustained, I wonder that the floor does not give way under the visitor while he is admiring the gewgaws upon the mantelpiece, and let him through into the cellar, to some solid and honest though earthy foundation." There were other warnings. In 1845 the New York playwright Anna Cora Mowatt produced *Fashion*, in which the head of a nouveau riche family is told: "You must sell your house and all these gew-gaws, and bundle your wife and daughter off to the country. There let them learn economy, and home virtues. . . ." As for the businessman: "Let moderation in future be your counsellor." Two years before, Charles Dickens had brought out *A Christmas Carol* in which a London businessman is forced to confront his social irresponsibility. Scrooge's dead partner Marley warns him that he now knows it was not enough to be "a good man of business." "Mankind was my business. The common welfare was my business; charity, mercy, forbearance, and benevolence, were, all, my business."[10]

Searching for antidotes to the growing materialism, thinkers found various solutions. Karl Marx and Frederick Engels imagined proletarian revolution, while George Fitzhugh envisioned universal slavery of the working classes to bring back a sense of paternalism on the part of the overlords. "All concur that free society is a failure," he argued. "We slaveholders say you must recur to domestic slavery, the oldest, the best and most common form of Socialism." But by far the greatest number of commentators found hope for the salvation of society in the home and in the central figure there: the child-bearing woman cast as the "angel in the house" or the "light of the home." *Godey's* magazine said in 1860: "The perfection of womanhood . . . is the wife and mother, the center of the family, the magnet that draws man to the domestic altar, that makes him a civilized being, a social Christian. The wife is truly the light of the home." Thomas Gentry, writing in the same journal thirteen years later, portrayed the mother as "a being around whom clusters all that is eminently good and truly grand," and urged young women to "occupy that station in life which your Creator has designed you for, where characters are moulded which shall sway sceptres or shape the destinies of worlds."[11]

Why was woman seen as a savior of character? First, the industrial revolution had encouraged separation of the sexes. Many men spent less time in the home, women spent more. Men were characterized as being in the vicious maelstrom of the public world, the marketplace, where they were calloused by competition. Women, conversely, were increasingly out of the rush of things and in a purer, if more naive, atmosphere. James Fenimore Cooper proclaimed that there was "everywhere the utmost possible care to preserve the females from undue or unwomanly employment." When man retired tainted to his home "to seek consolation from one who is placed beyond influence," woman was ready, within the "sacred precincts of her own abode . . . preserved from the destroying taint of excessive intercourse with the world." "Women, are literally, our better halves," he concluded. This stereotype hardly fit the millions of working women who were farm, factory, or domestic employees. Nor did the image of savagely competitive males fit their noble lordships lolling about their country estates. Nevertheless, even if the concept distorted reality, we can readily see how it came about.[12]

The Victorian home, a solidly built place with plenty of cushions within, might possibly keep away the horror of the swiftly changing world without. Woman as mother seemed to offset man's weak points. If he was selfish, she was self-sacrificing, risking her life to give life each time she bore a child. Where the male was acquisitive, the female was nurturing, giving of herself and her time to the household. Unfortunately, this seemingly perfect model was flawed. Not all women wished to be mothers; these were often forced to become "old maids," held in pity or contempt. In making men and women assume stereotypical roles, Victorian society created a distance between the genders. Some males and females came to see each other not only as different but as alien species, who thought oddly, acted peculiarly, and couldn't be trusted. The sexes became, to a degree, victims of the roles they had invented. Women often depicted men as poor, potentially vicious creatures to be saved from themselves. "Do not, my dearest James, be led away by gay companions to follow the vile and bad habits of men," wrote a southern woman to her nephew at school. "The more I see and know men the more I dislike them and think they are a vile set of animals."[13]

Some men came to feel that in order to be respected a woman had to be inhumanly pure, an angel in fact as well as theory. On her rested the total onus for moral good in society. "You are my good influence to keep me pure in heart," wrote an American to his betrothed in 1887.

Another young man wrote to his girl: "You are the very incarnation of purity to me . . . and you shall help to cleanse me." A woman who failed to live up to this divine mission might be labeled a whore. William D. Valentine wrote in 1837 that he had been shocked to meet a beautiful woman who enjoyed sex: "Vice has warped her notions of propriety—she was deficient in one quality and that quality is it which renders the fair sex so ethereal, so much the angel—the virtue of a woman. . . ."[14]

The angelic concept of women was given scientific authentication by medicine, which is to a degree culturally based. Male doctors could be disturbed by female sexuality and wish to control it. Overt sexual behavior could end in women being diagnosed as abnormal. Even clitoral castration was sometimes employed to dull physical desire. "I should say that the majority of women (happily for them) are not very much troubled with sexual feeling of any kind," wrote William Acton, an influential medical author. "What men are habitually, women are only exceptionally." Though animal passion was accepted in men, they were warned that too much indulgence could lead to insanity. According to Dr. Edward Jarvis, writing in 1850, male inmates of lunatic asylums were habitual masturbators. Man's difficulty, he said, lay in his "stronger passions and more powerful appetites and propensities." Some men sought sexual pleasure with prostitutes or servant girls. But others heeded medical advice and chose alternative physical activities for enjoyment.[15]

The bulk of this activity was athletic and it could be violent. The privileged nineteenth-century male pursued with obsessive ferocity the killing of other animals. The highest animal was man and therefore man killing was sometimes seen as the finest game of all. Killing was thought to be healthy for the individual and society. The capitalist was often pictured as selfish, putting private gain before public good. One antidote was the ministering mother figure. Another was the soldier, because the soldier, like a mother, put the good of others before his own life. In theory, his acts were essentially unselfish and in the interests of a cause greater than his own material well-being. Thus, ironically, the Victorians came to exalt the life-giver and the life-taker, the child-bearer and the man-killer.

These roles for men and women were stated by Theodore Roosevelt: "The woman who, whether from cowardice, from selfishness, from having a false and vacuous ideal shirks her duty as wife and mother, earns the right to our contempt, just as does the man who, from any motive, fears to do his duty in battle when the country calls him." These roles could in some degree account for the remarkable fame of Florence Nightingale. Perhaps she is an androgynous figure, combining the nurturing qualities of the female with the stern, soldierly facets of the male. Ordinary British soldiers excited her highest praise: "Their world was not ruled by money, and she detested materialism. The supreme loyalty which made a man give his life for his comrade, the courage which enabled him to advance steadily under fire, were displayed by men who were paid a shilling a day."[16]

Thus was the soldier cherished as an outstanding model of male civic virtue. And war had its adherents as a cleansing experience, good for a nation's physical and spiritual health.

PART I

SEPARATION OF THE SEXES

In 1857 Thomas Hughes published *Tom Brown's School-Days*. It achieved immediate popularity and became a classic tale for boys. The book is about Rugby, a public school, and part of its appeal was to the graduates of such institutions. But it also enjoyed a wider audience because it captured widespread male values. These values, sometimes in modified form, were embraced by many across the Atlantic.

Who are the Browns, the family from whom Tom springs? "The Browns," it says early in chapter one, "are a fighting family. One may question their wisdom or wit or beauty, but about their fight there can be no question." This is essential to Hughes's view of life: you don't have to be too bright but you have to be a fighter. He asks, "What would life be like without fighting, I should like to know? From the cradle to the grave, fighting, rightly understood, is the business, the real, highest, honestest business of every son of man."[1]

It follows that a primary aim of boyhood training should be to produce lads who are manly. "We're in the hands of our countrymen, you know," says Tom. "Must fight for the Schoolhouse flag, if so be." Academic achievement may be slighted so long as hardy character is developed. Squire Brown says of his hopes for Tom: "If he'll only turn out a brave, helpful, truth-telling Englishman and a gentleman and a Christian, that's all I want."[2]

Given the aim of the school to turn out a boy who accepts implicitly the value of the established order, the child who questions authority, or who is not a fighter, who is eccentric or intellectual, finds that he is rejected and victimized. East, an older boy, explains to Tom at the start of his school career: "A great deal depends on how a fellow cuts up at first. If he's got nothing odd about him, and answers straight-forward and holds his head up, he gets on."[3]

Pluck, the fighting spirit, is inculcated by manly competitive sports. Hughes comments of a Rugby football match that "a battle would look much the same to you, except that the boys would be men, and the balls iron. . . ." The captain of the team is the equivalent of the army commander: "His face is earnest and careful as he glances a last time over his array, but full of pluck and hope, the sort of look I hope to see in my general when I go out to fight." The children act like soldiers achieving a pitch of excitement in battle: "Meet them like Englishmen, you School-house boys and charge them home. Now is the time to show what mettle is in you. . . ." Hughes teaches that life is best when the blood is up and the adrenalin flowing: "This is worth living for; the whole sum of school-boy existence gathered up into one straining, struggling half-hour—a half-hour worth a year of common life." When applied to the battlefield, this concept was to convince some young men that it was better to be killed at fever pitch than live long in lower key.[4]

According to Hughes, death is preferable to life on any but the most manly terms. Boys are to be fastidious and to shun any impurity, including drunkenness, lying, masturbation, and impure thoughts about girls. After a boy dies of fever, Dr. Arnold, the headmaster, lectures the boys on sinfulness. They should live purely "because we then feel what it is to live that death becomes an infinite blessing. . . ." Good boys, that is, the ones who are plucky and don't masturbate, go to heaven when they die.[5]

Death in youth as the fulfillment of life makes sense when two factors in the book are considered. First, there is immense dwelling on young health and cleanliness. Age comes to represent decay and corruption in various forms. Second, the values of the group to which Tom belongs exclude the bulk of capitalist trades as legitimate life pursuits. A private career in building personal gain is almost criminal. Your life must serve the public good, even if that means sacrifice. "Keep the latter before you as your only object," a master tells Tom, "and you will be right, whether you make a living or not; but if you dwell on the other, you'll very likely drop into mere money-making, and let the world take care of itself for good or evil." The perfect self-giving server of the public is the soldier. When Tom's friend East becomes an officer, the same master comments, "He will make a capital officer." Yes, says Tom, "no fellow could handle boys better, and I suppose soldiers are very like boys."[6]

Tom Brown's School-Days is a male world throughout. It is one of violent challenge and male camaraderie. Women play a minor role. Part

Tom Brown sees Arthur's mother for the first time as she enters the sickroom. Appropriately, the Light of the Home carries two candles. (Thomas Hughes, *Tom Brown's School-Days.* New York: Thomas Y. Crowell, n.d.)

of the pollution of age is implied to be the loss of male virginity through sexual intercourse. Yet there is an image of women, a powerful sense of the female as mother. Images of their mothers float before the boys' eyes as angels beckoning them to visions of purity. Tom writes home to his mother rather than to both parents, he prays at night in deference to his mother's wishes, and after he faints during a torturing by Flash-man, his first word upon recovery is "Mother."[7]

Mothers may be worshipped. Tom takes a sickly boy, Arthur, under his wing, combats his shyness and studiousness, gives him pluck. Arthur's mother is grateful. When Arthur falls ill she comes to the school and enters the sickroom where Tom and Arthur are sitting together. The mother is typically Anglo-Saxon, with the looks of an angel: "Tall and slight and fair, with masses of golden hair drawn back from the broad white forehead, and the calm blue eyes meeting his so deep and open,— the eye that he knew so well, for it was his friend's over again,—and the lovely tender mouth that trembled while he looked." There is some-thing sensual here, a mood that deepens when "Tom held her hand, and looked on straight in her face; he could neither let it go nor speak." Going out, she "gave him her hand again, and again his eyes met that deep loving look, which was like a spell upon him." This situation is very Victorian; it looks like a ménage à trois but yet is pure and uplifting because its underlying dynamics are unacknowledged. Arthur says, "I have realized one of the dearest wishes of my life,—to see you two to-gether."[8]

The importance of mothers in *Tom Brown's School-Days* complements rather than contradicts the essential maleness. For mothers in Victorian society were by definition pure and unattainable—those who were not might be seen as whores. Boys could grow up without a realistic sense of females but with an idealized view of motherly purity that sometimes made balanced relations with women of actual flesh and sweat difficult. Thus the cult of motherhood reinforced the importance of males to males.

The following three chapters will examine the male world of the nine-teenth century. Men will be considered in their relation to women, then as males engaging with males. Finally, they will be described playing games, often violent, with other men. Overall, it will appear that the century emphasized separation of the sexes and that manliness came to be identified with exclusion of the female as soft and sentimental.

ONE | Men and Women

The Judeo-Christian tradition has always placed sex within firm boundaries and our culture has always treated free indulgence as a sin and crime. But the nineteenth century appears to have been particularly restrictive. Why? It was partly because of spermatic theory and the belief that orgasm was physically draining. This idea was current in medical circles as early as 1700. In 1758 the eminent Swiss physician Samuel Tissot published *De l'onanisme,* cataloguing the ill effects of "self-pollution." He asserted that the production of one ounce of semen cost the body as much effort as the manufacture of forty ounces of blood. Subsequent physicians warned that masturbation and excessive sexual indulgence could lead to spinal degeneration, brain damage, physical deformities.[1]

This conventional wisdom appealed to Victorians because they sought control and feared the loss of it. The nineteenth century was a period of chronic change and there was fear of being adrift on uncharted seas. At any point in the surge one could lose control, including self-control. The consequences of material excess haunted people with more goods and comforts than ever seen before. It was tempting to go too far, especially when stress could be assuaged in the forgetfulness of pleasure. Greedy self-indulgence, with all its problems for the public good, was a major horror.

Self-indulgence also raised the specter of romantic revolution. Wasn't the French terror partly a matter of excess, of going too far? Wasn't that why the world had gone mad in the revolutionary era? A correspondent for the *Public Ledger* wrote in 1816: "That the French Revolution, with all its constant horrors, was preceded by a total revolution of decency and morality, the virtuous qualities of a mind being sapped and undermined by the baneful exhibition of pictures, representing vice in the most alluring and varied forms, is a truth that unfortunately will not admit of doubt." The conclusion was that civic stability required control of sexuality. Hence, even the attempt to limit caning in English schools was opposed as a Jacobinism which would loosen society's hold on the boys' passions.[2]

COLORADO MOUNTAIN COLLEGE
Alpine Campus - L. R. C.
P.O. Box 775288
Steamboat Springs, CO 80477

The views of Thomas Malthus added to the concern about sexual habits. In 1798 he published his formative *Essay on the Principle of Population*, in which he argued that population had a natural tendency to increase faster than the food supply and therefore some people were always at the subsistence level or below. This theory influenced public policy on such issues as wages and employment while also encouraging a private trend toward smaller families: in such a situation it would be irresponsible to increase unduly the mouths to be fed.[3]

Some progressive Victorian social thinkers threw their weight behind the drive for continence. They opposed frequent sexual indulgence partly because of the risk to women inherent in childbirth, but also because the educated and sensitive craved the spiritual, a renunciation of the carnal. Angelina Grimké admitted that she had "been tempted to think marriage was *sinful*" because "instead of the higher, nobler sentiments being aroused, and leading on the lower passions *captive* to their will, the *latter* seemed to be *lords* over the *former*." Her husband, Theodore Dwight Weld, was equally determined to master passion, saying that "I have acquired *perfect self-control*" in matters of the heart. He berated his son for having nighttime emissions, claiming: "All authorities agree that this drain upon the seminal fluid will lead ultimately to *insanity* or *idiocy*." Such an authority was Weld's friend Henry C. Wright, who in *Marriage and Parentage* assailed the "UNNATURAL AND MONSTROUS EXPENDITURE OF THE SEXUAL ELEMENT FOR MERE SENSUAL GRATIFICATION."[4]

The concern for control was most pronounced among those in the middle reaches of society. This was partly a result of the Evangelical movement which in Britain and America had touched their ranks, producing piety and fastidiousness. But behind the religious rigidity stood other needs. These people, rather than the aristocracy who were cushioned behind ancient walls and privileges, felt the brunt of change, were most vulnerable to it, and least sure of their grip. All around them in the plastic middle zone of society the struggle to rise was going on, with demanding males pushing their way up and weak ones going to the wall. It was they who adamantly denied the sensuality of woman and insisted that she be the savior of the race. For if man was lustful and grasping, she had to be pure and spiritual in her mothering of all. Frederic Hamilton, looking back on a Victorian youth, praised "the average clean-living, clean-minded wife of the average British professional man, together with the strict ideals as to the sanctity of the marriage-tie, the strong sense of duty, and the high moral standards such wives usually possess." Note the importance here accorded to being average or conventional. The sexual point was put frankly by an Edwardian physician during a conversation at Oxford: "I can tell you that nine out of ten women are indifferent or actively dislike it; the tenth, who enjoys it, will always be a harlot."[5]

There was an equal expectation of purity on the part of American women. They formed the backbone of the Evangelical, churchgoing population and, early on, Tocqueville noted that they were "cold and virtuous," their purity being "the highest security for the order and prosperity of the household." Prominent American men attributed their salvation from moral decline to good women. Ulysses S. Grant wrote to his wife, Julia, "If I feel tempted to do anything that I think is not right I am sure to think, 'Well now if Julia saw me would I do so,' and thus it is absent or present I am more or less governed by what I think is your will." Henry Adams claimed that he had been rescued a number of times by women, including his sister and Mrs. Cabot Lodge, a person significantly older than himself. Women, he believed, were the guardians of morality and motherhood should be venerated. One biographer states: "In the modern world, with its great material temptations, it was even more important for women to remain at home and uncorrupted; only then could they temper male avarice with gentleness and altruism."[6]

The placing of southern womanhood on a pedestal was intended to fulfill the same function of social preservation. "The men are not all fools yet," wrote Daniel R. Hundley in 1860, "and they know that woman's one sole Inalienable Right, is to be a Teacher; for whatever may be said in praise of Public, or Free, or High, or Select schools, or any other kind of school, we maintain there is one greater and more praiseworthy than these all, for it is God's school, and is called THE FAMILY. And it is in this school that woman finds her proper sphere and mission." It followed that women had to be kept free from the corruption of the world. "For since to the family belongs the education and gradual elevation of the race, it is most important that mothers should be pure, peaceable, gentle, long-suffering and godly—which they never can be, if permitted to enter the lists and compete with selfish and lustful man for the prizes of place and public emolument."[7]

The liberalizing that took place by the turn of the century can be overstated. In social intercourse, the battle between the sexes intensified as the new century opened on a struggle for women's public rights. Walter Heape, a Cambridge professor, said bitterly that man's view of woman "as an integral component of society can never be the same again." Sexual closeness also did not necessarily advance. Some suffragists attacked contraception as allowing lovers "to indulge their passions" without fear of the consequences. *Herland*, the Utopian novel published by Charlotte Perkins Gilman in 1915, argued that sex should be strictly for procreation. When American males attempt to introduce carnal desire into Herland they provoke horror, because "the one high purpose of motherhood had been for so long the governing law of life. . . ." A Herland woman responds to lovemaking with frigidity: "that remote clear look as if she had gone far away even though I held her beautiful body so close, and was now on some snowy mountain regarding me from a distance."[8]

The Victorian emphasis on difference in nature and role between male and female meant that children were to a large degree segregated from each other. Little girls who wrote love letters to boys were treated as harlots. In one English school, letters had to be read by a mistress "in case any of the girls should be so wicked as to write to boys." In 1897 three girls were expelled from one establishment for writing love letters. Frances Trollope noted that in a distinguished American boarding school a girl of fourteen was reduced to hysterics by finding a man in the receiving room. She "put her hands before her eyes, and ran out of the room again, screaming 'A man! a man!'"[9]

L. E. Jones, remembering his Edwardian youth, said that his family was "chaster in thought than, on looking back from this age, appears quite human. . . ." His relations with girls were platonic. In college he did not kiss a date: "In those days such innocent pleasures were taboo." Frank Richardson recalled that his schooldays had been spent under watchful eyes. Walking arm-in-arm with a girl was prohibited and the headmaster lectured on "the sin against the Holy Ghost" which "somehow drained an important reservoir behind the heart." Richardson thought he meant masturbation. When Colonel Valentine Baker, a successful soldier, forced a kiss on a girl in a railway carriage, he was dishonorably discharged, fined, and sentenced to a year in prison. Said Mr. Justice Brett, the judge presiding, "The kiss of a daughter by her father is a holy one," but "a kiss that gratifies or excites passion is undoubtedly indecent." Baker died a mercenary in the Turkish service.[10]

Sex education was often inadequate. In 1912 Arthur Ponsonby said of the better English classes: "Parents still refuse as a general rule, whether out of shyness, false delicacy, prudishness, laziness, or stupidity, to inform their children of fundamental biological truths." Sex "remains unexplained, and boys are left to gather from whisperings, jokes, and foolish, promiscuous, childish gossip among themselves the first knowledge of the greatest of all mysteries. . . ." In America, Eleanor Abbott, growing up in the 1870s, received from her elders only the insight that "men in general, were reputed to be turned into 'wild beasts' by the slightest departure on the female's part from a 'mien or deportment of modesty.'" Finally she found out from a physician's daughter how babies were conceived. She first rejected the knowledge as "silly," then accepted the "horrible secret" but was "troubled" and "bewildered." In Derbyshire, Vera Brittain, aged eighteen in 1914, was asked by a girlfriend what being with a boy meant. "I was quite unable to enlighten her." At length, "half-knowledge engendered in me so fierce an antipathy to the idea of physical relationship" that when a boy proposed marriage, "my immediate and only reaction was a sense of intolerable humiliation and disgust."[11]

Members of the opposite sex might grow away from each other, separated by damaging ignorance. Some remained shy and ill at ease physically. Alice James noted the typical genteel Englishwoman's sexual immaturity. In 1858 Evelyn Wood's sister married Lieutenant-Colonel Thomas Steele. When she found that he expected sex, she left him. Marie Stopes, an American girl, realized several weeks after her wedding that her husband didn't know they should consummate.[12]

The most famous case is that of art critic John Ruskin, whose marriage to Effie Gray was unconsummated and finally ended. Effie admitted that "I had never been told the duties of married persons to each other and knew little or nothing about their relations in the closest union on earth." But Ruskin had the main problem. Her naked body repulsed him: "Though her face was beautiful, her person was not formed to excite passion. On the contrary, there were certain circumstances in her person which completely checked it." Yet doctors found her normal. Ruskin must have meant the evidence of puberty. Historians have wondered how an art critic could be so naive. But exposure to nude art is not knowledge of sexuality or a guarantee of a healthy attitude. William Etty, a celebrated artist, "was a devout celibate who spent his life painting naked women. . . ." Lord Leighton, another famous painter, "declares he has never seen a girl he could marry," said his mother. "Of course this shows he is unreasonably fastidious."[13]

Ruskin found prepubescent girls more attractive than mature women, like a youngster in Turin who was "half-naked, bare-limbed to above the knees, and beautifully limbed . . . her little breasts, scarce dimpled yet—white—marble-like. . . ." Victorian male involvement with young girls, including child prostitutes, had several sources. They were less likely to be diseased. Also, they were less threatening than grown women and, with scarce-dimpled breasts, resembled boys, allowing men a familiar association with their own gender.[14]

Ruskin was sheltered by parents he adored and his exposure to life was limited. He embraced the angelic concept of women, writing in 1868: "The man's work for his home is, as has been said, to secure its maintenance, progress and defense; the woman's to secure its order, comfort, and loveliness." The home must be stress free: "This is the true nature of home—it is the place of Peace; the shelter, not only from all injury, but from all terror, doubt, and division." If sexuality elicited terror or doubt it must be avoided. Ruskin said of his marriage: "I believed that she loved me, as I loved her, with little mingling of desire."[15]

Physical diffidence could be paralleled by emotional distance. One Victorian recalled having an idealized fantasy as a young man about a girl he never spoke to: "Anna was an intangible angel, entirely inaccessible to any mortal." Girls were then "supposed to be caskets of all sorts of precious virtues, to be admired but not touched." Love was sometimes a silly game, parodying courtly love with sighs from afar. Ettie Mosley, an English society queen, was credited with a number of love affairs but they were not consummated. Letters were passed protesting undying devotion and pretended wounds. One of Ettie's circle, Maurice Baring, wrote the novel *C*, in which the lovers barely touch "and then at moments of near fantasy—on a moonlit night, or in a garden redolent with jasmine."[16]

Men and women could fail to find lasting rapport together. Mary Chesnut, wife of the distinguished South Carolina senator, confessed after twenty years of marriage that she could not fathom her husband's thoughts. She believed he lacked feeling and he thought she needed to contain emotion, typical gender stereotypes. General Oliver Otis Howard was so conversationally lost with a woman that he could only ask "if she had reflected on the goodness of God during the past night." Henry James did not stretch credibility with "The Beast in the Jungle," about a man who spends his whole life unable to tell a woman that he loves her.[17]

Incomprehension of the opposite sex could produce indifference or hostility. Women might see men as little boys and sexuality "as one more method used by men to debase women to their own level by seducing them, and to keep them dependent by forcing them into parasitism," as Elizabeth Blackwell, an American physician, argued. "Why are men such animals?" asked Margaret Fountaine. Hating her father's values, she dreamed of driving nails into his coffin. Alice James also fancied hurting her father or committing suicide to escape him. "I used to sit immovable reading in the library with waves of violent inclination suddenly invading my muscles taking some one of their myriad forms such as throwing myself out of the window, or knocking off the head of the benignant pater as he sat with his silver locks. . . ." She retreated into illness. Henry Adams's wife took her life.[18]

Men could be shocked to find that the angels they courted might on further acquaintance become too real. Lord Dundonald wrote of the wives he saw at close quarters on a sea voyage: "What I could not understand then and now is how the soft pud of a female kitten can later develop such sharp talons, or why it is that the female of our species becomes so malicious against its male partner." Men retreated to their clubs to avoid the intimate company of women. Here they might indulge violent dreams. On the walls could be paintings which showed a desire to strip woman naked and do her damage. In *Idols of Perversity* Bram Dijkstra has pointed to the enormous amount of fin-de-siècle male art attacking, even visually raping women. Earlier examples include John Everett Millais's 1870 "The Knight-Errant" in which a warrior rescues a damsel in distress. He is clothed from crown to toe in steel plate, has a sword and freedom of movement; she is naked and tied to a tree. Ostensibly the lady is being saved from violation, but Millais has given her to the viewer frozen in time when she is most vulnerable and least threatening to the mailed knight.[19]

Sadism toward woman came partly from resentment of her place on the moral pedestal. Woman was seen as more virtuous than man, yet

Millais's well-protected knight encounters a female. (John Everett Millais, "The Knight-Errant" [1870], by permission of the Tate Gallery, London/Art Resource, New York.)

he was head of the household and she was not to challenge his temporal authority. The Victorian failure to resolve this paradox led to tension. A clergyman, male receptacle of virtue, could begrudge the moral pretension of women. Francis Kilvert, a cleric fond of young girls, wrote in his diary for January 4, 1872, an enthusiastic description of a painting he had just seen in a London gallery: "The beautiful girl stripped naked of her blue robe and stabbed in the side under the left breast is sailing through the air and reclines half standing, half lying back, supported tenderly in the arms of her lover who has been stabbed in the same place. The naked girl is writhing and drawing up one of her legs in an agony— but her arms are thrown back and clasped passionately around her lover's neck." The scene is sexual and the lovers are joined through their wounds, but she is naked and he is not. In other works, judgement is passed on naked women either through religious tribunals which torture them on the rack or Roman magistrates who have them butchered in the arena.[20]

Violence to women could come from fear that they reciprocated male hostility. In Edgar Allan Poe's "The Fall of the House of Usher" the hero buries his sister alive, destroying his feminine part. But she returns to drag him into the ruin. Terror lay in the threat that woman might break out of her sphere entirely and invade the male. Balance would be lost; the sexually or politically aggressive female would overload the already threatened male. Hence, suffragettes were harshly treated in British prisons. In 1910 W. Lyon Blease noted the nightmares experienced by politicians who saw the demand for the vote as feminine madness. "Perhaps the most striking proof of their failure to grasp the true nature of the problem was their constant fear of being blinded by vitriol, the weapon of the injured wife or the discarded mistress. The spectacle of Cabinet Ministers going about the country in dread of ferocious cruelty of this kind would have been almost ludicrous did it not indicate such a perilous ignorance of the facts." Suffragettes were beaten on the streets and sometimes stripped by mobs. They had forfeited social protection; by challenging their role they had become whores.[21]

Male fear of the female could also originate in childhood contact with the Victorian matron who took seriously her role as moral guardian. She was an awesome, intimidating figure. E. F. Benson noted that the great lady of his Victorian youth had great dignity because "she had power, she mattered, and that was her unsought reward in the performance of her duties." Millicent Fawcett remembered that her father was in awe of her mother. "It was really he who bent to her more than she to him. . . ." Her grip on the home was immaculate: "In domestic affairs she was orderly and methodical; every department of her big household was well organized and thoroughly under her control." Margaret Fountaine said that her mother had dominated everyone in her life through "rowing" with them. "There were 'rows' with the servants, with all of us children, in fact with anyone who has ever come into contact with my mother for the last seventy-four years."[22]

Woman was the crucial figure on the domestic scene. She took more responsibility for child-raising as men withdrew, leaving the burden of the child's emotional life on the mother. Fathers who were increasingly bound up with the manly virtue of the stiff upper lip distanced their children with stern aloofness. This fell hard on sons who needed care from an older male. "It was his relationship with his mother that carried the emotional current in a young man's life," says one historian. When fathers did take a hand with their boys it was often to toughen them through harsh discipline for the hard world outside the home. The upshot was that children "often were seething with hatred toward their repressive fathers," even though "they had to pay them extravagant forms of deference at all times." Even sex education was often left to mothers by men who were uncomfortable with the subject. "Mothers became the conduits through which were discharged much vehement expostulation from troubled men who baulked at themselves addressing boys. Mothers were instructed how to terrify boys into 'virtue' with warnings of lethal danger. . . ."[23]

Children were now at home and in school longer than they had been in the eighteenth century when even the offspring of well-to-do parents had been apprenticed at an early age. The Victorians invented adolescence because part of the meaning of plenty was that children were not needed in the marketplace and parents could afford to keep them unproductive. So they might be under the home influence longer at a point when the father's presence was receding. Men who feared their boys were too much molded by women could pack them off to boarding school. Charles Francis Adams, Jr., wrote to Endicott Peabody, principal of Groton, asking him to take his sons: "They have been almost wholly under female control," as "I have been so much occupied of late years that I have been wholly unable to give that time and attention to my two boys which every boy ought to receive from his father."[24]

Boarding schools subscribed to the cult of motherhood so that boys sent away to this masculine arena retained an idealized mother portrait. James McLachlan estimates that, "although 99 percent male institutions, boarding schools did not ignore the role of the woman and the mother, so important in romantic educational thought. If the school was truly to fulfill the familial image, women had to enjoy a conspicuous spot in the organization."[25]

Fiction for children made the same point. In *Little Women*, the central character is Marmee whose "gray cloak and unfashionable bonnet covered the most splendid woman in the world." This modest and self-sacrificing being is central to her children's world. She must wave them off to school because "somehow it seemed as if they couldn't get through the day without that." When she is away all is unsettled until her return, then the children "closed their weary eyes, and lay at rest like storm-beaten boats, safe at anchor in a quiet harbor." Everyone needs a mother. Laurie, the boy next door, twitches when he says he has lost his mother and he confesses that he enviously watches Marmee at night through the window. Fathers are more dispensable. Marmee's husband is a distant, anemic figure, a weak man going to the wall in modern cut-and-thrust; he has lost his money by signing pledges for friends.[26]

The death of the mother "is the great, irreparable, painful loss," said Eton master William Cory. He confided that "I was a young man when I lost my mother, and since then I have always been wishing to dream of her as I did once, eighteen years ago." Dreams could involve mothers erotically because, unlike waking fantasies, they are beyond our control and we are not accountable for them. Stanley Hall, a distinguished American psychologist born in 1844, feared and was covertly hostile to his brusquely masculine father. He idolized his mother, particularly after her death in 1887. In 1902 he wrote a story called "How Johnnie's Vision Came True." At the climax, a boy falls asleep, dreaming of a woman with "the mingled charm of mother, sister, and bride." She "resembled no one he had ever seen before, unless it was a nude woodcut of the Holy Mother that he saw in a Catholic church he had visited months ago in a little village." They embrace and "his lips met hers in a moment of such ecstacy as he had never dreamed of before."[27]

Mother-need could be obsessive. Ian Hamilton, whose mother died when he was young, held this loss crucial. "Often I have wondered what I should have been had she lived, and felt that another and a better being would have made his number in war and peace." He carried a lock of her hair with him and cherished this sacred token, saying that when he died, "It will have to be burnt, strangers must never handle it." Also he kept his mother's Bible by his bed. Reflecting his horror at her burial, he confessed "that I do not allow anyone to put anything on the top of it . . . not for a moment."[28]

Fixation on the mother cannot be entirely healthy for the child. Dorothy Dinnerstein pointed out that woman has been the primary parent and also the most available target for the child's anger because she represents the social authority against which the child naturally rebels. The male child may be especially resentful for he knows he is different from the female and will at some point inhabit a wider social sphere; therefore it is she who stands between him and freedom. Even while a Victorian male enjoyed the care of his mother, he could resent the implied subjection to her will. And woe betide a woman who attempted to exercise a similar authority without the mother's license to intrude! There occurs here "the creation of woman as villain," to use a phrase coined by Judith Fetterley. Also, since the mother is the only desirable female, and the fantasy of love with her must remain unfulfilled, love becomes associated with chasteness. A woman who is attainable is by definition unworthy.[29]

In these circumstances, men could distrust women to the point of only being comfortable with them at a distance. William Walker, the American adventurer shot in Nicaragua, is an example. The only important female in Walker's life was his invalid mother whom he served and doted on in his youth. So sacred was the relationship that he could not replace it. He only fell in love with one girl, whom he never kissed. "She was someone to be cherished and protected, perhaps even worshipped." Like his mother, she was physically handicapped. Ultimately, Walker could not relate to women of his own social standing, and though he occasionally visited prostitutes when his sexual need was great, he developed a moral Spartanism, refusing to allow his men to associate with women while in the field. He restricted his emotional life to soldiering, building upon a fastidiousness which, as class valedictorian at the University of Nashville, had led him to speak on "The Need for a More Firm Code of Morality." His biographer says that at no "time in his life were women really important to him" and he exorcised the "hidden, ferocious side" of his nature through exotic schemes of conquest. The man sometimes described as a Victorian rake was in fact a "sad swashbuckler."[30]

TWO | # Men Together

Years ago there was a saying among men that "a woman's a woman but a pipe's a smoke." The idea was that women have their uses, in their way, and in their place, but they are not satisfying companions and do not give lasting comfort. A pipe is a friend and won't disappoint you; a woman will.

This distrust of, and turning away from, the opposite sex was true of some women also. Carroll Smith-Rosenberg notes that nineteenth-century American culture was characterized "by rigid gender-role differentiation within the family and within society as a whole, leading to the emotional segregation of women and men." In this situation women, like men, turned to their own sex for intellectual and emotional closeness. "These relationships ranged from the supportive love of sisters, through the enthusiasms of adolescent girls, to sensual avowals of love by mature women. It was a world in which men made but a shadowy appearance." Women sought men as marriage partners but their trust and love, even physical intimacy, were reserved for each other."[1]

Men too drew together. Richard Cabot, an American undergraduate, wrote: "The men friends which I am beginning to get now will give me something far deeper than I can get from women." An English student noted that "girls were out of the picture at Oxford" and "the notional gap between man and girl made it difficult for either to regard the other as a simple fellow creature." Some men, embittered by failures with women, came to see them as bloodsuckers, all teeth and claws. The point is made imaginatively in F. G. Loring's story "The Tomb of Sarah" (1900). A vicar nearly succumbs to the lure of a vampire but is saved by a friend who cries, "in the name of all that you hold sacred, have done and play the man." Playing the man means rejecting the female. As Ronald Pearsall observed, desire, when suppressed, leads to its opposite, fear.[2]

Male distancing from women is evident in the condescension shown toward supposedly female traits. Men professed to admire the woman who was meek, giving, pliant, but they rejected such qualities for themselves. To be soft like a woman was to play the coward. Charles Gordon labeled the Arabs "cowardly, effeminate, lying brutes." J. F. C. Fuller thought the French "gross, cowardly & essentially effeminate."[3]

Men should be manly; tough and activist. Timothy Flint, an American advocate of hardiness, wrote in 1831 that "shrinking and effeminate spirits, the men of soft hands and fashionable life," should follow the pioneers, for "there is a kind of moral sublimity in the contemplation of the adventures and daring of such men" with their "manly hardihood." In 1888 General Horace Porter asked his audience to compare two lads: "Let one remain in a quiet city, playing the milksop . . . leading an unambitious namby-pamby life, . . . while the other goes out on the frontier, runs his chance in encounters with wild animals, finds that to make his way he must take his life in his hands, and assert his rights, if necessary with deadly weapons. . . ." He will "become the superior of the lad who has remained at home."[4]

This is an all-male world of brawn and physical power. Lew Wallace said of the settlers in frontier Indiana: "Instead of taking their quarrels into court, they settled them on the spot, resorting to their fists." No man could refuse: "If the party affronted hung back, or quailed, no allowances were made for him; he must fight." The British had the imperial frontiers where their manhood could be tested too against nature and in small sporting contests against military opponents like the Masai of Africa, whom the British admired as "brave, disciplined, and indifferent to women."[5]

The rejection of softness, the inculcation of toughness, is a rejection of woman. Also, it is a turning away from self-indulgence, from the material. By being ascetic, by not "spending oneself," one controlled both the allure of woman and the temptations of getting and using wealth. Be continent, said Thoreau, and you will be good. Heroism and manliness flow from this. If we have "a command over our passions," then "the spirit can for the time pervade and control every member and function of the body, and transmute what in form is the grossest sensuality into purity and devotion. The generative energy, which, when we are loose, dissipates and makes us unclean, when we are continent invigorates and inspires us. Chastity is the flowering of man. . . ."[6]

To be masculine was to be unemotional, in control of one's passions. Michael Barton has postulated that the American Civil War may be seen partly as an attempt by northern gentlemen to control the license of southerners, portrayed as voluptuous and sensually indulgent fellows, wallowing in steamy exotic settings and surrounded by half-naked, dusky maidens. Colonel James Fowler Rusling wrote in 1865, "We all remember one type of the traditional Southerner," a "fiery-eyed, long-haired, negligé individual, great upon juleps and cocktails, fond of fast horses and faster women, a barbaric compound of ignorance and cruelty." They had been taught the error of their ways through a sound thrashing at the hands of disciplined northerners.[7]

In fact, men on both sides strove to show a dispassionate front to the world. Robert E. Lee was famous for his rigid control over "strong passions." Young northern intellectuals like Oliver Wendell Holmes, Jr., deliberately cultivated a cold, clinical approach to the fighting. So did their elders. When Holmes was badly wounded at Antietam, his father came to find him. The parent must have been riven with anxiety but he did not allow himself any demonstration of feeling. When the two met, they merely exchanged the usual formal greetings. Said the senior: "Such are the proprieties of life, . . . decently disguising those natural impulses."[8]

If anything, the well-bred Britisher was even more removed from his feelings. John Stuart Mill thought that England was the most self-controlled culture in the world. "England is the country in which social discipline has most succeeded, not so much in conquering, as in suppressing, whatever is liable to conflict with it. The English, more than any other people, not only act but feel according to rule." The rule or formula was called "good form."[9]

An American woman said of English gentlemen that "they had worn the conventionalism of England so long that it had become a sort of easy uniform, which they didn't know they had on." Herman Melville captured the type in *Moby Dick*. Captain Boomer, master of a whaling vessel, like Ahab has lost a limb to the white whale. But his way of dealing with the trauma is different. Where Ahab fails to master his aroused passions, Boomer uses the wit and affected indifference of good form to preserve equanimity. He makes light of the wound and complements in a sportsmanlike way the whale's dexterity. An admirable form of manliness, Melville suggests, lies in masking emotion and using robust conventionality to push forward.[10]

Good form allowed a proper Englishman to block out the feminine, associated with free expression of sentiment. It also excluded from the club of insiders those men who could not learn the proper etiquette, the right demeanor. The parvenu, for example, could buy his way up the ladder but could not acquire "that look of deliberate indifference that I have noticed so many English gentlemen carry about with them—as if, although they are bodily present, their interest in life has been carefully put away at home."[11]

The male portrait that emerges is of someone without emotion who confronts unpleasantness stoically. The danger is that the man can become so removed from his feelings that he is truly coldblooded, a well-groomed machine. General George John Younghusband was concerned to defend the British ruling class against this charge. Take the young imperial administrator: he is "clean-bred, perfectly honest and unbribable," ruling thousands of natives "not by force, but by strength of character and moral rectitude." Some might say this noble fellow is dehumanized by his sterilized outlook: "travellers and new-comers often consider Englishmen in India unsympathetic, even hard and arrogant." But this "is only a superficial view, the Englishman is really the kindest person in the world. . . ."[12]

So there it is: the Englishman rules millions because he is morally clean and hardy. This fastidiousness was reflected in frequent communal bathing, an activity at whose heart was an essential ambivalence. On the surface, strong clean men are getting cleaner. But other, unacknowledged motives are in play. First, as Paul Fussell pointed out, bathing was a symbolic foil to industrial sootiness and the moral smudges of business. Also, men bathing together allowed for an unadmitted sensual sharing. L. E. Jones, a Victorian youth who was shy with girls, found out the meaning of puberty from his tutor with whom he and his brother swam nude in a local pond: "We learnt from him, as we bathed together, stark naked in a sheltered pool, the insignia of manhood. This interested us much. Mr. Meneer was definitely hirsute." Later, at Eton, Jones fagged for and hero-worshipped Sam Cockerell, a sports hero who rowed in the Eight. Jones remembered, "My heart leapt up when Cockerell . . . told me after prayers to put a can of water in his bath. . . ."[13]

Thomas Wentworth Higginson was an American who believed deeply in manliness. According to Francis Parker, a youthful acquaintance, he had "an attraction for younger men, as they had for him, and a great

Men are purified by immersion together in war and water: U.S. troops invade Cuba. (Picture by Howard Chandler Christy, *Leslie's Weekly*, August 28, 1898.)

facility in impressing and influencing them." Higginson appreciated
physical beauty in males, noting of one young man that he was "so handsome in his dark beauty that he seemed like a picturesque oriental."
Higginson said "he was like some fascinating girl." For such a man military service in the Civil War had real compensations in the companionship of males. He thought the satisfactions of men together in regimental
camp "reminiscent of the felicity of Adam before Eve appeared." In writing about his soldiers he said that "I always like to observe them when
bathing." He swam a good deal at night. After one dip he emerged before
a sentry with "not even a rag to which a button by any earthly possibility
could be appended. . . ." The private's coolness in going through the correct military motions amused him. A similar stunt was pulled in the
Great War by three British subalterns who timed their showers to coincide with an inspection by Prime Minister Asquith, "so that we all three
welcomed Asquith dressed only in an identity disk." It doesn't matter
if there was latent homosexuality in such actions. The point is that men
have created an all-male world which is physically, intellectually, and
sensually apart from women.[14]

The importance of rugged masculinity was reflected in the education
of boys. American and British private schools subscribed to the prevailing
idealization of motherhood but involvement with the other gender stopped
at this point. One boy arriving at prep school in 1863 was told that "Before the likes of you—a snivelling little beast—dare try and make friends
with US, you've got to drop Henriette, Aunt Cam., Gramama; all those
stupid old women must be dropped, and jolly quick too!" At Wellington
a dormitory captain stamped on the flowers with which a boy had deco-
rated his room, saying, "There is no room for this rotten effeminate stuff
here."[15]

American and British institutions were not identical in character
or situation: the American never achieved the homogeneity of approach
or exclusive position of the British public schools. But there was much
congruence of mission and message. Both drew faculty who looked askance
at the marketplace and inculcated a traditional view. James McLachlan
said of the American boarding school: "The gentlemanly ideal to which
it has attempted to mold its students has been a conservative one." In
a materialistic world pupils learned "self-restraint, rigid self-control,
severe frugality in personal style. . . ." Boys were encouraged to avoid
a business career. A Groton alumnus recalled that the principal, Endicott
Peabody, repeatedly "urged the boys to go into the professions and keep
away from Wall Street."[16]

In Britain boys from the nouveau riche were absorbed into the public
schools and taught to turn their backs on their fathers. Where capitalism
stressed personal profit and suggested that what was good for the individual was good for society, the schools put group solidarity above personal
advancement and intimated that individual brilliance could well be prob-

lematic. Brilliant types rocked the boat: they produced the change jarring society. So the schools stressed fitting in. Alec Waugh said of the system: "It is inclined to destroy individuality, to turn out a fixed pattern; it wishes to take everyone, no matter what his tastes or ideas might be, and make him conform to its own ideals." A recent study notes that "clever men" are still seen as outsiders who "because of their cleverness are probably dishonourable and possibly cowardly."[17]

Emphasis on the group over the individual stifled the expression of individual feeling, seen as female. Any permitted emotion was focused on the male group. Rupert Wilkinson says, "Even more than the British nation as a whole, the public schoolboy was both reserved and sentimental. Emotional expression he quietly reserved for the group, in other more personal spheres he cultivated the 'thick skin.'" In other words, good form reigned but with occasional outbursts on behalf of the house team or the regiment.[18]

The emphasis on being of service to the group led boys toward lives of public utility. Honor and duty were the goals. "Honour is real manliness, which is able to look every one full in the face; not from the possession of vulgar brass, but from a free conscience that has nothing to fear because there is nothing to hide." So said the distinguished American educator Henry Augustus Coit. In England they sang E. W. Hawson's "Here, Sir!"

> So to-day—and oh! if ever
> Duty's voice is ringing clear,
> Bidding men to brave endeavour,
> Be our answer, "we are here!"[19]

A code that emphasized dedicated self-sacrifice and manliness pointed to a career in the civil service or the military. The British public schools almost became army training colleges. Though they prided themselves on being above vocational training, associated with industry, they acquired Officer Training Corps. A graduate of Wellington recalled: "It was primarily an Army school, purposing to turn out a hardy and dashing breed of young officers." Percival Marling, a Harrow graduate, wrote that at a court-martial in 1881 "the sergeant of the escort was an old Harrovian, one of the witnesses had been at Eton, the President of the court-martial had been at Charterhouse, and the prisoner had been, I think at Westminster, and the orderly to the court at Winchester."[20]

In addition to West Point, the United States sprouted military schools throughout the nineteenth century, and there was a distinct toughness to boys' training. Augustus Kinsley Gardner, a medical writer, advocated military schools for boys, saying that many parents "seem to forget that a boy without a true, noble, manly character had far better be dead." He thought "there are too many like ancient Greeks, that will not permit their sons to get into the water until they have learnt to swim. They are not willing that their sons should have guns, until they have learned to use them." In their boys' book *Hero Tales from American History* Henry Cabot Lodge and Theodore Roosevelt wrote that "America will cease to be a great nation whenever her young men cease to possess energy, daring, and endurance, as well as the wish and the power to fight the nation's foes."[21]

Patrick Howarth's study of adolescent literature points to a consistent pattern in the genre: heroes are clean-cut, tough but sportsmanlike, they eschew money and women. Sanders of the River, the creation of Edgar Wallace, says he has "no use for women any way," though he respects them as mothers. In *Dr. Fu-Manchu* by Sax Rohmer, the hero Noyland Smith comments to his sidekick, Dr. Petrie, who is susceptible to female charms, "A woman made a fool of me once, but I learned my lesson. . . . If you are determined to go to pieces on the rock that broke up Adam, do so! But don't involve me in the wreck." In *The River Pirates* by Herbert Strong, an adventure tale about English schoolboys, there are no women at all. All the tales take place away from the complexities and commercialism of modern culture.[22]

The books reflected the authors, men like R. M. Ballantyne who was exceptionally shy with girls and, like William Gladstone, accosted prostitutes for Christ. He wrote that "boys are intended to encounter all kinds of risks in order to prepare them to meet and grapple with the risks and dangers incident to a man's career with cool, cautious self-possession." G. Manville Fenn, the Victorian biographer of popular writer G. A. Henty, said that "there was nothing namby-pamby in Henty's writings," and he "never made his works sickly by the introduction of what an effeminate writer would term the tender passion." Henty was apparently like his characters: not very introspective, physically brave, fastidious. He was "an ideal comrade—a brave man, amiable, happy in temper, straightforward, and ready at a pinch to dare danger to the very death."[23]

The production of boys' books reflects an absorption in children's moral training which permeated the period. The comparative abundance of the times kept privileged children out of the job market. Their productive labor was not needed and their parents could afford to keep them in school longer. Childhood was extended; we could say invented. And just as motherhood was a subject of analysis, so childhood became a topic for serious study. Moreover, just as motherhood was associated with purity because it was out of the public sphere, so childhood became a beacon of innocence shining forth amidst adult murk. One English educator said that aping adult patterns "is a tendency which in a schoolboy should be strongly checked" and to this end "the period of boyhood pastimes has been prolonged for as long as possible."[24]

It was hoped that childhood innocence might help to overcome some social evils. Harvey Green notes that in American Victorian literature children are increasingly the saviors of adults. The preservation of this innocence into maturity became a major aim. This meant keeping the sexes apart. But that raised the twin specters of masturbation and homosexuality. According to Harold Nicolson, "so convinced were the authorities that Satan was lying in wait for any unoccupied little boy, that some precise occupation was devised for every hour." Prefects told boys that if they masturbated they would go blind or mad. Boys' publications chimed in. Sir Robert Anderson told in one magazine about an Eton boy who went insane after masturbating over an obscene photograph flashed by a scoundrel in a railway carriage.[25]

This harrying put tremendous pressure on children. A few even mutilated themselves to avoid sexuality. The tragedy was that in striving to preserve innocence and youth, each child was fated to lose. One could grow up a virgin but one had to grow up anyway and to be adult was by definition to enter the corrupt world. Perhaps it was best to die before losing youth's bloom. An old student said of Principal Coit that "it was the strength of innocence for which he strove in himself and in his boys." His ideal image was of the boy who died "never knowing any other life but the growth in loving obedience." Child suicides increased and adolescents might never shake guilt about their thoughts or bodies. Ian Hamilton remained haunted by the features of his headmaster torturing him into admission that the boys used bad words: "The face of a clergyman changing into that of a werewolf which, in one second, could bury its fangs in the throat of a child."[26]

Here is a paradox: children were held up as crucial to society's salvation yet were also harassed and frequently ill-treated. They could respond with similarly ambivalent feelings. Adolescents often embraced the importance accorded their role in theory while resenting the adults who dictated their lives in fact. If the nineteenth century invented childhood, it devised the generation gap also. Frances Trollope saw the point. In a clash between father and son in one of her novels, the senior denounces "the presumptuous folly of self-sufficient young men, who must needs proclaim themselves to be better and wiser than their fathers. . . ." Herman Melville observed the behavior of midshipmen who had a "boyish and overweening conceit of their gold lace." They bullied the sailors. "It would almost seem that they themselves, having so recently escaped the posterior discipline of the nursery and infant school, are impatient to recover from those smarting reminiscences by mincing the backs of full-grown American freemen."[27]

Childish conceit was made inevitable by the aims of Victorian education. When the thrust of education is to promote change and improvement in society, the concentration and energy of the child are directed toward external problems. But when the goal is only to preserve what is, then the energy turns inward upon itself and becomes narcissistic. This led to an unfortunate equation: children had a growing self-importance and yet, due to sheltering from adulthood, they were increasingly immature. Douglas MacArthur said of his classmates at West Point: "They were thrust out into the world a man in age, but as experienced as a high school boy. They were cloistered almost to a monastic extent." If their society entered a crisis, these young people might not have the maturity to help avoid a tragedy.[28]

The army, like the academy, sheltered males against the worlds of business and women. The officer corps of the western nations made up the most exclusive male social club in the world. Commitment to woman was replaced by loyalty to the military unit. "'The regiment' is mother, sister and mistress" wrote General Sir Garnet Wolseley. Reluctance to engage with women partly reflected a notion that family ties damaged a soldier professionally. Sir Henry Lawrence held "that soldiers have no business to marry; under the idea that anxiety for their wives' welfare and safety often induces men to hesitate to run risks which they would otherwise cheerfully undergo." Colonel St. Leger Grenfell, on the staff of Confederate General John Hunt Morgan, believed that marriage robbed the sharp edge from his chief, saying that "Morgan was enervated by matrimony, and would never be the same man as he was."[29]

Some soldiers were naturally clumsy with females. "I am no use at all with women," admitted General Dunsterville. General Ulysses S. Grant said he only lost his presence of mind "when thrown in strange company, particularly of ladies." Colonel Robert Gould Shaw, forced to address a gathering of ladies, was petrified: "I was brought forward to the slaughter in a terrible perspiration," he wrote.[30]

Soldiers' discomfort with the opposite sex mirrored that of the society at large. It is striking that a large number of prominent military men came out of relationships with strong mothers. General Sir Horace Smith-Dorrien remembered his father as a nice but disinterested man who probably rarely "entertained hope of my ever becoming a useful member of society. ..." On the other hand, his mother was "a wonderful woman of strong personality, full of activity to within a few days of her death. ..." Evelyn Wood's mother was a powerful figure who influenced the children more than did the father. It was "my mother, to whom I owe any good qualities I may possess. ...." Basil Liddell Hart, looking back in 1924, spoke of the supreme power of mothers in molding the character of the race. "How gifted in this respect were the women who inspired us in boyhood to a sense of the nobler and more spiritual aims of life." Such a woman was Lady Randolph Churchill, of whom Winston wrote, "My mother always seemed to me a fairy princess: a radiant being possessed of limitless riches and power." Idealization of motherhood permeated soldiers' language. When Dwight D. Eisenhower described the sanctity of the honor code of West Point he "likened it to the virtue of a man's mother."[31]

The mother could exert great pressure on a young man. Douglas MacArthur's wrote to him at West Point:

Like mother, like son, is saying so true;
The world will judge largely of mother by you.
Be this then your task, if task it shall be
To force this proud world to do homage to me.

Mother's demands could evoke a sinister image in the male mind. In World War I Arthur Conan Doyle saw a great gun called Mother, "which sat squat and black, amid twenty of her grimy children who waited upon her and fed her."[32]

Men could feel like slaves to mothers holding captive the male ego. L. E. Jones, who became a cavalryman, resented being forced to bow to his mother's will. She dominated the children and servants, even her husband: "There were two minds with but a single thought, but the thought was hers." Later, she interfered with his developing interest in girls. If he tried to strike up a conversation with one, he saw "the stiff, indifferent poker-face imposed upon me by my mother's company." Trips to art galleries were only permitted "provided her grown-up son averted his eyes, as she averted hers, from the occasional nude goddesses. . . ."[33]

Those who gave prime emotional allegiance to the mother could find that this alienated them from other women. The poet Wilfred Owen, his mother's favorite child, was possessive of her and could not break away to form close contacts with girls of his age. Baden-Powell's father died young, leaving his mother to raise the children. The boy never outgrew his mother-love. In the Matabele campaign of 1896, aged thirty-nine, he kept a diary for her as he needed a daily talk still. Other women scarcely concerned him. He married late, at fifty-five, a woman whose gait (while walking a spaniel) he admired.[34]

Distance from women could come from their inability to measure up to the idealized mother figure; from a rejection of sexual thoughts about women which, for mother-fixated men, could be incestuous; and from a fear that closeness to the mother meant the son was effeminate. A man might reject women and seek out males to reinforce his sense of masculinity. Perhaps some officers who idolized their mothers needed to affirm their maleness through killing. George Cabot Lodge was not close to his eminent father, Senator Henry Cabot Lodge, who awed the boy and was too often absent to be a companion. George was nearer his mother but this made him worry that he could not make it in a male world. He confessed to his mother, "I do so want to do something that will last—some man's work in the world,—that I am constantly depressed by an awful dread that perhaps I shan't be able to." He had also "my crying inability to adapt myself to my time and become a moneymaker." He found a place in the male milieu as a naval cadet in the Spanish-

American War. In his *Poems*, written at this time, woman appears as the supreme consoler but also as a danger for she uses "love's euthanasy" to lure the hero from his true role in mortal combat.[35]

Herbert Kitchener, Britain's leading soldier after 1900, rejected female companionship. He adored his mother, who was the strong parent, her husband depending heavily on her. When her son became Earl Kitchener of Khartoum in 1899, he chose as his second title her birthplace. No other women entered his life and at times he even objected to having married officers in his command. Though he chose bright, handsome young aides, he probably didn't have homosexual relations. He practiced a regimen of strict self-denial. "The development and elevation of the character of a people depends mainly on the growth of self-control and the power to dominate natural impulses," he wrote. This self-discipline had a price: Kitchener became unfeeling. Arthur Conan Doyle, who knew him in Africa, said Kitchener was "inhuman in his cool accuracy." When told that an accidental dynamite explosion had killed forty workers, Kitchener asked, "Do you need more dynamite?"[36]

John Nicholson was less cool. He was deeply attached to his mother and allowed no other woman in his life. According to Michael Edwards in *Bound to Exile* (1969) he was a repressed homosexual who was disgusted by his inclination and sought release in manic violence. He could not conceive of sexual relations with the female, the angel mother. The thought of Indian mutineers killing, even touching, white women made him frenzied. He advocated "the flaying alive, impalement, or burning of the murderers of the women and children at Delhi." It may have been a blessing when Nicholson was killed, for he was mentally unbalanced.[37]

Padraic Pearse was a leader of the 1916 Easter rebellion in Ireland and his case is worth a brief digression. Deeply attached to his mother, Pearse could not embrace female sexuality. When a friend commented on a girl's legs in a musical review, he replied lamely, "They were the limbs of an angel." Perhaps because sexuality made him feel unclean, he made a fetish of purity. He neither drank nor smoked and encouraged the Irish Volunteers to avoid women. In some ways he remained a child and he celebrated children. William Irwin Thompson says, "Throughout his plays, poems, and stories, he celebrates children and fools, for in them he is steadfastly resisting maturity."[38]

Pearse left a legal career to open a school. Here he taught boys to die for Ireland. "Bloodshed is a cleansing and sanctifying thing," he said, "and the nation which regards it as the final horror has lost its manhood." In his cause, Pearse pursued a fiercer love than that of woman, "the sharp, transfiguring love of death." In his poem "Renunciation" he turns away from the beauty of woman, "And I blinded my eyes / For fear I should fail," in order that he may go "To the deed that I see / And the death I shall die."[39]

William Butler Yeats helped to sow the seeds of rebellion with his play *Cathleen ni Houlihan*, in which Mother Ireland calls on her sons to leave their wives and free Eire. Later in life Yeats was troubled by the violence; in the rebel leadership he saw a fanaticism fed by single-minded love of the cause where love of woman should have been: they "have suffered through the cultivation of hatred as the one energy of their movement, a deprivation which is the intellectual equivalent to a certain surgical operation." They had castrated themselves. No wonder that a woman said, of a rebel she knew, that under fire "I have never seen him look happier—he was like a bride at a wedding."[40]

Male disjunction from the female could lead to overt masculinity expressed in violence. When the British took Pearse out to be shot, his regret was in parting from his mother; his joy was in the words written over his schoolhouse door:

I care not if my life have only the span of a night and day
If my deeds be spoken of by the men of Ireland.[41]

THREE | Male Games

In 1898 the United States engaged in a sporting little contest with Spain and Britain admired the manly spirit of the Dervishes slaughtered at Omdurman. That same year, Stephen Crane published "The Bride Comes to Yellow Sky." In this tale there appear to be three main characters, two males and a female, but it is really about the relationship between the men; the woman is an intrusion.

Jack Potter, marshal of Yellow Sky, has just taken the drastic step of marrying without consulting his cronies who have a large stake in such a public figure as the peace officer. His bride "was not pretty, nor was she young," and "it was quite apparent that she had cooked and that she expected to cook." Jack Potter has settled for humdrum domesticity. This makes him the butt of humor to other men on the train to Yellow Sky, who "covered them with stares of derisive enjoyment."[1]

Scratchy Wilson waits in Yellow Sky. He is a survivor from the open west before steam tractors and traveling salesmen, a holdout against modernity. Scratchy goes on drunken sprees, shooting up the town. Then he and Potter engage: the marshal "fights Scratchy when he gets on one of these tears." This violent game is central to both men and so neither ends it by killing the other. Wilson is an expert gunman; "the long revolvers in his hands were as easy as straws." Yet Potter isn't touched and he has only "shot Wilson up once—in the leg," seemingly almost by accident.[2]

Now Potter has spoiled things by introducing a woman into the sanctum of male values, the game arena. When Scratchy comes to fight, only to find that the marshal is unarmed on his wedding day, Scratchy is lost, "like a creature allowed a glimpse of another world." "I s'pose it's all off now," he gasps, and trudges away. Scratchy's world centered on the rejection of woman and modernity. He lived for violent games.[3]

Games played a prominent role in the lives of many nineteenth-century men. Leading activities included rugby, polo, cricket, American football, hunting and shooting. Games provided physical exercise. But they also divided the leisured and privileged from the workers. They excluded women from a self-sufficient male milieu. And they gave meaning and sharpness to lives which often had little focus. For some men who were divorced from their emotions, aggressive physical encounters with other men and animals became a primary form of communication. As the educational anthropologist Jules Henry commented, "All cultures offer through prescribed channels, some outlet for the emotional problems they create." Victorian games were such a channel.[4]

The games encouraged in childhood training were largely team sports, though a proper English education included rabbit-shooting ("if they are to be an ornament to their country 'tis surely wise to take measures to develop their instincts for slaughter," said Alice James) and American boys quickly learned gun-handling. British headmasters increasingly valued sports so that by the 1860s they were prominent in the curriculum. Only sportsmen got ahead at Eton, said one old boy. "It would have been good," he thought, "if boys of intelligence, wit and originality, however inept at games, had been allowed to achieve prominence and leadership." E. C. Wickham, head at Wellington, told a father concerned that his boy should be studying more and playing less: "I look on his present purpose of getting into the eleven as, in itself, a considerable part of his education here." His parents should "not vex themselves that he does not work *very* hard while he is cricketting." George F.-H. Berkeley, a Wellington alumnus, defended the accent on sports as a valuable teaching aid, saying that a boy could only respect a master who "was as good a man as he was at the game he loved best."[5]

The absorption in organized sport which dominates American school life began before 1900. James McLachlan says: "In American colleges and secondary schools by the turn of the century organized athletics—particularly football—almost buried all other aspects of school life." Civil War veterans, convinced that physical testing made men, boosted the trend. General Francis Walker said that the student of his youth had been a sickly, moody fellow. He "not infrequently mistook physical lassitude for intellectuality, and the gnawings of dyspepsia for spiritual cravings. He would have gravely distrusted his mission and calling had he found himself at any time playing ball." Sports cured this: on the playing field "patriotism and public spirit is developed" to offset "the selfish, individualistic tendencies of the age." Henry H. Arnold, a 1907 graduate of West Point, remembered a lack of academic pressure: "I had time to play football . . . the polo squad, place in the shotput at interclass track meets, and with the rest of the Cavalry fanatics ride furiously. . . ."[6]

Sports offset the less desirable tendencies of industrial culture. Amateur games demanded leisure and thus reproved those who labored too hard for gain. Sports occurred in fields away from sooty factories. "When fathers of families saw huge towns suddenly springing up around them they said: soon every Englishman will be a townsman; the race is losing its virility. Our only hope lies in fostering out-of-door sports and games." Cities corrupted. "Anything that will help to counteract the disintegrating forces of city life," said Professor Richards of Yale, "is to be welcomed as an ally of the best education. I maintain that the system of athletics existing at our colleges and athletics clubs . . . does this."[7]

What seemed missing in modern life was a responsible attitude that put the public good above private profit. Team sports looked like a solution because, to win, the individual had to subordinate himself to the group. True, games did not build knowledge, but if this were not the end, if civic character was the aim, then they were as good as if not better than scholarship. Endicott Peabody of Groton "instinctively trusted a football player more than a non-football player, just as the boys did." Edward Bowen, a Harrow master, asserted in 1884 that "I had rather regenerate England with the football elevens than with average members of Parliament."[8]

Given the determination to keep boys sexually innocent, games appealed also as a physical outlet. J. A. Mangan comments that "the elements of sexual identity and legitimate sensuality are inseparable from the worship of games during the period under discussion. To be manly was a condition that exuded the physical, but, at the same time, it was an asexual physicality extended into early manhood in which sexual experience and knowledge were taboo." Augustus Kinsley Gardner urged athletics upon men and boys to control sexual impulses. Urbanites in particular were warned that "the imperfect air and light of the city, coupled with the city-dweller's dangerously stimulating food and inaptness for exercise, encouraged one to pour out energy in sexual excess, which in turn merely worsened appetites and derangement." In the sweeter air of Groton, Endicott Peabody rejoiced that athletics kept "pure and clean and righteous living in the school."[9]

Underlying the educational veneration of sports was a dubious philosophy: thoughts do not necessarily shape acts, but acts can and do shape thoughts. "You cannot have a firm will without firm muscles," said American psychologist G. Stanley Hall. Kicking a ball can make a people moral. "Action fills a nobler sphere of being than . . . thinking," said Yale President Timothy Dwight. Thus the answer to multifaceted problems could be the application of a formula based on the rules of the game. In Harold Begbie's book for boys, *The Story of Baden-Powell*, sports are a paradigm for life. Three officers killed at Mafeking "had run a great race." Baden-Powell holding that city against the Boers is "the intrepid Goal-Keeper." He is an educational paragon: a leading sportsman but not too bright, "a hero but no prodigy," a fellow who despises "a fast, raking life," and who always says, "Play the game, play that your side may win."[10]

This sounds wholesome, yet boys are being told not to think for themselves and that physical toughness beats mental acumen. In the boy's world there is no place for the sensitive, unaggressive child. Shelley was hounded at Eton for refusing to fight. In R. M. Freeman's 1891 story *Steady and Strong*, the headmaster states: "I want each of my boys to

Allardyce had raced through.

The race across the rugby goal line prepares youth for the struggle across No Man's Land—for many, their last team effort. (P. G. Wodehouse, *The White Feather*. London: Adam & Charles Black, 1907. Courtesy of the Lilly Library, Indiana University, Bloomington, Indiana.)

be foremost in braving pain and facing danger, to take a licking without flinching, to stop the most violent rush at football. . . . to 'funk' nothing." Theodore Roosevelt told a college audience: "As I emphatically disbelieve in seeing Harvard, or any other college, turn out molly-coddles instead of vigorous men I may add I do not in the least object to a sport because it is rough." Such accents brutalized boys, crushed sensitivity and independent thought.[11]

Sports maintained a central place in the adult lives of educated males. Hunting to hounds was popular, and almost obsessive among the British officer corps. General E. A. H. Alderson commented at the end of the Matabele campaign of 1896: "I had thus hunted in June, fought till the end of November, and then taken hounds again. What more could a soldier possibly want?" Put another way, he had the pleasure of killing through half a year. General Lyttelton subtitled his autobiography "Soldiering, Politics, Games." He told the story of an eager officer who went to see "the great Holman Hunt picture," hoping to see a meet, but was disappointed to find "a picture of our Lord riding on a donkey," by Hunt the artist. He "had not felt his time and money quite wasted, as somebody was riding something."[12]

Riding to hounds was traditional to the upper echelons of society. Alexis de Tocqueville said that the southern planter, despising labor, turned to games and soldiering: "he covets wealth much less than pleasure and excitement; and the energy which his neighbor devotes to gain turns with him to a passionate love of field sports and military exercises . . ." In like vein, *Punch* commented that cavalry's role in war was "to give tone to what would otherwise be merely a vulgar brawl."[13]

The other great male game was shooting. The number of animals killed on a shoot could be astonishing. General Wolseley and party once killed over 900 game; his gun shoulder was black and blue. In two days' shooting, Percival Marling and six others bagged 991 game. Americans too hunted as though at war with nature. In 1871 General Philip Sheridan and party undertook a western hunt, escorted by two companies of cavalry. They killed 600 buffalo, 200 elk, and many smaller animals.[14]

India and Africa were great playgrounds for sportsmen. Here British officers had "pig-sticking, antelope, duck, snipe, and quail shooting," as General George Richard Greaves recalled. He admitted that "I thought very little about Britain's affairs in those days, I was so busy with my shooting and fishing and the hounds and cricket, racquets, and what not." Pig-sticking was a popular but cruel sport whose aim was to spear the creature. Clean kills were difficult. "I can recollect one very foggy morning when Wilson's hands and mine were so frozen that we could not drive our spears home hard enough to do much harm, and it took us about twenty thrusts to kill," said General Francis Howard. He once killed ten boars in a day. "It is a grand sport," said Field Marshal Lord Birdwood. "The more you do of it, the more strongly it seems to grip you."[15]

The West tugged at the imaginations of young American gentlemen like Francis Parkman, Richard Henry Dana, and Rufus Sage of Connecticut, who in 1841 set out for three years' adventure trapping in the west. Inevitably, the British turned up there too. In 1869 the Earl of Dunraven dragged his bride out to the frontier on their honeymoon, as "he had always dreamed of going to the western United States because of the exciting tales he had heard." To exploit this traffic, dude ranching developed, offering visitors a home while they roamed and slaughtered.[16]

The wilds provided an escape from modernity. Douglas MacArthur was depressed when in 1890 he left Oklahoma for Washington. "It was my first glimpse at that whirlpool of glitter and pomp, of politics and diplomacy, of statesmanship and intrigue. I found it no substitute for the color and excitement of the frontier West." In *The Rogue Elephant*, Elliott Whitney described a hunting party readying itself for the bush: "The luxuries of civilization, where everything was done for them, soon grew monotonous. When they had gone over their beloved guns, oiling every inch, and received instructions for the use of the few simple medicines taken along, there was little to do." Normal life is reduced to monotony between shoots.[17]

This is the perennial appeal of Huck Finn, the male desire to pushoff and leave the complexities of organized society behind. Likewise, Rip Van Winkle wandering off into the mountains with gun and dog (where he observes magical men playing magical games). Both Huck and Rip are escaping from women, as were some sportsmen. "All the explorers and big game hunters that I have known have been what you call solitary men," said Baden-Powell. More bluntly, Mervyn Herbert, a Balliol man, allowed no women on shooting trips because he "was passing through a phase of hostility toward young women, whom he regarded as spoilsports. . . ." The violence of male sports guaranteed the exclusion of women and also that the feminine in man would be muted. "This vaunted age," said an American boxing fan in 1888, needed "a saving touch of honest, old-fashioned barbarism, that when we come to die, we shall die leaving men behind us, and not a race of eminently respectable female saints."[18]

J. F. C. Fuller believed that sports kept the British officer corps physically and morally clean. They also enhanced professional skills: "Our English games & sports create a quick eye & what is more essential to an officer than this." Sports as war games had many promoters. Men and boys felt that they were in training, keeping themselves steely-limbed for some great violent test. The *Cheltonian*, a school magazine, asked "How many a charge through the ranks of the foe / Have been made by a warrior who years ago / Hurried the leather from hand to hand?" "Battlefield seems the right word," said popular author Anthony Hope, observing American football in 1903. "The defensive armour worn by the combatants . . . had a grim appearance; and a row of substitutes sat in readiness to take the place of any comrade killed or wounded in the battle. . . ." Football, said Raymond G. Gettell of Amherst, afforded a chance for "physical combat" and satisfied the "primitive lust for battle," while also training the would-be leader through "organization, cooperation, and the skilled interrelation of individual effort directed to a common purpose."[19]

A comprehensive case for sports was put by British General E. A. H. Alderson, who pronounced that "I honestly do not know of *any* instance of a good sportsman not being a good *active* service officer." Fox hunting was most beneficial for the young officer because "it can continue to educate him in a way that nothing else, except actual experience of active service, or work under conditions very nearly akin to those of active service, can possibly do." In hunting, "the handling of horses cultivates the qualities required for the handling of men" because "boldness, judgment, and self-reliance are required to lead them successfully, just as they are to ride horses properly." Hunting also developed courage, for at the huntsman's cry "the funkers pale, and the 'right sort' glow as they do at the sound of battle."[20]

Writing in 1900, Alderson had to admit that barbed wire had made hunting and soldiering more difficult: it was a new "fence" for the rider. Also "prominent among the new 'fences' which the soldier has to face are an effective shrapnel shell, smokeless powder, the magazine rifle with a flat trajectory, a perfected machine gun, high explosives, and quick-firing guns." So the general was schooled in new developments. But this was his answer: "It is only by having resolute men fully imbued with the all-important 'get on' feeling . . . that we can hope to win." The "get on" spirit came from hunting. Modern smokeless weapons, fired from cover, "will try the soldier's nerves much as the suspected presence of wires in the fences tries those of the rider across country." But the practiced man will come through: nerve will allow flesh to triumph over steel.[21]

Whatever the intrinsic merits of hunting, their specific application by Alderson to the European military situation of 1900 made no sense; charging ahead against barbed wire and machine guns was anachronistic. Alderson exhibited professional dyslexia of social origins. Basic was an educational system that substituted a simple formula (in sport and in life, said the General, "the only safe thing to do is to *always play the game*") for preparedness to match new solutions to new problems. Herbert Branston Gray, an educational critic, noted that the public schools turned out "a useless drone trained only to wield a willow or kick a bladder," a harsh charge but one with foundation. The sporting ethic was part of an anti-intellectual milieu in which World War One was possible because the formula did not provide any vehicle for questioning the validity of the game.[22]

The sporting ethic also helped to make war feasible by failing in its central claim: it did not produce true sportsmanship always. The accent on hunting, killing, and beating could produce insensitivity to suffering. Violence permeates the literature of the period, from children's books that stress aggression to the private writings of polished adults. Beating people is normal. If a worker on a military railway crossed Lieutenant G. A. Henty, "a muscular athletic English gentleman," he would "give the scoundrel, to the intense delight of the lookers on, a thoroughly solid and manly thrashing." Theodore Roosevelt retained his own boxer in the White House. He enjoyed killing animals, telling his children how he finished a cougar by "thrusting the knife you loaned me right into his heart. I have always wished to kill a cougar as I did this one, with dogs and the knife." Roosevelt was said to be "not in the least sensitive about killing any number of men if there is an adequate reason." George Armstrong Custer told his wife how his dogs had broken every bone in a wolf's body: "Each time they closed their powerful jaws I could hear the bones crunch as if within a vice." The trophies of death adorned hunting rooms everywhere. When General Francis Howard retired in 1907, he mounted 200 animal heads in his home and sold 600 more.[23]

Sport included the maiming and killing of people. Howard remembered fondly a prizefight between Tom Sayers and "Heenan the Bernicia Boy" which left Heenan blind. Baden-Powell mounted as a trophy the club of a native he killed, alongside a photograph of the body. Major William Hodson, a hero of the Indian Mutiny, was "a beautiful swordsman, he never failed to kill his man." He played cat-and-mouse with opponents, "laughing, parrying most fearful blows, as calmly as if he were brushing off flies, calling out all the time, 'Why, try again now,' 'What's that?' 'Do you call yourself a swordsman?'"[24]

What makes this unfeeling possible is a blurring between sport and war, so that the killing of men can be sloughed off as tribute to athletic prowess. The enemy, reduced to a hunting quarry, is stripped of humanity, leaving the killer free to destroy without guilt. "War is a business as natural to man as hunting," said Virginia soldier David Hunter Strother. "Man the peace lover is simply a poltroon and coward. Roll your drums, flaunt your banners, and advance to the battlefield."[25]

Language merging sport and war characterized the military vocabulary. William O. Gulick, an Iowa cavalryman in the Civil War, described hunting guerrillas as "the best game I ever saw." J. E. B. Stuart's men saw chasing Union cavalry as "a fox chase." "It was rather like pig-sticking" said a lancer after the 1884 Suakin campaign. "Most excellent pig-sticking ... the bag being about sixty," said an officer after a Boer War charge (the pun on Boer and boar was inevitable). "I've been snipe-shooting, and got five of 'em," said an officer after killing Fuzzie-Wuzzies. Erskine Childers, a gunner going into action against Boers, had "the same sort of feeling that one has while waiting to start for a race, only with an added chill and thrill." Exchanging battery fire was "a game of skill" and a near-hit was "an excellent running shot for the sportsman who fired it."[26]

Why did otherwise civilized men enjoy killing? Dearth of intellectual stimulation and the crude physicality of manliness kept some emotionally immature. This was evidenced in a penchant for insensitive practical jokes. General Custer, a veteran prankster, "with rollicking glee worthy of a school-boy," pegged a box on top of a sleeping man to enjoy his terror upon waking up buried alive. General Freyberg, when a junior officer on the western front, as "a glorious joke" made his sergeant-major stand about the trench line with a placarded message for the enemy. Also he "picked up a particularly dangerous German bomb which fell into the trench unexploded, and marched off to headquarters with it; much to the amusement of everyone, except H. Q. itself."[27]

These antics represented attempts at expression by men without more developed communications skills. Male education in Britain and America emphasized strict adherence to forms of behavior, suppression of feeling, action over thought. Little that was spontaneous or original was allowed, save in games. These became a primary emotional as well as physical outlet; killing, with its intense feeling, became the most climactic sensation of all. Continually, men who killed referred to the felt excitement. Battle, said General John Younghusband, was "more exciting than any of our schoolboy games." Custer kept as a trophy the sword of a rebel officer he pursued to the kill. It was "the most exciting sport I ever engaged in."[28]

Whether "killing rats with a terrier, rejoicing in a prize fight, playing a salmon, or potting Dervishes," killing "is a big factor in the joy of living" said Oxford don Ernest Bennett. "Man shooting is the finest sport of all" announced General Wolseley. "There is a certain amount of infatuation about it, that the more you kill the more you wish to kill." "I have had more enjoyment, a more vivid sense of the delight of living, with every faculty at full stretch, when pursuing and killing birds and beasts, than in any other activity," wrote L. E. Jones.[29]

The feeling toward the gun, the killing piece, sometimes became sensual: "To sniff the little wisps of smoke that oozed from the breech as I broke the gun to re-load" made it "good to be alive that winter morning, in the Old Square Wood, and to see the rabbit turn head over heels, stone dead. . . ." "Such a sweet little thing, . . . lovely smooth-working locks; in fact a perfect beauty," said General Greaves, describing his shotgun like a lover. "I remember how my heart began to beat" when he sighted a rare makhor. He killed it; "my elation can be imagined."[30]

One of the few to recognize the underlying emotional dynamics of killing was Ernest Crosby, an American lawyer. Leo Tolstoy turned him against war and he became an advocate of peaceful arbitration between disputing nations. He wrote *Captain Jinks: Hero*, a satirical attack on the American war with Spain. In it he also took a couple of swipes at

British officers. One says, "I didn't object to pig-sticking in South Africa [killing Boers], and I believe that man-hunting is the best of all sports. . . ." Another character remarks upon the short cut of the officers' mess jackets, ending above the buttocks: "Convenient for spanking, I suppose." Spanking, a popular sexual practice of the period, is often associated with homosexuality. The masochism of the infliction can be explained as guilt and a need to be punished. But, as female prostitutes often did the beating, it may also be related to mother fixation. The mother is the earliest authority figure and the first to administer discipline to the child; it is fitting that she should spank the culprit while also giving illicit sexual pleasure. Whatever the needs fulfilled, spanking reflected a violent, inarticulate form of expression, like killing.[31]

Ultimately, violence was an effort at communication. Richard Slotkin, who studied violence on the early American frontier, said: "Aggression was not just a rupture but a relationship, serving men who could not express mutual affection more openly and vulnerably." This is the bond between Marshal Potter and Scratchy Wilson. Union Colonel Higginson said: "Yonder loitering gray-back leading his horse to water in the farthest distance, makes one thrill with a desire to hail him, to shoot at him, to capture him, to do anything to bridge this inexorable dumb space that lies between."[32]

War became a Victorian game and, like other sports, it provided some men with a missing sense of vitality and community. This helped to make the enthusiasms of August 1914 possible. "For war by any other name," ran a patriotic song of that time, "is just another British game."

PART | II

WAR AND MALE
FULFILLMENT

Undergraduates regularly describe Stephen Crane's *The Red Badge of Courage* (1895) as the first modern antiwar novel in English. Though hallowed by repetition, this opinion misreads the viewpoint underlying the text. It fails to acknowledge that Henry Fleming, the hero, is made a man through war.

Students believe that the book is antiwar because it is relatively realistic in its depiction of battle and they assume that a writer would only describe slaughter to condemn it. Crane did present war candidly, as in this description of a wounded man dying: "He was invaded by a creeping strangeness that slowly enveloped him. For a moment the tremor of his legs caused him to dance a sort of hideous hornpipe. His arms beat wildly about his head in expression of implike enthusiasm." In Victorian fiction and art, the dying usually lay down as if to sleep. The dead did not become food for worms, save in a poetic way. Crane gave the lice real bodies and colors. Henry, coming unexpectedly upon a dead soldier, finds that "the eyes, staring at the youth, had changed to the dull hue to be seen on the side of a dead fish. The mouth was open. Its red had changed to an appalling yellow. Over the gray skin of the face ran little ants. One was trundling some sort of a bundle along the upper lip."[1]

Character is also portrayed naturally in many ways. Crane studies the psychology of fear as exhibited by the soldiers. They sweat, they get crabby, they become ridiculous. When the young lieutenant is hit in the foot, he does not strike a heroic pose but, as a man used to swearing, he "produced from a hidden receptacle of his mind new and portentous oaths suited to the emergency."[2]

Some critics have supported the antiwar argument. In searching the book for Crane's larger philosophy of life, they see the battlefield in abstract terms as a symbolic plane upon which the forces of good and evil grapple. R. W. Stallman thinks that "Crane's book is not about the combat of armies; it is about the self-combat of a youth who fears and stubbornly resists change, and the actual battle is symbolic of this spiritual warfare against change and growth." If the battle is only symbolic, we can avoid the uncomfortable thought that Crane saw fulfillment through war. The problem is, however, that Crane modeled the action on a specific battle, Chancellorsville, May 1863. Why go to this trouble if the battle is only a backcloth?[3]

The fact is that *The Red Badge* is about how boys achieve manhood by facing violence. Why else would Crane choose the title of the novel, which bluntly states that men earn the prideful badge of courage through fighting? When the soldiers of Henry's regiment beat back a particularly strong rebel attack, they felt a special self-respect: "They gazed about them with looks of uplifted pride, feeling new trust in the grim, always confident weapons in their hands." Crane states simply, "And they were men."[4]

Shortly after the book appeared, an incisive review was penned by George Wyndham, British Under Secretary for War and a professional soldier. Wyndham felt that Crane saw war as the great tester of men and he cautioned against being misled by the vivid accuracy of the battle scenes. "The terrible things in war are not always terrible; the nauseating things do not always sicken. On the contrary, it is even these which sometimes lift the soul to heights from which they become invisible." There are many, he says, "to whom danger is a strong wine," and for these men battle is the ultimate expression of life, the equivalent of motherhood for women. "The woman in love, the man in battle, may each say, for their moment, . . . 'I was made perfect too.'"[5]

Henry, Crane tells us, is a boy who dreams of war. The church bells tolling news of battle "made him shiver in a prolonged ecstacy of excitement." By joining up he wants to be a hero to his mother (his father is already dead). This role proves disappointing. Mother fusses about him wearing fresh socks and not getting into bad company. "It had not been quite what he had expected, and he had borne it with an air of irritation. He departed feeling vague relief." Important as she is, the mother is stifling, doesn't grasp male joy, and is best left behind. After a brief pause to be admired by girls at the railroad depot, Henry is whisked off into the world of men.[6]

His first exposure to the military is deflating. He endures months of drilling and daydreams of sword-waving glory dissipate. Battle too is not as Henry had imagined. It is anonymous mass slaughter produced by modern technology, in which he felt "he was in a moving box." Were Crane's story truly antiwar, it might end here. But it continues. "The youth perceived that the time had come. He was about to be measured." This is the great trial by battle, and the boy fails. He runs away. But he receives a second chance through his red badge of courage which allows him to reenter the company of men. At this crucial moment of rebirth, Henry appropriately thinks about his mother and about his male friends engaged in the ritual of bathing together. "He saw his clothes in disorderly array upon the grass of the bank. He felt the swash of the fragrant water on his body." These associations, like the red badge, are at the heart of life.[7]

From this point, Crane intimates, Henry "was now what he called a hero." "He had slept and, awakening, found himself a knight." Knights belong to the revival of chivalry, part of the Victorian positive view of war. In the final fights, the men of the regiment, and Henry in particular, are transcendent in battle. "It is a temporary but sublime absence of selfishness," a passion "tuned in strange keys that can arouse the dullard and the stoic." Henry and his friend Wilson even capture the rebel colors, a melodramatic and symbolic act of manliness. By taking the enemy's flag or gun, one unmans him, robs him of these phallic symbols. Henry is now part of a select few: those who have risked death and taken life. "He felt a quiet manhood, nonassertive but of sturdy and strong blood. He knew that he would no more quail before his guides wherever they should point. He had been to touch the great death, and found that, after all, it was but the great death. He was a man."[8]

This ending is consistent with Crane's philosophy. He pursued adventures to give life an edge. His liking for the English sporting style led him to buy a Sussex estate. Morally ascetic, Crane rejected most passions. He drank little, was shy and chivalrous with women of his class. Like Prime Minister Gladstone, he related to fallen angels, rescuing women of the street. One of these, Cora Howarth Stewart, estranged wife of a British soldier, he took to Sussex with him. Such acts earned Crane a reputation as a profligate but, like other Victorian swashbucklers, he was essentially chaste. His rescues of fallen women revealed his inability to relate to females of his station. His passion was for adventure. He went gun running to Cuban rebels, missing death when his ship sank. And while suffering from tuberculosis, he rushed off as a correspondent to cover the Spanish-American War.[9]

In this section of three chapters, male philosophical involvement with war will be considered. War was viewed as an abrasive to cleanse and toughen a society dissipated by material consumption. To cushion the inhumanity of modern total war, its adherents dreamed of chivalry and, like Henry Fleming, woke up as knights. War first and foremost served the purposes of the modern national state but some who were ill at ease with aspects of modernity found comfort in the promotion of war. For individuals stressed or bored by the tempo of contemporary life, war offered a temporary escape. Some preferred taking a bullet to the slow decay of aging or cancer. In 1900 Crane died of tuberculosis. Just over a year earlier he had experienced "the best moment in anybody's life." It was watching the American attack go in at San Juan hill.[10]

FOUR | # A Little Bloodletting

Throughout the period, some people prescribed a little bloodletting as good for the body politic as well as for the individual. War scrubbed clean national arteries clogged with wealth and ease, produced a trimmer, fitter culture. Deep in western society is a basic paradox. We are to work hard and try to prosper, but when we do this we inevitably become guilty of enjoying our profits, spending for pleasure. We lose in success the hardness we needed in striving. We supposedly become soft, decadent, irresponsible. Then must come hard periods of retribution, scourings to make us strong again.

Fears of decadence were present in the United States from the beginning. Here were people imbued with the Protestant ethic, who had the virgin resources of a continent to practice industry upon. A querulous John Adams asked Thomas Jefferson: "Will you tell me how to prevent riches becoming the effects of temperance and industry? Will you tell me how to prevent luxury from producing effeminacy, intoxication, extravagance, vice and folly?" The softness of wealth carries a negative association with the female.[1]

War is masculine, hard. The 1812 conflict was welcomed in this light. Samuel Putnam Waldo wrote that, after the Revolution, "sudden wealth was the result of the exertions of the different classes of Americans. The voluptuousness and effeminacy, usually attendant upon the possession of it, were rapidly diminishing that exalted sense of national glory, for which the *Saxons* . . . were always celebrated." The war brought rejuvenation. Andrew Jackson, complementing the citizens of New Orleans on defeating the British in 1815, stated: "Inhabitants of an opulent and commercial town, you have by a spontaneous effort shaken off the habits, which are created by wealth, and shown that you are resolved to deserve the blessings of fortune by bravely defending them."[2]

Years of peace brought renewed fear. Alexis de Tocqueville, visiting in the late 1820s, warned that in a democracy the military spirit was quenched because the only passion was for getting rich. "The ever increasing men of property who are lovers of peace, the growth of personal wealth which war so rapidly consumes, the mildness of manners, . . . all these causes concur to quench the military spirit." Success in the Mexican War brought relief that the rot of prosperity had not gone deep. J. Frost commented in a popular history: "Europe has long contemplated us as a mere commercial and business-loving nation, smothering our former military abilities, in inordinate love of wealth." "The war in Mexico has dissolved this vain dream." But only for the present: anxiety always returned with renewed peace.[3]

In Britain the tonic effect of the Napoleonic Wars was followed by a long era of peace and booming material growth, especially in the commercial-industrial sector. A raised standard of living for many made optimists assert that humanity would be liberated soon from the age-old inheritance of toil and want. To some, progress had a marvelous symmetry. In pursuing his self-interest, a man added to the general stock of goods and thereby benefited everyone. Similarly, nations pursuing profit through commerce would be bound to each other by mutually beneficial ties of trade. Belligerence would help nobody and war would be rendered obsolete. Such were the views of the Manchester school of economists and some Utilitarian thinkers.

But progress had its shadows. Industrial cities were ugly, the workers condemned to a world of crowding and grime which they rarely escaped. The Utilitarian philosophy seemed to argue for a standard of judgment relying on the lowest common denominator of popular taste: the vulgar mass dictating to the polished few. Such a triumph seemed discernible in the success of new, powerful additions to the middle class; men who had gained social command through their wealth earned in business and political power through the Reform Act of 1832.

The businessmen were attacked by Charles Dickens in *Hard Times*, published in 1854. Dickens accused them of judging everything by the profit and loss columns of a ledger. Their philosophy is laid out by Bounderby in a lecture to school children on modern social management: "We hope to have, before long, a board of fact, composed of commissioners of fact, who will force the people to be a people of fact, and of nothing but fact. You must discard the word Fancy altogether." When a little girl tries to talk of nonprofitable issues, love of nature and art, she is reprimanded. The kudos go to a nasty boy called Bitzer, who has absorbed the lesson. In life, he says, "What you must appeal to is a person's self-interest. It's your only hold. . . . The whole system is a question of self-interest."[4]

War was one of the proposed antidotes to selfishness. The value of bloodletting appeared to have scientific endorsement. Victorian doctors took blood to rid the system of poisons; why shouldn't the same work for society which by analogy was akin to a living organism? There was also religious sanction. In Christianity, doesn't sin require a sacrificial act of atonement, a crucifixion? The sacrifice came during 1854 in a war with Russia. The onset of hostilities was greeted with great enthusiasm.

Justin McCarthy noted that the war "was popular partly because of the natural and inevitable reaction against the doctrines of peace and mere trading prosperity which had been preached somewhat too pertinaciously for some time before." He felt "it was like a return to the youth of the world when England found herself once more preparing for the field. It was like the pouring of new blood into old veins."[5]

The allies won the Battle of the Alma but then the war settled into a drab siege while rumors of inefficiency drifted back to Britain. Then in October came electrifying news: in response to a bungled order, the light cavalry had made a suicidal charge against heavily supported batteries. No matter that the attack was militarily absurd: British character stood redeemed. Tribute was paid by the Poet Laureate, Alfred Lord Tennyson. In "The Charge of the Light Brigade" he celebrated the "noble six hundred" who performed a sacrificial act of honor from which they could reap no utilitarian benefit: "Was there a man dismayed? Not though the soldier knew / Some one had blundered."[6]

Critics are uncomfortable with Tennyson as a man of war. They write off "The Charge" as a sop to Victorian sentimentalism, a gesture by Tennyson to earn his official salary. James D. Kissane says that "martial fervor, whatever might be said in its behalf, seems awkwardly framed in Tennyson's finely-tuned numbers" and Stopford A. Brook sees the war poetry as "artistically unfortunate." Allan Danzig says that Tennyson did not serve "any propagandist purpose" because he is talking not about real war but a symbolic struggle between good and evil. What Tennyson's hero "does is enroll himself on the side of the warrior saints, who war in this life for the good."[7]

In fact, Tennyson was addressing real war and he was not pandering to the crowds. Like Dickens, he was disgusted by the self-interest of the Manchester school. He was shocked by the unpatriotic response to a threatened French invasion in 1852 and wrote of the "niggard throats of Manchester":

> The hogs, who can believe in nothing great,
> Sneering bedridden in the down of Peace,
> Over their scrips and shares, their meats and wine,
> With stony smirks at all things human and divine!

True peace and liberty, he argued, are bought with blood. "Peace of sloth or of avarice born, / Her olive is her shame. . . ." Young men, that element which must fight wars, seemed indifferent. "Alas, our youth, so clever yet so small," dilettantish, "an essence less concentrated than a man." The goading of youth toward death is a theme of patriotic literature which runs into the Great War.[8]

The poet stated his philosophy at length in *Maud*, also written in 1854. The poem has three parts. The first shows the hero, a young gentleman, alienated from the materialism of the age. He cannot fit in, "when only the ledger lives, and when only not all men lie." He contemplates suicide. Then, in Part II, he glimpses salvation with Maud, his childhood friend and now his lover. But vulgar betrayal intervenes: her brother plans to marry her off to a nouveau riche coal baron to recoup the slipping family fortunes. Maud acquiesces. In anger, the hero kills Maud's brother and must flee abroad. Hope of finding meaning with a woman has failed. He sinks into madness. But he is saved by the start of the war. He is at last one with his people, a nation "that has lost for a little her love of gold / And love of a peace that was full of wrongs and shames, / Horrible, hateful, monstrous, not to be told; / And hail once more to the banner of battle unrolled!"[9]

The soldiers again showed great heroism at Inkerman, fought in November 1854. The *Times* concluded: "The nation is still in its essentials the same as it was forty years ago, sound to the core, true to itself, animated by a spirit . . . which has neither been contaminated by unexampled prosperity nor degraded into a mere power of calculating profit and loss by the sordid doctrines of a shallow and ungenerous utilitarianism."[10]

Meanwhile, in America, the Mexican War had failed to bring permanent faith in national virtue. For one thing, greed could be seen in the desire to grab Mexican lands and extend slavery, an exploitative labor system. Henry David Thoreau, who refused to pay taxes to finance the war, blamed commerce, which "curses everything it handles," for tying the free north to the slave south's immoral policies. In "Slavery in Massachusetts" he attacked the New England military's role in Mexico and in enforcing the Fugitive Slave Act. "Is this what all these soldiers, all this *training*, have been for this seventy-nine years past? Have they been trained merely to rob Mexico and carry back fugitive slaves to their masters?" The Massachusetts soldier "is a fool made conspicuous by a painted coat."[11]

The fear of lessened manhood was acute in the northeast because urban industrialization was most advanced here and therefore the rot of materialism would be most extensive. Since the Revolution, Yankee agents, selling manufactured goods throughout the Union, had gained an unsavory reputation for putting profit before honest dealing. The price of prosperity appeared to be moral decline. Stung by unanswered attacks on northern manhood, such as the beating of Senator Charles Sumner by Preston Brooks of South Carolina, New York lawyer George Strong asked if anything could "stiffen up the spiritless, money-worshipping North? Strange the South can't kick us into manliness and a little moderate wrath. Southerners rule us through our slaves of Fifth Avenue and Wall Street."[12]

Northeastern male insecurity also reflected the democratic revolution which had swept common men into power and gentlemen out of it, patricians like John Quincy Adams, New England's favorite son, slaughtered by Andrew Jackson in 1828. The men who survived were manipulative machine politicians like Martin Van Buren. East coast gentlemen retreated from politics. One told Francis Grund, a visiting European, that the time was past when respectable people could be in politics, where only blackguards succeeded. But as they brooded in their studies, gentlemen wondered what was wrong with them that they couldn't hold their own. "Has nature grown sterile of men? Is there male and manly virtue left?" asked Theodore Parker, the famous New England theologian and reformer.[13]

John Brown's Harper's Ferry raid gave hope. Thoreau thought it more sublime than the Charge of the Light Brigade, for while the one man chose to die for freedom, the others were killed merely obeying a stupid order. But the real jubilation exploded when Fort Sumter was attacked and the north became united for war. The Bostonian George Ticknor recorded: "I never knew before what a popular excitement can be. Holiday enthusiasm I have seen often enough, and anxious crowds I remember during the war of 1812–15, but never anything like this." There was jubilation in the south too, tired of being morally condemned over slavery. Now was the time for a showdown "between the gentlemen and the Yankee rowdies," as a naval officer put it.[14]

There was satisfaction in the willingness of the volunteers. Wendell Phillips, a Boston abolitionist, cried, "Why this is a decent country to live in now," and he apologized for having thought Massachusetts too "choked with cotton dust and cankered with gold" to fight. "A nation hath been born again, / Regenerate by a second birth!" wrote W. W. Howe. There was little bitterness about the destruction to come. "Let no one feel that our present troubles are deplorable, in view of the majestic development of Nationality and Patriotism which they have occasioned," said the New York *Tribune*. "But yesterday we were esteemed a sordid, grasping, money-loving people, too greedy of gain to cherish generous and lofty aspirations. To-Day vindicates us from that reproach, and demonstrates that, beneath the scum and slag of forty years of peace, and in spite of the insidious approaches of corruption, the fires of patriotic devotion are still intensely burning."[15]

Northern gentlemen hoped to make two related gains through the fighting. First, they would prove to themselves and the nation that they were still manly. They applauded such incidents as the gallant death of Colonel Robert Gould Shaw, leading his black regiment against Fort Wagner. Henry Ward Beecher said, "Our young men seemed ignoble; the faith of old heroic times had died . . . but the trumpet of this war sounded the call and O! how joyful has been the sight of such unexpected nobleness in our young men." Emerson wrote proudly, "When Duty whispers low, *Thou Must*, / The youth replies, *I can*." The death of young men is again urged to make their elders proud.[16]

The second gain for gentlemen would flow from the first. If patricians showed that they still had leadership capabilities, then surely America would welcome them back into leadership. Such was the dream of Francis Parkman, who despised common-man democracy. "Our position is not to be lamented," he wrote in September 1861. "A too exclusive pursuit of material success has notoriously cramped and vitiated our growth." With no crisis to call it forth, "the best character and culture of the nation has remained for the most part in privacy, while a scum of reckless politicians has choked all the avenues of power." But the time had come "when, upheaved from its depths, fermenting and purging itself, the nation will stand at length clarified and pure in a renewed and strengthened life." He meant that the patricians would regain power.[17]

Unfortunately, rather than purifying society, the war in some ways seemed to make things worse. Huge government contracts for arms and equipment made even more new fortunes and scarred the landscape with boom towns like Detroit and Chicago. Not only did the northern gentleman not gain back his prominent status but his natural allies in the postwar world, the southern planters, were wasted in the trenches before Atlanta and Petersburg. Union Colonel Theodore Lyman wrote: "It is not a gain to kill off these people. . . . They are a valuable people, capable of a heroism that is too rare to be lost."[18]

One of the north's very successful generals, and the one who would ultimately make the most political capital out of the war, was Ulysses S. Grant, a rather dull and unprepossessing commoner from Ohio. Polished New Englander Richard Henry Dana, Jr., wrote of him: "He had no gait, no station, no manner." New York patrician Colonel Charles S. Wainwright called him "stumpy, unmilitary, slouchy and western-looking; very ordinary, in fact." Grant's victory over Lee was not seen as a result of superior generalship but a grinding use of larger numbers, a victory of quantity over quality, of vulgar mass over finesse. Thus the western general represented everything gentlemen despised in the modern milieu. Francis Winthrop Palfrey, an eastern veteran, wrote in 1882: "As for Grant, with his grim tenacity, his hard sense, and his absolute insensibility to wounds and death, it may well be admitted that he was a good general for a rich and populous country in a contest with a poor and thinly peopled land, but let any educated soldier ask himself what the result would have been if Grant had had only Southern resources and Southern numbers to rely on and use."[19]

Revelations of graft and corruption during Grant's second presidential term, from 1872 to 1876, made it seem clear that the cancer had not been cut out by war. "The world after 1865, became a banker's world," wrote Henry Adams. Making money, without regard to ethical restraint, ruled the hour. "Grant's administration outraged every rule of ordinary decency, but scores of promising men, whom the country could not well spare, were ruined in saying so. The world cared little for decency." In such a milieu, the man to admire was materially ruined by doing his duty. When he came to write a novel about the postwar political scene, Adams made his hero an ex-Confederate, a Virginian whose sense of honor had impelled him into the rebel army, even though "he had seen from the first that, whatever issue the war took, Virginia and he must be ruined."[20]

In 1876 there was a hopeful little bloodletting, an atonement for national sin. George Custer's command died game at the Little Big Horn. In military terms, the defeat was as questionable as the Charge of the Light Brigade. But it appealed for the same reasons. "The underlying thought in this massacre of Custer and his command is duty and valor," thought the New York *Herald*. "It will be remembered as long as the charge of the Light Brigade has an eternal freshness in the memory of Englishmen." Laura Webb, musing on "Custer's Immortality," pictured "how our glorious dead / Rode straight 'into the Jaws of Death, / Into the Mouth of Hell.'"[21]

Custer's defeat was a minor setback in America's inexorable conquest of the continent. By 1890 the frontier was officially ended and with it went internal opportunities for little wars to keep the national mettle burnished. Inevitably, attention turned overseas, to the Pacific and South America, obvious potential spheres of interest. The expansionist urge was encouraged by Social Darwinism, which fed already existing fears of losing fitness and going to the wall in nature's struggle. Darwin had reminded his materially comfortable age that beneath pleasant surfaces the eternal struggle went on: "We behold the face of nature bright with gladness, we often see superabundance of food; we do not see, or we forget, that the birds which are idly singing around us mostly live on insects or seeds, and are thus constantly destroying life; or we forget how largely these songsters, or their eggs, or their nestlings, are destroyed by birds and beasts of prey. . . ."[22]

Applying this argument to human society, Leonard Wood, one of America's leading soldiers, asserted that ending war "is about as difficult as to effectively neutralize the general law which governs all things, namely the survival of the fittest." "War," said Rear-Admiral S. B. Luce, "is one of the great agencies by which human progress is effected." It "purges a nation of its humors . . . It tries a nation and chastens it, as sickness or adversity tries and chastens an individual." Alfred Thayer Mahan similarly applauded "the strong masculine impulse" and attacked "that worship of comfort, wealth, and general softness, which is the ideal of the peace prophets of today," disciples of "the Manchester school . . . who consider the disturbance of quiet as the greatest of evils."[23]

Not only military men but writers and thinkers argued for a bloodletting. Owen Wister thought America was too prosperous and needed chastening. Ambrose Bierce, another author and a Civil War veteran, welcomed "war, famine, pestilence, anything that will stop people from cheating." Even William James thought a fight might "hammer us into decency." A conflict with Spain was the perfect sort of exercise to keep the national muscle firm. Whipping up war sentiment in 1897, Theodore Roosevelt roared, "There are higher things in life than the soft and easy enjoyment of material comfort. It is through strife, or the readiness for strife, that a nation must win greatness . . . a rich nation which is slothful, timid, or unwieldy is an easy prey for any people which still retain those most valuable of qualities, the martial virtues. . . ."[24]

The problem with splendid little wars was that, while they provided temporary hardships, they also increased the victor's possessions and potential wealth, guaranteeing that opulence would increase and further purgings would be needed. The Spanish-American War gave the United States overseas territories and interests to protect against foreign enemies. And as the economy continued to grow, external opponents were aided by internal foes, abundance and complacency. Homer Lea, a soldier of fortune and military theorist, warned America of both the Japanese "yellow peril" and German imperial ambitions. He reminded this most wealthy nation that "opulence, instead of being a foundation of national strength, is liable to be the most potent factor in its destruction." It "produces national effeminacy and effeteness, hence there springs up whole tribes of theorists, feminists, and, in fact, all the necrophagan of opulent decadence." Note that the feminine and women's rights are associated with social decay. You must remain masculine, warlike, for "deterioration of military strength or militant capacity in a nation marks its decline. . . ."[25]

Lea's writings had some influence, particularly in the British service where Field Marshal Lord Roberts thought highly of them. British soldiers similarly saw themselves as lean centurions trying to protect an opulent empire that valued too highly the benefits of peace and social progress. At times they could be positively paranoid about British ability to respond to overseas threats. Coming largely from a class and school system whose roots and power were traditionally in the rural estate, the officer corps tended to be horrified by huge modern industrial cities and to see them as reducing the race to consumptive wretches. General Sir William Butler felt that the peasant born in the glen was more courageous than the man born in the slum court, and between them was "that gulf which measures the distance between victory and defeat." Writing in 1889, he was convinced that urban industrialization was destroying the British, who had once been "soldiers of a type and bearing now rarely to be seen, men of tall stature, sinewy frame, well-chiselled features, keen glance, and elastic figure, the pick and flower of a population still largely a rural one."[26]

General Napier blamed the manufacturers, who were "uncontrolled despots," depriving the workers and producing "corrupt morals, bad health, uncertain wages." J. F. C. Fuller, in 1897 a junior officer, wrote that in "this age in which we live the generality of people are cold, unfeeling, unloveable. And why? Simply because Mammon at present 'bosses the show.'" The "parvenu plutocrats . . . like vermin stink more in proportion as their coat grows finer thicker & more glossy."[27]

Popular politics added to the low tone, with liberals like Gladstone opposing extension of the empire, Irish home rulers gaining seats, socialists organizing the industrial proletariat. Fuller said in 1906: "To me the name politician is in most cases a synonym to 'canailleo'. . . ." General Evelyn Wood was openly contemptuous of political democracy, especially as it prevented the introduction of peacetime conscription, a volatile issue at the polls. "In a long life I have known only two or three Ministers who led the nation; most show their ability by saying to-day what they think a majority of the electorate will want in a short time."[28]

The answer, as always, lay in a little bloodletting to stiffen everyone up and bring a better class of leaders to the fore. Speaking on July 2, 1904, to the boys of Beaumont College, Wood declared: "War is always grievous, often terrible, but there is something worse, and that is the decline of enthusiasm, manliness, of the spirit of Self-Sacrifice. Peace is blessed, but if the price to be paid for it is that 'wealth accumulates and men decay,' then the bloodiest wars are lesser evils."[29]

Britain's most admired soldier before World War I was Garnet Wolseley. His views were typical of the officer class and his popularity says much about his countrymen's mood (he was the model for Gilbert and Sullivan's "very model of a modern major general" in *The Pirates of Penzance* 1880). Born into the gentry class, Wolseley had no sympathy for ordinary people: "How pleasant it is to be born a gentleman." Those who achieved this status through money and not birth elicited his contempt: "Lady Lymington," he commented after a dinner party, "is a sort of inferior kitchen maid, with a pink—rather red—face, a bad, servant girl sort of figure and is shy, dull, gauche, plain vulgar looking without any redeeming point except youth and I believe money from her tradesman father." He despised business and was eternally grateful that he had been a soldier and not had "to embark upon trade which would wean me from all the lofty ideas of honour and noble, soul-inspiring patriotism in which I had been reared. . . . I thank Heaven that I never allowed myself to stoop down and drink from the slimey pools from which the trader, the money grubber and the politician draws his daily sustenance."[30]

Wolseley fought for, and took rewards from, an industrial empire whose military products gave his armies their winning edge over native opponents. Yet his England was a romanticized rural conception and he was shocked in 1881 to discover the industrial towns of the Midlands. "I would not have imagined that the United Kingdom possessed such unredeemingly hideous houses and streets as those of Hartlepool, Hull &c." Racist, anti-semite, national chauvinist, Wolseley inevitably despised the progressive attitudes of men like Gladstone, who "would not I believe fight for the Isle of Wight." In general, he hated "all the depths and shoals of that abominable pit in which party politics seethes and emits its degrading gases."[31]

Periodic wars kept democracies from ruin. "On both sides of the Atlantic wise men as well as weak men fly from the wiles of the demagogue to the strength of the soldier." He noted, "There is an epoch in the history of nations when man becomes so absorbed in the pursuit of wealth and the enjoyment of ease, that the drastic medicine of war can alone revive its former manliness and restore the virility that had made its sons renowned." War "is the greatest purifier to the race or nation that has reached the verge of over-refinement, of excessive civilization." Such purification was necessary because there were always modern Spartas like Germany waiting to devour the soft and feeble.[32]

The flaw in the little bloodletting theory was that its demands for gore could never be satisfied. Commercial opulence, spiritual and physical decay, called for war to cleanse the system. But wars inevitably increased the possessions and the prosperity of the empire. Therefore, the original problem was compounded and another war called for. This was a conundrum the soldiers never worked out: their wars actually served the purposes of the commercial interests they affected to despise and upon whose strength the army was itself dependent financially and technologically. The brightest and more honest admitted this. Sir William Butler, though eager to fight, confessed that most modern wars lacked high purpose. Politicians fabricated pretexts for wars to get "a new frontier, an outlet for trade; a bigger vote at the polls, a higher place in the cabinet. Then comes the great financier, the man of many millions, the controller of vast enterprises. He is really the final factor in all this business." Butler concluded that "the soldier of today has to be content with what he can get, and the gift war-horse which the Stock Exchange is now able to bestow upon him must not be examined too sincerely in the mouth."[33]

The soldiers embraced the chance to see action in the Boer War but they saw some mundane motives at work in the desire of financial interests to net the diamond resources and other riches of South Africa. Butler loathed the commercial interests that followed the army into Johannesburg, which "has more prosperity in it, as that word is understood in modern life than any place in the world." And so the last British fight before 1914 failed to fulfill its mission of redemption. Referring to the British public, Frederick Maurice wrote, "We had hoped that this campaign had taught it something of the meaning of war and the needs of an army, but apparently it is still ignorant of the very rudiments." Thus a new cleansing teaching the value of military sacrifice would be called for.[34]

In "His Last Bow," Sherlock Holmes matches wits with a German spy. The story is set in August 1914, "the most terrible August in the history of the world," when "one might have thought already that God's curse hung heavy over a degenerate world, for there was an awesome hush and a feeling of vague expectancy in the sultry and stagnant air." The air is fetid, remarks Holmes, but it will be cleansed. "There's an east wind coming all the same, such a wind as never blew on England yet. It will be cold and bitter, Watson, and a good many of us may wither before its blast. But it's God's own wind none the less, and a cleaner, better, stronger land will lie in the sunshine when the storm has cleared." Many an Englishman must have agreed with Conan Doyle on that sultry Bank Holiday in August 1914 that a bloody purging would be good for the country.[35]

| # Knights and Their Dragons

The nineteenth century is the modern age. Its innovations and technological advances appear to separate the epoch from all that had gone before. This is the time of steamboats and railroads, the telegraph, gas and electric light, mass production and standardization in everything from off-the-peg clothing to revolving pistols. Humanity could stand in a bright material present and confidently anticipate a better future. Yet some in this modern age with all its improvements were obsessed by the past of knights and chivalry.

In the American Civil War, a modern mass slaughter, the combatants often posed as knights. Rebel lieutenant John Chamberlayne referred to Lee and "his round-table of generals," while Mary Boykin Chesnut thought John Bell Hood had "a sad Quixote face, the face of an old crusader who believed in his cause, his cross, his crown." Varina Howell Davis was reminded of Arthur being taken to Avalon when her President husband left for prison: "As we looked, as we thought our last upon his stately form and knightly bearing, he seemed a man of another and higher race."[1]

Northerners, despite their factories, called themselves "knights of chivalry." To George Hughes Hepworth, a Boston man, the bells ringing news of Fort Sumter "told us that the days of chivalry were at hand, and that every willing knight was needed for the contest." George Freeman Noyes, a staff officer, found that on a night march during the Antietam campaign, "all that was commonplace and mean about us lay transfigured by the witchery of the moonlight. . . . No longer Yankee soldiers of the nineteenth century, we were for the nonce knights of the ancient chivalry, pledged to a holier cause and sworn to a nobler issue than Coeur de Lion [sic] himself ever dreamed of."[2]

The bloodshed did not end knightly fashions. Before and after the war, Americans staged medieval tournaments, wore Robin Hood style outfits to go hunting, and threw balls like the one attended by Julia Dent Grant where "we had kings, knights, troubadours, and every other character pretty and gay." As late as 1911 the Detroit Society of Arts and Crafts threw a dinner party where the guests, all in medieval costume, included "a Princess of France wearing her coat of arms with royal dignity; and a Prioress who might have stepped straight from the pages of an illuminated missal."[3]

Across the Atlantic, Philip Gibbs recalled that before World War I "there was an epidemic of pageantry in England." At one show, in Saint Albans, "the bowmen of England let loose their arrows in thick flight which screamed through the air." Boys like L. E. Jones read books on Crécy, Agincourt, and Poitiers, and had crushes on Joan of Arc "with the face of an angel and wavy golden hair, clad in shining armour." Young Frederic Hamilton pretended that his pet mouse was a knight called Sir Bevis. The children played Camelot: they "knighted each other dozens of times."[4]

Englishmen romping out to kill animals were seen as knights errant. A gossip columnist said of Willy Grenfell, a leading hunter, "that such a man should for ever be performing heroic deeds such as slaying dragons or killing giants." Big game hunters "were all knights in shining solar topees!" and Africa a mysterious place where "some all-powerful evil genius held sway over the land and kept some lovely damsel or great treasure deep hidden in the interior, surrounded by a land teeming with horrors and guarded by the foul monsters of disease, of darkness and savagery." British soldiers fighting natives were the reincarnation of the crusaders. General Smith-Dorien recalled his commanding officer in 1880 "charging up and down the parade-ground with a billiard cue, imagining he was a knight-errant of old."[5]

Though their men carried modern rifles, army officers were to each other companions of the Round Table. Field Marshal Lord Birdwood described Sir Dighton Digby as "entirely *sans peur et sans reproche* and a model of all manly and knightly virtues." General Napier called Major James Outram "the Bayard of India, *sans peur et sans reproche*." General Wolseley said of Sir William Butler that he had the "most chivalrous of hearts, had he lived in medieval times, he would have been the knight errant of every one in distress." Arthur Conan Doyle felt that Colonel Crabbe of the Grenadier Guards, soldiering against the Boers, was in "his bearing a medieval knight-errant."[6]

The question is, why did people living at the hub of modernity, using each day the latest technology, riding on street cars and wearing spectacles, recur to the Middle Ages for inspiration? Why would Conan Doyle, physician, scientist, inventor of the ultra-modern detective, Holmes, care more about *The White Company* (1890), his tribute to medieval chivalry, and see *Sir Nigel* (1901), another novel of knighthood, as his masterpiece?[7]

Partly, there is the enormous influence of Walter Scott and other historical novelists whose popularity is now hard to imagine. At West Point, cadet Ulysses S. Grant read Scott and Bulwer in addition to Cooper. Mary Lincoln read Scott to Abraham and their son Robert during long winter evenings. Henry Adams read Scott in his youth. Siegfried Sassoon absorbed Scott's *Ivanhoe* and Longfellow's *Excelsior*. Allusions from chivalric literature colored every facet of daily life; steamboats plying American frontier rivers had names like *Lady of the Lake*. So convinced was Mark Twain of Scott's impact on the southern states that he blamed him for the Civil War: "Sir Walter had so large a hand in making Southern character, as it existed before the war, that he is in great measure responsible for the war."[8]

Yet these romantic writers were as much symptom as cause of the medieval mood. There are other factors. To find these, we must ask what dragons these latter-day knights hoped to slay. Key is the centrality of change in Victorian experience: it infiltrated every arena and while it stimulated it also frightened. Take as a metaphor one of the era's remarkable inventions, the London underground railway. This marvel was described in 1891 by Sara Duncan, a visiting American. The subway gave her "an odd, pleasurable sensation of undermining the centuries and playing with history." It could shoot under "old London, with its Abbey, and its Tower, and its Houses of Parliament" as though it were a time machine. But it discomfited her for the same reason. The cars set off "with a scream and a rush into the black unknown." She felt disoriented: "It seemed to me in the first few minutes that life as I had been accustomed to it had lapsed, and that a sort of semi-conscious existence was filling up the gap between what had been before and what would be again." The fast pace of change, exciting as it might be, was also stressful.[9]

Tearing through time generated a need to hold on, to cling to ancient verities. The medieval past provided these. From the underground, Duncan went to Madame Tussaud's wax museum where she would only view "English history, with its moated castles, and knights in armour, and tyrant kings and virtuous queens. . . ." She refused to look at the figures of modern "American Presidents in black with white ties. They had intelligent faces, but beside your Plantagenets I don't mind confessing they didn't look like anything."[10]

Democratic politicians marching in overfed solidarity with heads of business were depressingly mundane compared to heroic kings. It is a paradox that while the modern pace is swift and stress a common problem, it also brings complaints about the unending monotony of existence. Chivalry, "the unbought grace of life," was much needed to offset the grossness of modern life, thought Frances Trollope: "Knightly sensitiveness of honourable feeling is the best antidote to the petty soul-degrading transactions of every-day life. . . ."[11]

The knight, who lived in a precapitalist age and held the money lender, the financier, in contempt, offered a lesson to moderns absorbed by profit. American writer Brooks Adams "found a fascination in the middle ages when men were 'emotional,' priests or peasants or knights or artisans, but never businessmen." By emotional he meant they were not human calculating machines. John Ruskin, denouncing materialism, cried out: "How many yet of you are there knight-errants . . . who still retain the ancient and eternal purpose of knighthood, to pursue the wicked and to aid the weak?" Amidst the gloom of false, rotten prosperity, Englishmen needed heroes to "show them how, there, to live, or to show them even how, there, like Englishmen to die."[12]

Science contributed to the instability permeating modern life; the science, for example, of evolutionists who had shaken traditional faith in the biblical account of creation and even questioned the existence of a benevolent personal God. The simple fundamentalist creed of the crusading knight was partly an appeal to ancient usage to dispel the disquiet caused by the geologists. Science also meant industrial technology and this too was bewildering enough to knock people back into the Middle Ages.

Henry Adams, visiting industrial Birmingham, where he took "the plunge into darkness lurid with flames; the sense of unknown horror in this weird gloom," understood why Englishmen recoiled to "exquisite country" estates where one became "an ecclesiastic, and a contemporary of Chaucer." For Adams, the dynamo symbolized modernity. Its electric energy had become society's ruling force and "to these gigantic engines modern citizens dedicated their genius and money, as society eight hundred years earlier had lavished its intelligence and wealth on cathedrals." But there was a difference, for medieval religion had unified the community whereas the dynamo did not. "Rather, it created confusion as it drove machinery and altered life in ways that none understood and none were prepared to handle."[13]

The inability of some to appreciate science was compounded by their education which, in the more elite schools in America and Britain, tended to neglect this area. Adams said of his education: "in the concepts of all science, except perhaps mathematics, the American boy of 1854 stood nearer the year 1 than the year 1900." At Eton in 1884 there were twenty-eight classics masters but no scientists. The aim of the schools was to teach not technical knowledge but worthy character, and here the precepts of medieval knighthood seemed as relevant as those of physics. The result, according to Douglas Goldring, could be a graduate whose "mental equipment for withstanding the schock of experience was as useless as the imitation suit of armour, the dummy lance and shield of the actor in a pageant." His education "preserves him as an intellectual adolescent living in a fairyland of chivalrous illusion."[14]

The immaturity fostered by the cushioning illusions of chivalry was also noted by the French historian Elie Halévy, who thought the British treated the nasty guerrilla war against the Boers as a tournament, "almost a child's game," and came out of it with "an institution for children." He meant scouting, which Baden-Powell developed from his experience of irregular war in South Africa but which, paradoxically, he also based on "the general principles in the ideas underlying the orders of chivalry." Scout projects included "The Quest of King Arthur" in which boys undertook digs to find Camelot. Across the Atlantic, boys could join groups with names like The Knights of King Arthur, who met at a Round Table and were pledged to revive "the spirit of chivalry, courtesy, deference to womanhood, recognition of the *noblesse oblige*, and Christian daring."[15]

Girls embraced chivalry in dreams of knights coming for them. Mary Bulkley, in 1870s Saint Louis, had "a romantic notion, as to the only sort of man who would be good enough" for her. "He was a beautiful combination of Sir Lancelot, Sir Galahad, and Robert Elsmere." In New York, Emily Smith addressed her beau as "My Knight," and Caroline Drayton inscribed her diary, "Dedicated to my Knight," the ideal suitor who appeared in "her vision of what true love must be."[16]

Through the revival of chivalry women could expect at least a modicum of decent treatment from men in an age that left them legally vulnerable to abuse. Elizabeth Custer approved of the chivalrous attitude toward women in the 7th Cavalry: "Though army women have no visible thrones or sceptres, nor any acknowledged rights according to military law, I never knew such queens as they, or saw more willing subjects than they govern." Officers, like knights, went on patrol "wearing all sorts of love-pledges," and saw retaking white women Indian captives as rescuing damsels in distress.[17]

Always, man's role is to fight. Chivalry allowed males to talk about killing without appearing barbaric. The playwright W. S. Gilbert wrote that man was "A being strongly framed, / To wait on woman, and protect her from / All ills that strength and courage can avert." He was to toil for her and "To fight and die for her, that she may live!" This elaborate concern with protecting women meant that you could distance them by spending your time working on their behalf and fending off villains. The revival of chivalry emphasized the courtly rather than the carnal element in medieval love and contributed to the Victorian concern with control of passion. W. R. Greg wrote in the *Westminster Review* (1850) "that all of [the] delicate and chivalric which still pervades our sentiments towards women, may be traced to *repressed*, and therefore hallowed and elevated passion." "And what, in these days, can preserve chastity, save some relic of chivalrous devotion?"[18]

Chivalry kept flirtations from going too far. The Confederate cavalryman J. E. B. Stuart was a noted sex symbol but his dalliances meant little. One biographer concludes: "Stuart seemed to practice some nineteenth-century variant of courtly love. He idealized women, placed them upon pedestals, and strove to please them." He played charades in Richmond on January 8, 1864. On stage was a shrine at which pilgrims, "a peasant, priest, knight," came to worship. Then in strode "Stuart, in full uniform, his stainless sword unsheathed, his noble face luminous with inward fire." He placed his sword on the altar and then, to stress that it was spotless, he was joined by nuns "to bless the sword laid there." The scene is emotionally charged but sensually safe.[19]

The ideal relationship between knight and lady in Victorian chivalric literature is without physical significance. In Anthony Hope's smash hit *The Prisoner of Zenda*, a gothic adventure complete with castles, counts, and sword fights, the hero, Rudolf, falls in love with Princess Flavia. She calls him "My lover and true knight!" but they do not consummate. Rather, each year they exchange roses with the note, "Rudolf—Flavia—always." Meanwhile, Rudolf concentrates on the good stuff, his inevitable confrontation with the evil Prince Rupert of Hentzau: "therefore I exercise myself in arms, and seek to put off the day when the vigor of youth must leave me."[20]

To make sure that the ideal is not spoiled, Rudolf is killed in the sequel. "To me it seems now as though all had ended well," comments a soldier friend. Dying for a woman is a more satisfying imaginative resolution than living with her. When the princess sends a young and adoring lieutenant on a mission, "The service seemed so great and the honor so high, that he almost wished he could die in the performing of his *rôle*. It would be a finer death than his soldier's dreams had dared to picture." Virgin death as ideal love is a common theme. When in *Little Women* Amy dreams of Laurie, the boy she will marry, she sees him as "the effigy of a young knight asleep on his tomb." Chivalry allowed

Rudolf, clutching Flavia's rose, finds an admirable—and virgin—death. (Anthony Hope, *Rupert of Hentzau*. New York: Henry Holt, 1983.)

for the graceful elimination of the other gender from one's most intimate life scenario.[21]

In this, knighthood might encourage homosexuality. Frederick Farrar, a Harrow master, worried that the knight-squire relationship overly encouraged hero worship of older by younger boys. "I used to fancy that a big fellow would do no end of good to one lower in the School and that the two would stand to each other in the relation of knight to squire." But, "when a boy takes up a little one, *you* know pretty well that those are not the kinds of lessons he teaches." Perhaps so, but there was little conscious urge toward homosexuality in chivalry. Rather, it reinforced a strong male fastidiousness: knightly heroes were clean, they did not use bad words, and cheating at cards could ruin a man for life. The real passion of modern knighthood was for physical challenge.[22]

Inevitably, the chivalric renaissance had great currency in the officer corps. It complemented the soldiers' professional style, which on both sides of the Atlantic emphasized character and athletics over scientific study of war. Knighthood helped soldiers cope with, even deny, the impersonal in modern mess war, where the individual was of minimum consequence. "The soldier of today," said Secretary of War Elihu Root in 1899, was "part of a great machine which we call military organization; a machine in which, as by electrical converters, the policy of government is transformed into the strategy of the general, into the tactics of the field and into the action of the man behind the gun." It was Adams's dynamo applied to the army.[23]

The modern war machine bewildered Frederic Remington, used to individualistic frontier fights with Indians. Below decks on a steel battleship in the Spanish-American War, "through mile after mile of underground passages I crawled and scrambled and climbed amid wheels going this way and rods plunging that, with little electric lights to make holes in this darkness." The ship's engineering "stuns me. At last when I stood on deck I had no other impression but that of my own feebleness, and, as I have said, felt rather stunned than stimulated."[24]

Soldiers could not afford a self-image as mere insects crushed by the anonymous power of mighty machines. Character still had to count. George H. Hodson said that British valor in the Indian Mutiny proved "that even the Enfield rifle has not reduced all men to a dead level, but that there is still a place to be found for individual prowess, for the lion heart, and the iron will. One seems transported back from the prosaic nineteenth century to the ages of romance and chivalry, and to catch a glimpse, now of a Paladin of old, now of a knightly hero *san peur et sans reproche. . . .*" At Ulundi in the Second Zulu War the British did not use their Gatlings because, as Lord Chelmsford put it, "we must show them that we can beat them in a fair fight." The same explanation has been offered for Cutser's refusal to take Gatlings to the Little Big Horn. To downplay war as a massacre machine and stress its character-building qualities, the exploits of individualists like Charles Gordon were highlighted. He was "the mirror and measure of true knighthood," even though (and perhaps because) most of his career was spent on detached service in backwater campaigns unindicative of modern battle conditions.[25]

The machine itself was coopted in the interests of chivalry. In 1913 Basil Liddell Hart wrote a science fiction story about an Anglo-German air war. He predicted zeppelin bombing of London, armed aircraft, midair radio communications, parachutes, camouflage. yet the war is fought like a medieval tournament. British flyer Denis Harcourt performs feats of chivalry, such as saving an enemy machine by keeping his wing under its damaged tail. The fighter plane has become the knight's charger.[26]

The horse was central to the soldiers' involvement with knighthood and their refusal to confront the nature of modern war. The final dragon was any weapon or tactic that might unseat them. By the American Civil War, modern rifles and artillery had made cavalry charges too costly. Yet mounted charges with lance and sabre remained in use. In 1900 Conan Doyle called for reform but was rebutted by Colonel F. N. Maude, who asserted: "The advantage of either sword or lance in cavalry work is that a severe wound drops the man at once. A man may be mortally wounded by rifle or revolver bullet and still fight on for a couple of hours." Maude didn't explain how the trooper could get close enough to use his medieval weapons. Neither did Theodore Roosevelt, who justified the peculiar decision to raise cavalry for fighting in Cuban jungles by saying, "My belief was that the horse was really the weapon with which to strike the first blow. I felt that if my men could be trained to hit their adversaries with their horses, it was a matter of small amount whether, at the moment when the onset occurred, sabers, lances, or revolvers were used." On the eve of the Great War, Evelyn Wood, umpiring a mock battle, gave a victory to cavalry over concealed infantry, even though they had "their lances entangled in the branches and their spurs in the bracken."[27]

Since mounted Norman knights had ridden over Saxon infantry at Hastings in 1066, the cavalryman had been the symbol not only of military but of social elitism in western civilization. Confederates took the connection literally, boasting that they were descended from Norman knights, born to ride and rule over Yankees spawned by Saxon churls. To surrender the horse meant the end of a world. Winston Churchill remembered glorious mass maneuvers in his early days with the cavalry. He admitted occasionally "wondering what would happen if half a dozen spoil-sports got themselves into a hole with a Maxim gun and kept their heads" but said that everybody avoided this for the cavalry represented the flower of European military society. Looking back in the 1930s he thought it a shame that war had lost its pageantry "and should turn instead to chemists in spectacles, and chauffeurs pulling the levers of aeroplanes or machine guns." It was this that knighthood had protected the soldier against: admission that war had passed into the hands of organization men and scientists.[28]

The blindness to what a modern war would entail later troubled Sir John French, Chief of the Imperial General Staff and first commander of the British Expeditionary Force on the western front. After the slaughter of 1914–18, he could not "help wondering why none of us realized what the most modern rifle, the machine gun, motor traction, the aeroplane, and wireless telegraphy would bring about. It seems so simple when judged by actual results." None of his experience, he said lamely, had led him to expect a war of fixed positions dominated by defensive weapons. His social values had blinded him, for the evidence was there.[29]

It was clear to George Bernard Shaw, a progressive civilian with no time for chivalry, who in 1898 published *Arms and the Man*. This novel portrays a fictional war between Serbia and Bulgaria. The story opens with a successful cavalry charge by Bulgarians against a machine gun battery, seemingly standard chivalric fare: the triumph of spirit over steel. But the Serb officer points out that his guns had been sent the wrong ammunition, otherwise the cavalry would have been slaughtered. "Is it professioanl to throw a regiment of cavalry on a battery of machine guns, with the dead certainty that if the guns go off not a horse or man will ever get within fifty yards of the fire?" asks the Serb.[30]

This officer, Bluntschli, is the bourgeois son of a parvenu candy manufacturer, and he has no aristocratic illusions about war. He describes a colleague's fate: "Shot in the hip in a woodyard. Couldn't drag himself out. Your fellows' shells set the timber on fire and burnt him, with half a dozen other poor devils in the same predicament." Technology kills randomly and meanly. Sergius, the Bulgarian cavalry officer, is Bluntschli's complete opposite. Contemptuous of the mundane world of work and trade, he lives in a chivalric fantasy, boasting that "I have gone through the war like a knight in a tournament." He is shown to be an anachronism when he challenges Bluntschli to a duel and the saner man chooses Maxims for weapons.[31]

Shaw's only failure was in not recognizing that, while chivalry was a disaster militarily, it worked psychologically for the military. Through chivalry, soldiers could avoid confronting disturbing elements in their own makeup and the work they did, such as their brutality toward weaker peoples, their use of the machine to kill when it did not threaten their own social position. Their actions often were not knightly. The defense of womanhood was an excuse for savage reprisals in the Indian Mutiny, including blowing captives from the muzzles of guns. General Wolseley, fighting in South Africa, berated the native because he would not "come out in the open *'like a gentleman'* and fight it out." A manly challenge, but the warriors were armed with primitive weapons and the fight would not be a "fair" one. Sometimes the truth was a slip of the pen away. Winston Churchill was imbued with the chivalric spirit but when he and brother Jack played toy soldiers, "he was only allowed to have coloured troops; and they were not allowed to have artillery." Play mirrored life.[32]

The British might talk about the Boer War as a tournament but they ruthlessly burned Boer farms, drove livestock, and relocated the population in a determination to win at any price. J. F. C. Fuller, frustrated by chasing Boers, wrote: "The more boers we can wipe out now the better for the future there is no doubt about that." Because Fuller can rely on his correspondent to know that, according to the formula, we are the chivalrous ones, he can invert language to blame the enemy for ruthlessness. "An uncivilized or semicivilized people do not understand kindness and consideration and one has to leave one's mark on them before they will recognize one."[33]

Soldiers who spent much of their time in brutal police actions could justify each swing of the club through chivalry. George John Younghusband, patrolling imperial boundaries, saw his fellows as "true knights and British Officers, walking brave and debonair, maybe towards glory, and maybe towards the pleasant fields of Heaven, where warriors rest." On one scout his men fired a thousand rounds trying to bring down one wretched native bandit. Having cornered the man, Younghusband cried out: "Who art thou, O Warrior, and whence comest and whither goest?" Scott could have done no better in *The Talisman*. Younghusband was so impressed that he forced the man to enlist instead of hanging him.[34]

In America, soldiers saw little action at this time except against Indian raiders and in defense of corporate property. But they too colored their role. John Breckinridge Castleman, who in 1878 was head of the Kentucky State Guard, and whose duties were stopping lynchings and shooting railroad strikers, was described by intimates as a "Bayard, Sir Phillip Sidney, Prince Rupert, D'Artagnan."[35]

Chivalry veneered the naked use of force. That the code did not apply to those who were not in the club was shown imaginatively in a story called "The World of the War God," published by George Griffith in 1900. Rollo Lenox Smeaton Aubrey, Earl of Redgrave, and his American bride, Lilla Zaidie, take a spaceship honeymoon through the galaxy. As ambassadors of western civilization, they are equipped with four small cannon, two machine guns, two elephant guns "carrying explosive bullets," a dozen rifles. The couple are clean-cut, proper, handsome; she is feminine, he is gallant. They even have along their butler, Murgatroyd. When they land on Mars, having shot down several Martian ships which tried to intercept and quarantine them, the greetings go well until the inhabitants start to make suggestive noises, "half-human, half-brutish," about her ladyship. With no compunction, they shell and machine gun the lot: "The onward-swarming throng seemed to stop, and the front ranks of it began to sink down silently in long rows." The travelers continue on their way, satisfied that they have punished those who do not understand earth's chivalric etiquette. The story is told without a trace of irony.[36]

The Martians here fulfill the role of brown peoples on earth, such as the Sudanese, whom the British punished for Charles Gordon's death. Ernest N. Bennett, an Oxford don who accompanied the military to Omdurman, wrote with sensitivity about the flora and fauna along the Nile. Then he explained the necessity to use soft-head maiming bullets: "A civilized combatant, when he is struck by a bullet—even if the wound be a comparatively slight one, say through the shoulder—almost invariably sits down on the ground; but the nervous system of the savage is a far less delicate organism, and nothing short of a crushing blow will check his wild onset." Language is again inverted so that the use of barbarous dumdums is justified because not we but the enemy are uncivilized.[37]

What developed was a frightful combination: the presence of advanced military technology alongside a warrior code that willed combat as a high male endeavor and refined the butcher instinct by associating it with the aura of the search for the grail. The dynamics of the situation were explored in Mark Twain's *A Connecticut Yankee in King Arthur's Court*. Twain disapproved of the knightly fashion and tried to expose the medieval period as brutal and superstitious. But he also recognized that a King Arthur could have some noble, redeeming qualities. At the same time, the modern man, "the Boss" as he comes to be called, though bringing a certain enlightenment to Camelot, can also be dangerous in his determination to control and impose his own system. Here Twain reaches his climax: neither modern technology nor chivalric ideas are necessarily threatening in the proper context and taken separately; the danger arises when modern mechanics are placed down in a world with an Arthurian value system. In the climactic battle, technology is made the servant of an enormous war. The results are devastating: using mines, an electric fence and Gatling guns, the Boss and his fifty-four technicians kill 25,000 knights in no time. Churchill's spoilsports had got in a ditch with a machine gun.[38]

Ironically, chivalry was supposed to prevent the kind of butchery that Twain predicted: It was to set up codes between civilized men so that the slaughter of modern weapons could be limited and men on horseback could continue playing the game. But the premise was wrong. One cannot limit the destructive capability of military technology; one can only refuse to resort to war. Chivalry obfuscated the inhuman quality of modern war and in so doing it not only failed to contain slaughter but helped to encourage it.

| # Civic Claustrophobia

In 1910 H. G. Wells published *The History of Mr. Polly*, the story of how a man is finally true to himself, escapes intolerable drudgery, and becomes a hero. Mr. Polly is no conventional hero, no manly, strapping fellow. He is undersized, goes bald early, and has an owl-like expression. As Wells puts it, "He was a short, compact figure, and a little inclined to a local embonpoint." Though in his youth he dreamed that "he led stormers against well-nigh impregnable forts, and died on the ramparts at the moment of victory," he is not athletic and "had an instinctual hatred of the strenuous life. He would have resisted the spell of ex-President Roosevelt, or General Baden-Powell. . . ."[1]

Polly fails at chivalry. Like other youths, he adores young women from afar. "He would watch them going to and fro, and marvel secretly at the beauty of their hair, or the roundness of their necks, or the warm softness of their cheeks, or the delicacy of their hands. He would fall into passions for them at dinner-time, and try to show devotions by his manner of passing the bread and margarine at tea." This leads to an attempt at courtly love with a girl in an exclusive boarding school. Polly imagines her as "a beautiful maiden imprisoned in an enchanted school." "'You make me feel like one of those old knights,' he said, 'who rode about the country looking for dragons and chivalresque adventures.'" The girl thinks him a fool and brings friends to laugh at him.[2]

Polly is amusing because he is petit-bourgeois and has suffered a mangling education in a state school where he acquired a penchant for using long words which he mispronounces. Forced to be a white-collar worker, one of the millions caged by modernity into clerking away life in the service of commerce, he is a unit in the great process of consumerism. He goes to his first job, as a salesman, like a trapped animal: "A young rabbit must have very much the feeling when, after a youth of gambolling in sunny woods and furtive jolly raids upon the growing wheat and exciting triumphant bolts before ineffectual casual dogs, it finds itself at last for a long night of floundering effort and perplexity in a net—for the rest of its life."[3]

Polly's captivity is completed when he stumbles into marriage with

Miriam, his humorless, rigid, and demanding cousin. He runs a shop and develops indigestion. He sours inwardly from the grinding smallness of his life. He thinks about escaping to sea but knows he would not make a sailor. After fifteen years of strangling marriage and stupefying shop-keeping, he settles upon suicide. As he looks back, he thinks "that life had never begun for him, never! It was as if his soul had been cramped and his eyes bandaged from the hour of his birth. Why had he lived such a life? Why had he submitted to things, blundered into things? Why had he never insisted on the things he thought beautiful and the things he desired, never sought them, fought for them, taken any risk for them, died rather than abandon them? They were the things that mattered. Safety did not matter. A living did not matter unless there were things to live for."[4]

This is Polly's epiphany and the making of a hero. Dying is the easy way out. He realizes he has the courage to live and defy convention to find himself. Life becomes an adventure. He leaves Miriam, after making sure she is comfortably situated. He becomes a tramp and finds happiness as an odd job man at a rural inn, living with the jolly fat woman who runs the place. He has little money but finds pleasure in sunsets, solid pub food, and odd lots of old books he buys at auction. His digestion improves and he is a hero. He is not a hero by virtue of fighting, though he does have a mock-epic battle with an unsavory type who hangs around the inn. His real heroism is in challenging convention, rejecting the conformity of modern life where material acquisition passes for fulfillment.[5]

In creating Mr. Polly, Wells tried to indicate a nonviolent answer to a problem confronting citizens of developed countries: how to prevent sedentary, predictable lives from losing all lustre and adventure. For many men, breaking out of the pattern meant violence—in sports, hunting, war. Wells understood the attraction, commenting in 1908, "When the contemporary man steps from the street, of clamorous insincere advertisement, push, adulteration, underselling and intermittent employment into the barrack-yard, he steps on to a higher social plane, into an atmosphere of service and cooperation and of infinitely more honourable emulations." But he also saw that Britain's splendid little wars brought misery to weaker peoples. In 1898, the year of Omdurman, he tried to let his contemporaries feel what it would be like on the receiving end of a one-sided struggle. When the Martians land, in *The War of the Worlds*, British military technology is as useless as Sudanese spears or the Spanish fleet in the Philippines.[6]

Wells encouraged channeling the warrior instinct into war games played with toy soldiers but using adult rules for intellectual challenge. In *Little Wars* he argued, "Here is the premeditation, the thrill, the strain of accumulating victory or disaster—and no smashed nor sanguinary bodies. . . ." Real war, he said, was "not only the most expensive game in the universe, but it is a game out of all proportion." Wells had a point but most people disagreed with him and, if like Polly they found their daily round stifling, they did not have his courage to defy convention. For some, national crises like wars provided the major peaks in the flatness of their lives.[7]

The nineteenth century, in its attempt to manage the pace of change, controlled life in many ways. True, the period was materially expansive and there was more political expression for many common white men of the middling sort. But the Victorian world was spiritually constraining. Partly this was in reaction to the intellectual boldness of the eighteenth century, which produced a "moral panic" among the more conservative and an emphasis upon respectability. Social intercourse was guided by an elaborate hedge of etiquette. Marriage reinforced the precepts of propriety. Donald Mitchell, a champion of bachelorhood, asked: "Shall a man stake his independence and comfort upon the die of absorbing, unchanging relentless marriage?" In a story called "The Lady Automaton" (1901) E. E. Kellett invented a robot society woman whose repetitive polite conversation was so like the reality that nobody noticed the difference.[8]

The nature of work was changing as man shifted from a rural to an urban-industrial environment with business office routines. More people did uniform work in uniform surroundings. Herman Melville tapped a root of modern alienation in "Bartleby the Scrivener" (1853), about a man whose life has been spent sorting mail in the dead letter office and making copies of legal documents. He becomes paralyzed and dies. Melville commented on society: "Take mankind in mass, and for the most part, they seem a mob of unnecessary duplicates." Life became more systematized as government bureaucracy and business organization advanced. Julia Dent Grant's father, a midwesterner, got out of business because "the Yankees that have come west have reduced business to a system. . . . if we did any business now we would simply bind ourselves to a treadmill." He meant that the management methods of the industrially advanced northeast had taken the adventure out of trade.[9]

The nineteenth century was the age of mass production, so that people dressed better in ready-made clothing, had nicer homes with machine-made furniture, printing-pressed books, and pictures. But as a consequence they also looked more alike and lived in a more uniform environment. Lord Frederic Hamilton remarked that, except for language, even the capitals of Europe now seemed the same, "with big modern hotels, which bear such a wearisome family likeness to each other . . . all look alike, and even the cooking has, with a greater or lesser degree of success, been standardized to the requisite note of monotony." He predicted that shortly "everyone will be living in a drab-coloured, utilitarian world, from which most of the beauty and every scrap of local colour will have been successfully eliminated."[10]

The upshot of respectable uniformity was monotony. The representative modern American, Henry Adams said, was "bored, patient, help-less." Even Cambridge, with its Harvard faculty, congressmen, and other cosmopolites, was "a social desert that would have starved a polar bear." Thoreau had noted that "the mass of men lead lives of quiet desperation. What is called resignation is confirmed desperation." Perhaps the aim of education, said Alec Waugh, should be to prepare one for the ensuing long littleness of life.[11]

What could be done to stimulate a sense of adventure? Women had the fewest options, for any deviation from given norms could lead to ruined reputations. They could pursue charitable works or seek refuge from monotonous reality in invalidism. Both sexes took stimulating drugs, and addiction was significant. In the United States, consumption of opium rose from 24,000 pounds in 1840 to 168,641 pounds in 1872. Conan Doyle gave this emotional charge a permanent monument when he made Holmes an intense male, estranged from women, whose answer to boredom between cases is a seven percent solution of cocaine.[12]

Alongside of drugs and alcohol to relieve stress or provide excitement, there were sexual encounters. But like substance abuse, sex had risks. Conventional medical wisdom held that too-frequent sexual indulgence, even within marriage, could lead to such problems as consumption, heart stress, brain damage. Illicit liaisons had even more risk. They often had to take place under cover of night. Sex in darkness was thought to be more draining than when the sun's solar rays could replace precious lost vitality: "Sexual expenditure had to be in the presence of the sun. The copulators would be recharging their batteries even as they were discharging." The promiscuous also risked venereal disease, which drove mad and destroyed Lord Randolph Churchill. A. P. Hill, while a West Point cadet, contracted gonorrhea from a prostitute, which ruined his health permanently and lowered his efficiency on campaign. Those who broke marital rules could also get killed by angry spouses. Future Union General Daniel Sickles shot his wife's lover dead in the street and was released by a jury, as the "unwritten law" condoned killing "the defiler of his marriage bed."[13]

The dangers of night crawling were laid out imaginatively in two popular novels. In *The Strange Case of Dr. Jekyll and Mr. Hyde*, published in 1886 by Robert Louis Stevenson, an eminent London physician has a craving for low night life. He takes drugs which distort his personality and features, allowing him in this degraded form to prowl London's streets unrecognized to indulge his perversions. But such a wretch can come to no good end and he finally commits suicide to end his horrific double life.

In *Dracula*, by Bram Stoker, the creature of the night has charm and allure. He is of an ancient warrior family and shows some ironic nobility by declaring, "Blood is too precious a thing in these days of dishonourable peace; and the glories of the great races are as a tale that is told." In the night he is attractive to women and can arouse their passions, suggesting how easily men thought angels could descend into whores. This is his crime: he turns angels into devils and for this violation of moral taboo he is destroyed by sober, conventional professional men. They have a jolly time hunting him down and this gives us a clue to another cure for social claustrophobia. Dracula's pursuers never violate convention; they are superstitiously religious, punctiliously chivalric. But they get to chase and kill. Their adrenalin flow comes from the manhunt as, indeed, does Sherlock Holmes's. Danger, in the ritualized male game of hunting, is an allowable escape from normality. This is justified by the evil of the opponent: his violations of the rules excuse the right fellows' also becoming wild.

Life could be spiced up a little through flirting or voyeurism, for which Victorian society allowed considerable latitude. Though consummated sexual encounters were dangerous, men could visually ravish women whose evening wear was highly expressive. Art dealt extensively with erotic themes and British tourists in Paris were noted for "staring in the shop windows at the latest studies of nude women." But voyeurism aroused more than it satisfied and offered no genuine adventure. For men, a more satisfactory solution to dyspepsia was to get away from it all for a while. Wild nature could be challenged on the seas, as was recognized by Richard Henry Dana and Herman Melville, who shipped before the mast. Melville noted that on a Sunday New York's docks were crowded with "thousands upon thousands of mortal men fixed in ocean reveries." These poor creatures full of fantasies of freedom were "landsmen; of week days pent up in lath and plaster—tied to counters, nailed to benches, clinched to desks."[14]

The frontier also offered excitement and men from the more developed regions adventured there. In the Yellowstone Expedition of 1873 General David M. Stanley allowed two bored young Englishmen to accompany the troops: "They have had an Indian fight, have killed all kinds of game, and now they seek new adventures." Owen Wister captured a restless type in his Virginian, a man from a people who, historically, "have fought when we got the chance," and who left his nuclear family for the west because they never changed their habits or opinions. "I put on my hat one mawnin' and told 'em maybe when I was fifty I'd look in on 'em again to see if they'd got any new subjects. But they'll never. My brothers don't seem to want chances." The narrator, a clean-cut easterner seeking hardihood in the west, is duly impressed by this "slim young giant" with "splendor that radiated from his youth and strength."[15]

India and Africa similarly acted as escape valves. Travel accounts spoke of Britain as too safe, predictable, stifling. "The charm of a life of freedom and complete independence—a life in which a man goes as and where he lists. . . . Not back to the cage. Anything but that!" was a typical sentiment. Here one could practice the self-reliance missing in a world of insurance policies, pensions, and sound investments. "There is a charm in the feeling of independence which a farewell to civilization brings with it, and in the knowledge that henceforward one has to rely solely on one's own resources, and that success or failure depend on one's self," wrote a visitor to Africa.[16]

The military appeared to offer an alternate lifestyle, since most officers were not yet chained to desks. Elizabeth Custer said of the frontier garrisons: "The most contented people I ever knew lived in the very heart of the great American desert." They did not have the "carking care" of other professions: "In the short half-hour allowed for dressing, a business man must shake off all the cares and perplexities that have consumed him all day, and put himself into visiting trim. Our officers have not that to do."[17]

Most soldiers, in entering the army, made a conscious choice against the office world. Frederick Lugard, refusing a business job, explained that "the Lugards have been in the Army and in the Church, good servants of God or the Queen, but few if any have been tradesmen." J. E. B. Stuart thought it much better to be "a Bold Dragoon than a pettyfogger lawyer." General Ian Hamilton said that when soldiers were "summing up their lives, they feel they have no cause to envy the many who have sat like octopuses on one spot sucking gold out of anyone who touched them." "Society is now but one great horde / Formed of two mighty sects the bores and the bored," was J. F. C. Fuller's summation. Herbert Kitchener "made no attempt to conceal how bored he was by commonplace English house parties" and was happy to be abroad on duty, for Europe was "not worth living in."[18]

The period produced numerous soldiers of fortune, taking what work they could to stay away from civil life. Flamboyant Sir Percy Wyndham began a fighting career at fifteen in the French Revolution of 1848, served in the British, Austrian, Italian, and United States armies, was commander-in-chief of Burmese forces, and was finally killed in 1879 flying a hot-air balloon. Charles Gordon found sanctuary in foreign parts, writing from the Sudan: "I prefer it infinitely to going out to dinner in England; the people here have not a strip to cover them, but you do not see them grunting and groaning all day long as you see scores and scores in England, with their wretched dinner parties and attempts at gaiety where all is hollow and miserable."[19]

George St. Leger Grenfell could not stand the tedium of polite society. He left his wife in 1843, after ten years with this "nice, quiet steady woman," to go gun running to Tangier and fight in the Crimea and the American Civil War. He died in 1868, a federal prisoner trying to escape from the Dry Tortugas. His biographer states: "Grenfell's life was a continuing act of violence against the sanctities of Victorian life, and especially against its inmost essence, the family." Grenfell's own judgment on his choice of styles was this: "We have all got to live a certain time, and when the end comes, what difference will it make whether . . . I died in a four-poster bed with a nurse and phials on the bed table or whether I died in a ditch?"[20]

In America, military titles and paraphernalia provided a colorful alleviation to the uniform tones of republican life. As early as Jackson's presidency, visitors noted that men you met were "nearly all addressed by the titles of general, colonel, and major." General David S. Stanley recalled the monotony of growing up in Ohio. "The great event of the year" was the militia muster where you saw the color and glitter of the uniformed general and staff: "The curious country boy looked on in wonder and with a little awe."[21]

In war neurotic symptoms seemed to dissipate. Thomas J. Jackson's hypochondria cleared up when the Civil War came (he had believed one leg shorter than the other and that he only perspired on one side). "I think a little lead, properly taken, is good for a man," said Robert E. Lee, a soldier whose family life was sometimes strained. "I was much in the way of everybody, and my tastes and pursuits did not coincide with the rest of the household. Now I hope everybody's happier," he wrote after returning to active service. William McFeely says that the war ended U. S. Grant's personal sense of hollowness. Politics, business, marriage had lit no fires. "Only in war—and possibly, at the end of his life, in writing about the war—did he find the completeness of experience that, when engaged in it, was so intensely his."[22]

Soldiers agreed that civil life had no thrill to match fighting. "I thirst now not for the calm pleasures of a country life, the charms of society, or a career of ease and comfort, but for the maddening excitement of war," wrote Major William Hodson from India. "In the quiet hum-drum of home life with all its dull humanizing but often vulgar influences, we may moralize over the angry passions which war develops," but of the "wild pleasures," "war with all its sudden changes, and at times its maddening excitement was the greatest," said Garnet Wolselely. He described battle as one might also picture sexual climax. "It is only through experience of the sensation that we learn how intense, even in anticipation, is the rapture-giving delight which the attack upon an enemy affords. I cannot analyze nor weigh, nor can I justify the feeling. But once really experienced, all other subsequent sensations are but as the tinkling of a doorbell in comparison with the throbbing toll of Big Ben."[23]

You didn't have to be a career officer to enjoy the unaccustomed zest of a splendid little war. George Alfred Henty used the Crimean War to escape Oxford: "The quiet student life at the university became painful, the days passed in college seemed to be prison-like." Ernest Bennett, a don, barely finished grading papers before dashing off on the Omdurman campaign, saying, "I shook off the dust of these papers from my garments, and stepped upon the steamer's deck a free agent." Erskine Childers, Clerk of the House of Commons, joined a volunteer battery in the Boer War, eager for "the chance of a fight." "It is something, bred up as we have been in a complex civilization, to have reduced living to its simplest terms," he wrote. He had a new sense of being alive and involved: "Perhaps the best of all is to have given up newspaper reading for a time and have stepped one's self into the region of open-air facts where history is made and the empire is moulded. . . ."[24]

Francis Parkman, a scholarly and frail American, nevertheless could not get enough of things military. On a British troop ship he felt he was "carried about half a century backwards," away from modern comforts and social progress. "No one cants here of temperance reform, or of systems of diet—eat, drink, and be merry is the motto everywhere." He saw "no canting of peace. A wholesome system of coercion is manifest in all directions—thirty-two pounders looking above the bows—piles of balls on deck—muskets and cutlasses hung up below." How different, he thought, from the peace advocates "who when smitten on one cheek literally turn the other likewise—instead of manfully kicking the offender into the gutter." Even Nathaniel Hawthorne felt war's tonic effect in 1861: "The war, strange to say, has had a beneficial effect upon my spirits, which were flagging wofully before it broke out."[25]

Thomas Wentworth Higginson, a fellow New Englander, found periodic bouts with danger an essential antidote to conventional life. Raised mainly by his mother, a strong woman, Higginson was awed by females and had trouble relating to girls. For a while he was a peeping tom, spying on a favorite girl through her windows. When he married, his wife quickly became invalided and it has been suggested that she was avoiding a difficult relationship. Higginson's adventure was not to be in his marriage. A clergyman, he felt keenly the common view that ministers were effeminate and showed a need to demonstrate physical prowess through strenuous athletics and risk taking.[26]

He found adventure in violently opposing slavery, leading an attack on the Boston jail to free a fugitive slave. He financed John Brown and visited Kansas where he realized he liked carrying a gun. When he had to pack away his revolver as his train returned to Boston, "it fully came home to me that all the tonic life was ended, and thenceforward, if any danger impended, the proper thing would be to look meekly about for a policeman, it seemed as if all the vigor had suddenly gone out of me, and a despicable effiminacy had set in." Home to tending the invalid wife.[27]

Higginson's philosophy was now set: "Life is sweet, but it would not be sweet enough without the occasional relish of peril and the luxury of daring deeds. Perhaps every man sometimes feels this longing . . . when he would fain leave politics and personalities, even endearments and successes behind, and would exchange the best year of his life for one hour at Balaklava with the 'Six Hundred.'" He enjoyed his Civil War service: "Nothing can ever exaggerate the fascinations of war, whether on the largest or smallest scale." In dangerous situations, such as night patrols, "every nerve is strained to utmost tension; all dreams of romance appear to promise immediate fulfillment" (the Victorian use of romance to mean not love but adventure is revealing). For the rest of his life, Higginson promoted war's tonic effect and enjoyed tasting danger. At fifty-three he went to watch a fight between police and strikers; "find myself enjoyed this little danger as of yore," he confessed.[28]

War as a finishing school offsetting the constrictions and sheltering of modern society is a theme of John William DeForest's 1867 novel, *Miss Ravenel's Conversion from Secession to Loyalty*. The book opens with a portrait of modern youth, the product of urban refinement and plenty, a Harvard student: John Whitewood, Jr., was "thin, pale and almost sallow, with pinched features surmounted by a high and roomy forehead, tall, slender, narrow-chested and fragile in form, shy, silent, and pure as the timidest of girls. . . ." The hero, Colburne, is not in such a bad way, but he too needs to escape into the vital atmosphere of war. After four years of outdoor life and fighting, he returns "dark-red with sunburn; gaunt with bad food, irregular food, fasting and severe marching; gaunt and wiry, but all the hardier and stronger for it, like a wolf." Modern man's neurotic symptoms are gone from him: "His constant labors and hardships and his occasional perils have preserved him from that enfeebling melancholy which often infects sensitive spirits upon whom has beaten a storm of trouble."[29]

Oliver Wendell Holmes, Jr., like DeForest, went through the war as a Yankee volunteer officer. Despite being badly wounded several times, he looked on the war as perhaps the most stirring time of his life, writing in famous lines: "The generation that carried on the war has been set apart by its experience. Through our great good fortune, in our youth, our hearts were touched with fire." This message, passed down to young men, made them want to take part in the great male adventure which no civil success could match in intensity; in 1898 Theodore Roosevelt had no trouble recruiting Ivy League graduates with the best professional prospects. "They were to a man born adventurers," he noted proudly.[30]

Roosevelt went to Cuba with romantic notions of war which were rudely shaken by reality. Instead of heroic hand-to-hand combat, the field was swept by unaimed fire from unseen opponents, which killed men randomly. Men suffered horrible wounds and around their bodies "big, hideous land crabs had gathered in a gruesome ring, waiting for life to be extinct." He confessed that "charging these intrenchments against modern rifles is terrible." Yet when the campaign ended and Roosevelt was faced with return to political life, he was already nostalgic for the fading adventure, sighing, "So all things pass away. But they were beautiful days." Later he would say, "San Juan was the great day of my life."[31]

William James recognized that the horrible in war did not turn men away, because "militarism is the great preserver of our ideals of hardihood, and human life with no use for hardihood would be contemptible." War's advocates could argue that its "'horrors' are a cheap price to pay for rescue from the only alternative supposed, of a world of clerks and teachers, of co-education and zo-ophily, of 'consumer's leagues' and 'associated charities,' of industrialism unlimited and feminism unabashed. No scorn, no hardness, no valor any more! Fie upon such a cattleyard of a planet!"[32]

The problem for a pacific person was to find a "moral equivalent to war" that would provide manliness without slaughter, salutary pain to offset the increasing slide to a "pleasure-economy," "intrepidity, contempt of softness, obedience to command." James proposed to draft young men into a national civic force to fight nature in tough jobs; they would be sent "to coal and iron mines, to freight trains, to fishing fleets in December, to dish-washing, clothes-washing, and window-washing, to road-building and tunnel-making. . . ."[33]

Similar suggestions continue to be made but they come up against basic problems which James failed to address. Business and organized labor do not want a national youth army meddling extensively in the private capitalist sector, coopting jobs and potential profit. Psychologically, window-washing may inculcate hardihood and discipline but the glamor and adventure of the military are missing. The Peace Corps recently and the Salvation Army in James's time have tried to associate themselves with some of the military mystique through organized service, but with only limited success. Even suffragettes traded on the popularity of military styles, adopting military formations and marching steps. One feminist asserted "that militant suffragettes stand in an analogous position to soldiers." But these movements had only narrow appeal and their aims were often antithetical to the philosophies of those who lauded the martial virtues.[34]

To work, James's plan would have needed the active advocacy of educators, but most would have found degrading the notion that menial chores like clothes-washing were a beneficial activity for their students. The academy contained relatively few pacifists. More typical, perhaps, was Eton master William Cory who would stop his class to watch a file of soldiers go by, as "his eyes filled with gathering tears."[35]

Education, which played an increasingly significant role in the lives of middle and upper class boys, failed in large measure to help them adjust easily to the world they were growing into. Many teachers were in retreat from modernity with its noise, bustle, rapacity, and vulgarity. They encouraged childhood as a phase separate from, and in many ways antithetical to, adulthood. Their answer to the problem of living in the modern milieu was to avoid it as long as possible. G. G. Coulton recalled that his masters at Felsted "were little more than grown up schoolboys to the end." They could inculcate in the boys a jaundiced view of the world and a naive view of their role in it. Typical American prize essays in school competitions at the turn of the century bore titles like "The Search for the North Pole as a Training for Heroism" and "The Effects of Luxury on National Development."[36]

This reflected a broader tendency in the society, so that some adults were immature, striving to retain a boyish innocence. "You must always remember that the President is about six," said Cecil Spring Rice of his friend Roosevelt. Baden-Powell admitted that men like himself were "boys all our lives" and "we have our toys and will play with them with as much zest at eighty as at eight." Winston Churchill, arriving in Cuba to observe the dirty little irregular warfare there between Spaniards and guerrillas, "felt as if I sailed with Long John Silver and first gazed on Treasure Island."[37]

At times the desire to postpone full entry into the arena of adult work and civic involvement attained the dimensions of a death wish. Cecil Boyle, from an old English family, disappointed school chums by becoming a stock broker but redeemed his reputation by dying as a Boer War volunteer. Herbert Warren wrote in memorial:

Life's business came, you passed into the stress
Of gainful rivalry, and 'Lost' we cried . . .
Not so. Through lulling ease alert and trained
You kept your manhood's force and your desire;
Still quick, though slumbering, in your breast remained
The seed of sacred fire.

Better an early death than the long mundanity of city finance.[38]

Children can dream of dying in moments of glory; it is a way of dramatizing the developing self. L. E. Jones recalled having a recurring dream as a boy, "in which I died, shot through the chest, on the field of battle, in the moment of victory. I subsided into the arms of an officer; the anxious staff, red-coated and gold-braided, hung over me; I knew that the battle was won and that the credit was mine; and then I woke up." In some literature of the period we find this childish fantasy being encouraged as a satisfactory ambition, a good end to a life curtailed before age can win its victory.[39]

The Hill, a popular 1905 novel by Horace Annesley Vachell, is about three English public school boys. One of these, "Demon" Scaife, is a bounder. He does awful things like play bridge and drink an occasional Scotch. This is because his family is nouveau riche and thus he "lacked a soul." His batting at cricket is technically superb but is suspect because it is too consistent, like the products of his father's machines. "Scaife had been transformed into a tremendous human machine, inexorably cutting and slicing, pulling and driving—the embodied symbol of force, ruthlessly applied, indefatigable, omnipotent." We are reminded of U. S. Grant appalling his contemporaries by the grinding use of force and of Henry Adams's dynamo.[40]

To be redeemed, Scaife must reject his family's milieu and serve in the Boer War. He is encouraged and helped to find a commission by Harry Desmond, the best of the three boys. When Desmond is killed leading a charge, the headmaster of his old school, Harrow, speaks to the school, but his text is not about grief:

> To die young, clean, ardent; to die swiftly, in perfect health; to die saving others from death, or worse—disgrace—to die scaling heights; to die and to carry with you into the fuller, ampler life beyond, untainted hopes and aspirations, unembittered memories, all the freshness and gladness of May— is not that cause for joy rather than sorrow?[41]

The head has stressed five times the positive value of "to die." Now he concludes, starting with a disclaimer which he quickly leaves behind:

> I do not say—God forbid!—that you should desire death because you are still young, and, comparatively speaking, unspotted from the world; but I say I would sooner see any of you struck down in the flower of his youth than living on to lose, long before death comes, all that makes life worth the living. Better death, a thousand times, than gradual decay of mind and spirit; better death than faithlessness, indifference, and uncleanness.

The third boy is left admiring his war hero chums.[42]

If youth is real life and adulthood a sort of padded cell with occasional parole, if childhood is spring and maturity a monotonous winter, then early death is a blessed relief. The dead but unsullied youth is saved from becoming the gradually decaying man. In 1914, bright, idealistic young men, unprepared to know how to live successfully but schooled in dying well, would march to war convinced that in their sacrifice a glutted society would find redemption.

PART | III

PETER PAN'S GREAT ADVENTURE

In 1976 John S. Goodall began a series of delightful little books on Edwardian England. In pictures he takes us through an Edwardian Christmas, a family holiday, summer, and more. Sir Harold Macmillan wrote a foreword to *An Edwardian Summer*. He suggested that the Edwardian period "is not, perhaps, one of the most exciting periods" but it elicits "such indulgent nostalgia" because it had a timeless quality, a sense of eternal strength and verities. It was "our fond belief that our world, no doubt with continual if small changes for the better, would last for ever. . . ."[1]

Sir Harold noted that Edwardian England did have its darker side of privation and hardness, yet this "cast but the smallest of shadows" on his world. Macmillan was not wrong in remembering a gentle, civil time, but it was only a partial picture; a shining image with a dark, glowering mirror twin. The decency and fair play so precious to the English were one aspect of playing the game. But the same mentality also produced virulent anti-intellectualism, obsession with sports, stultifying conformity to team and social rules, callousness to the less fortunate. The stiff upper lip was an admired way to meet death but it was not a good way to live, stifling creativity and free expression. Britain in that golden age on the edge of war was part of a larger western society alive with alienation, boredom, hostilities bred by the anxiety of change, and ready to vent its frustrations in a blood bath deemed wholesome for society.[2]

Since many adolescents were about to fall in Flanders field, it is appropriate to begin this section with a work for children, one which has been immensely popular since it appeared in 1904—*Peter Pan*. Rupert Brooke saw the play three times. He "laughed and wept" and was so carried away that "all things were rose for three hours."[3]

Peter Pan is the lost child, "the boy who would not grow up." He fled his home when he overheard his parents discussing a career for him. "'I don't want ever to be a man,' he said with a passion. 'I want always to be a little boy and to have fun. So I ran away.' . . . " He escaped to an island where he had constant adventures, fighting pirates and Indians. He might be Winston Churchill landing in Cuba with *Treasure Island* racing through his mind, or Roosevelt dropping (Teddy) bears.[4]

Why did Peter fear growing up? A good idea is provided through the character of Mr. Darling, the only employed adult male in the book. He is a financier and works in the City (London). His life is mundane and boring. Darling is a wretched figure. Though always claiming distinction as the breadwinner, he is without stature in his own home, hasn't enough sense to knot his tie correctly, is a physical coward who can't take medicine, and is jealous of his dog's place in the family. No wonder Peter Pan ran away if this is what growing up meant. Better to be Captain James Hook, the "not wholly unheroic figure" who is Peter's antagonist. Hook somewhat represents the Englishman freed from the claustrophobic atmosphere of career and home which have stunted Darling (Hook and Darling are played on stage by one actor). Hook is a graduate of Eton and prizes above all good form, playing the game.

Hook and Peter are largely content playing games of hunting each other, except that Hook is pursued by a crocodile and both fellows want a mother. Not a real mother, however. Though Mrs. Darling is a finer character than her husband, and though she gives Peter the special kiss she has concealed from Darling, she is a mature woman and therefore intimidating. The ideal mother is prepubescent and not sexually threatening. She is Wendy, followed—when Wendy grows up—by her daughter. A good mother cooks and mends for the boys, utters inspiring sentiments, but doesn't get in the way of male games, and has no needs of her own. When Wendy hints to Peter that she wants him to act as her husband instead of her son, he rebuffs her, saying, "You are so queer."[5]

Much of this came out of author J. M. Barrie's experience. His mother found power through invalidism. She took to bed when Barrie was young and he served her, revelling in adolescent knight-errantry. She dominated the boy. He was conditioned to guard against impure thoughts, so that even at university his social life excluded girls and he was shocked by male sexual jokes. When he wrote about women, says his biographer, "they came out of his pen as romantic, self-possessed, sexless beings, set apart from common humanity, completely unreal."[6]

Because sex disturbed him, Barrie seemingly questioned his virility. His short height also bothered him. To compensate, he courted men of action like explorer R. F. Scott and future Field Marshal Bernard Freyberg, a man's man who chose the military over women: "If I find myself falling in love with a girl in this town, I won't stop running till I get on the train, for I know there'll be a war soon and I'll die of a broken heart if I can't go." Pan must finally reject Wendy. When Barrie did marry, he could not expunge his mother's puritanism. In *Tommy and Grizel* he wrote of a male character who might have been himself: "She knew that, despite all he had gone through, he was still a boy. And boys cannot love. Oh, is it not cruel to ask a boy to love?" Barrie's marriage was unconsummated and broke up.[7]

Barrie's view of women is not very nice. Tinker Bell is the female "cat" who is jealous of Wendy, hating her "with the fierce hatred of every woman." She manipulates the boys into shooting Wendy. The mermaids on the island play cruel jokes. Tiger Lily, the Indian princess, is adored by all the braves but she returns their affection with a hatchet. Woman is a rejecter.[8]

Animosity to women surfaces when Tootles shoots down Wendy, mistaking her for a bird. "Tootles' face was very white, but there was a dignity about him that had never been there before. 'I did it,' he said, reflecting. 'When ladies used to come to me in dreams, I said Pretty mother, pretty mother. But when at last she really came, I shot her.'" Such a fate might be justified, for woman is the betrayer. She is carnal and finally hurts those who would be her sons. Shortly after Peter ran away, he decided to go home but found that his mother had bolted the window and another boy was in his bed.[9]

Women must be left behind in favor of the great pursuit of male competition. Being a man is ultimately facing the challenge of death. All the male characters come through rather well here. When Peter believes he is going to drown, after saving Wendy, he behaves in the best stiff-upper lip tradition: "Next moment he was standing erect on the rock again, with that smile on his face and a drum beating within him. It was saying 'To die will be an awfully big adventure.'" In an age which wanted exciting exploits, the big adventure with death would be the formative experience for a generation which experienced the trenches.[10]

In dying well, young men are encouraged by the precepts of playing the game. When Hook is making the boys walk the plank, he allows Wendy "a mother's last words to her children." Wendy says, "I feel that I have a message to you from your real mothers, and it is this: 'We hope our sons will die like English gentlemen.'" Even Hook is at his best at the end. In the final fight, all of the seedy reprobate dissolves. He dies with good form, facing impossible odds, and this transfigures him: "His mind was no longer with them; it was slouching in the playing fields of long ago, or being sent up for good, or watching the wall game from a famous wall." How better to die than in battle, thinking of the Eton wall game.[11]

Dying well was a lesson boys heard a lot at the turn of the century. Barrie's friend, Captain Scott, wrote to him just before he died in the polar wastes. Scott had lost the expedition through poor planning and bad management. But, as he said, successful living mattered less than good form: "We are showing that Englishmen can still die with a bold spirit fighting it out to the end. It will be known that we have accomplished our object in reaching the Pole and that we have done everything possible even to sacrificing ourselves in order to save sick companions. I think this makes an example for Englishmen of the future." Future English men were then English boys completing their education. They did cherish the example and it led them onto the enemy barbed wire.[12]

Did all the killing change the attraction of the great adventure? In 1918 Theodore Roosevelt's son Quentin suffered the worst death known to an aviator: he burned alive over the lines. His father wrote: "Only those are fit to live who do not fear to die; and none are fit to die who have shrunk from the joy of life. Both life and death are parts of the same Great Adventure." Young men are fragile, they die, but Peter Pan lives forever.[13]

SEVEN | A Purpose for Living

Vivian Gilbert, a British actor who became a volunteer officer, began his war memoirs with a short fictional scenario intended to evoke the mood of 1914. He pictures a dreamy Edwardian summer of the kind captured by John Goodall. Under a balmy sky, in the shadow of Ivythorne Manor, Brian Gurnay, a boy of twenty, lies reading. Brian is "a typical product of the English public school," "keen on games and sports of all kinds," a good team player and careful not to outshine his pals academically. The son of an established county family, a secure place in the world is mapped out for him. He would like to be useful but isn't quite sure how. "There were many boys like Brian in England in 1914, drifting into manhood with no settled purpose in life but a vague resentment at the apparent futility of existence." Brian has a benevolent contempt for "the masses." They are to serve him, the tradesmen "who kept shops which supplied his needs." If Brian finds a purpose for living, it will not be in commercial fields.[1]

The book the boy is reading is about the Crusades. In it a knight, Sir Brian de Gurnay, prays that there may be a last holy crusade. Inspired, young "Brian streched out his arms in supplication towards the clear blue sky" and cried, "To fight in thy cause, to take part in that Last Crusade I would willingly leave my bones in the Holy Land! Oh, for the chance to do as one of those knights of old, to accomplish one thing in life really worth while!" But Brian realizes that, in the prosaic, progressive days of summer 1914, his wish for a great adventure is unattainable.[2]

Then Brian's mother calls to him. There is good news in the newspaper: Europe is going to war. "Dear little mother"—how appropriate that she should bring the tidings. "Her voice always struck a chord in his utmost being." Brian is covertly relieved that his father is dead because it has drawn him and his mother closer. "She depended on him for so much and was so helpless when he was not by her side to advise." Why isn't looking after mother a sufficient mission in life? Well, mother may be wonderful, but she is still female, and thus not man's mental equal as a companion. Brian condescends to her. Also, there is the incest taboo. Brian has taken his father's place but he cannot lie in his bed.[3]

The point is made when mother tells Brian about the war. He is exhilarated and feels manly. "Slowly he put his arm around his mother and led her into the hall. In his left hand he still held the paper, hard and crisp to the touch; with the other hand he felt the soft, silky lace of her scarf. How little and bent her shoulders seemed with his strong young arm about them!" The juxtaposition of the hard newspaper and the yielding mother suggests dangerous ground and Brian needs to escape.[4]

"He wanted to break out of the cage which held him, a cage whose bars were love and solicitude and peaceful security." He will go to war. The scenario is perfect. He has no career but the boy will now be useful to his society. Through war he can serve mother, sacrificing for her as she sacrificed by bearing him, while at the same time he can escape the magnetism of their relationship. And by fighting he will escape growing up. Like Peter Pan he will have great adventures outside society, dodging the mundane responsibilities normally associated with his upcoming twenty-first birthday. Triumph: "his eyes shone and he held his mother to him. Her hand trembled still, but Brian felt somehow his prayer was going to be answered, and he was glad."[5]

Speaking now in his real voice, Gilbert says he was working in the New York theatre when Britain declared war. "I realized that for the first time in my life, perhaps, the opportunity had come to do real work in the world, a *man's* work! I could with safety leave the stage to the care of women and boys and men too old to fight." Gilbert was not alone in dismissing the artistic life as "woman's work" or in feeling that war provided real men with their opportunity. American author Owen Wister thought Gilbert's ideas "remind us of the greatness in man at a time when his littleness seems chiefly to the fore."[6]

The story of the boy Brian is perfect evidence for Arthur Ponsonby's 1912 charge that English public schools and their patrons unfitted boys for the real world. "They have no remote idea of how the wealth of a nation is built up, how the business of a nation is carried on, or even how their own needs and requirements are satisfied." Such adolescents lacked purpose. "What may be called a project of life does not exist for them." Thus, as T. C. Worsely was to observe in retrospect: "The war arrived as something of a fulfillment for a large number of Public School boys. This is what we should expect. The nature of the training necessarily foreshadowed something of the kind."[7]

Malcolm Graham White, who left King's College, Cambridge, to join the Rifle Brigade, and who was killed in July 1916, wrote: "When a war breaks out, thousands of leisured young men, who have hitherto thought of little but of how to enjoy themselves, who have hitherto turned their backs on all that was unpleasant and all that provoked thought, suddenly discover that, though it was not 'up to them' to live for their country in peace time, yet it is absolutely their duty to die for it in war time, and fling away their lives with heroism. It is, apparently, easier to fight for one's country than to devote one's leisure to social problems."[8]

The privileged found meaning in war. Frederick Maurice wrote that fighting Germans "has been a wonderful experience," thanks to which "all my peace weaknesses seem to have disappeared. I think I was meant to be a soldier." In peacetime he had suffered headaches. "Now I never have a head or a trace of migraine. I never even use my spectacles."[9]

The sense of alienation from mainstream life was gone. "Did we forget in the days gone by," asked Isaac Gregory Smith, "Not for each other but for all, / The sacred bond of Brotherhood, / By which great empires rise or fall? / Nay! But that evil dream is past, / That strange aloofness healed at last." The aloof, critical intellectual pose of young men was shrugged off with ease and the role of loyal soldier embraced. Basil Liddell Hart brushed aside his parents' concerns about his taking a commission, saying, "If you have any real concern for me to strengthen & form my character & my health you will not withhold your consent." He confessed, "Before the war I, Basil Hart, was a Socialist, a Pacifist, an anti-conscriptionist." But now he believed in "compulsory military service because it is the only possible life for a *man* & brings out all the finest qualities of manhood." Also, "I have acquired rather a contempt for mere thinkers & men of books who have not come to a full realization of what true manhood means."[10]

William Edgar Oliver, a barrister, also embraced the authoritarianism necessitated by total war: "I really do think that from one point of view (i.e., the citizen's) militarism is a fine thing. Everyone ought to serve their State." Paul Jones, a public school graduate turned officer, asked his young brother, "Have you ever reflected on the fact that, despite the horrors of war, it is at least a big thing?" In peacetime, "one just lives one's own little life, engaged in trivialities, worrying about one's own comfort, about money matters, and all that sort of thing, just living for one's own self. What a sordid life it is!"[11]

A little bloodletting would be good for the body politic. Mr. Ward, a typical Church of England minister, preaching on August 30, 1914, declared the war a punishment for materialism: "God is calling us by this terrible calamity from our life of sensation & self-indulgence." In the sacrifice of youth, England would be redeemed from the taint of commercial success. "We were taunted with being a nation of shopkeepers," wrote literature professor Walter Raleigh. "That is a bad mistake to make about any nation, but perhaps worst when it is made about the English, for the cavalier temper in England runs through all classes." The British Expeditionary Force, dying where it stood to stop the German offensive into the heart of France, convinced Grace F. Tollemache that "we wronged thee much" when we thought "ENGLAND! that thou wast faint of heart."[12]

Though the United States was not yet involved in the hostilities, some well-off young American men found release from purposeless ease by volunteering for service. War correspondent Richard Harding Davis found that wealthy Americans in Paris were enjoying being useful in the medical corps. "Certain members of the American colony, who never in their lives thought of anyone save themselves, and of how to escape boredom, are toiling like chambermaids and hall porters, performing most disagreeable tasks . . ." The more adventurous, like Raoul Lufberry, Bert Hall, and Kiffin Rockwell, joined the French Foreign Legion. "If I die, you will know that I died as every man should—in fighting for the right," said Rockwell. Hall was emotionally overwhelmed by the inchoate power of the mobilization in Paris. "No! There never was a thrill like the early days of August, 1914, in Paris, . . . I wouldn't have missed it for all the money in the world." As the troops swept by, he realized that, "by God, I was shedding tears."[13]

As well as allowing men to escape from the sense of floating aimless in an alien materialistic universe, the war gave them the chance to do a "Huck Finn," to jump on the military raft to avoid the women left on the Blighty's shore. And they were waved on by ladies who enthusiastically gave white feathers to younger men out of uniform. There is a revealing image in *High Adventure*, the memoirs of James Norman Hall, an American in the French air service. As he flew over a French village, he saw "a mother vigorously spanking a small boy." He deliberately flew low to frighten her and the boy escaped. Hall said Tom Sawyer couldn't have done better. Indeed—for women's power over men and boys was weakened by war.[14]

Victor Chapman, a young Harvard graduate who joined the Foreign Legion in 1914, had trouble relating to women. After his death in 1916 his father recalled, "During the last few years, I was sometimes disturbed by his lack of interest in women and by his relations to them, which were either social or seraphic—for he was an angel in these matters of sex. He was untouchable. . . ."[15]

The one important woman in his life was his mother and a large motive for fighting was to live up to her expectations. So deep was the attachment that "to leave her out in any account of him would be to leave out part of himself." She was "the author of the heroic atmosphere, a sort of poetic aloofness that hung about him and suggested early death in some heroic form." She had raised him to fight for virtue and against sin. The father recalled: "He continued to the end of his life to make the sign of the cross in saying the same prayers that she had taught him, which ended with the phrase—'and make me a big soldier of Jesus Christ who is the Lord and Light of the world!'"[16]

The power of the mother-son relationship is a central theme in Horace Annesley Vachell's play *Searchlights* (1915). In this work, the war brings back together the members of a family whose lives have been soured by

DUTY CALLS

Although this should be a wrenching farewell, the soldier is waving
his hat exuberantly at the passing troops and the open garden gate
symbolizes the male's imminent escape to freedom and adventure
("Duty calls": 1917 print by G. Renesch, Chicago.)

peace. At the beginning, the relationship between mother and son is particularly close, though not entirely healthy. The boy Harry has a girlfriend but tells his mother: "I don't love her as much as I love you." Love for his mother has spoiled him for another. He adds, "As a matter of fact, I don't know that I could be madly in love with anybody. I'm a cool sort of cove." Mother revels in the intimacy. When Harry kisses her, Vachell's stage direction reads: "She has been lying back with her eyes half shut, as if she were gloating over his caresses." She compares Harry favorably to his father who, she says, has a head but no heart.[17]

This is a volatile situation and it is well that the war comes to whisk the boy away. Harry has been a bit of a "mommy's boy," spoiled, self-indulgent (a drive of the possessive mother is to stop the male child being hard and aloof like the father). He learns grit with the army at Mons and comes home a man. He is reconciled with his father who thought him a pampered waster and also felt threatened by him. Father pays off Harry's debts, "as you have borne arms for England." Harry still loves his mother but now that he has made his sacrifice to her and England, and is a man amongst men, he can safely control the relationship. War makes all come out well.[18]

The war seemed to justify the educational obsession with games. In peace, having no aptitude beyond a sporting bent might look frivolous, but in war sportsmen were seen as assets. Richard Harding Davis, the American correspondent, admired the sporting cut of British officers. "They talk of the war as they would of a cricket-match or a day in the hunting field. If things are going wrong, they do not whine or blame, nor when fortune smiles are they unduly jubilant." Sportsmen could stay the distance. Sir John French thought that the volunteer regiments benefitted from being "officered by county men of position and influence, accustomed to hunting, polo, and field sports."[19]

Sporting language obsessed the officer corps. Massing for attack was like waiting to bat, when you "would like to be knocking about the bowling." Heavy action meant the "hounds are fairly running"; the whole war was like a "hard game of polo." In the Royal Navy, chasing enemy vessels was "stalking warrantable game," fleet action was reminiscent of "when one goes in to bat at cricket," and ships sunk "were tabulated something like a cricket score."[20]

The sporting approach to war was not altogether harmless. Officer candidates were sometimes chosen on this narrow criterion while men from the working middle class with no games experience were passed over. Because there is no necessary correlation between athleticism and leadership in war, Britain got some officers of questionable ability. Hervey de Montmorency, a captain in the Dublin Fusiliers, at first thought the regiment lucky to have rugby players for officers: "I regard an Irish gentleman as the salt of the earth, and when he is a Rugby football player he is the supreme type of what a man should be." But the stereotype didn't hold up: "The three greatest cowards in battle whom I ever met were men who, gauged by their peace-time pastimes, might have been expected to be heroes: one was an international polo-player and the other two had been public school and county cricketers. On the other hand, some of the bravest I have ever known were youths who had never possessed the leisure or means to be sportsmen."[21]

The stressing of sports led to the slighting of expert professional knowledge in favor of a vague accent on "the right stuff" in officers. Guy Chapman's brigade major in France was an unscientific officer of the old army who hunted twice a week, kept fit, and knew so little of the real world that he never checked his bank balance and bankrupted on the eve of the war. "By Jove," he said, "I should have been in the soup if the war hadn't started and let me get straight." He disapproved of Chapman's heavy reading, saying "I only carry two books, the Bible and Jorrocks [on hunting]."[22]

Slighting of professionalism could produce the kind of general who mistook a range finder for a Lewis machine gun. It meant that cavalry was kept in the field as an offensive weapon despite its vulnerability to modern fire power. Worse, "the machine gun was for long belittled," as Major-General Ernest D. Swinton remembered; "few battalion commanders detailed their best officers and men to machine gun duty, which in some units was regarded as a fatigue." As late as the Somme (1916) L. E. Jones was reprimanded because the men of his dismounted machine gun squad were not wearing swords.[23]

Chivalry still found a special place in the lexicon of war. Henry Newbolt wrote, "However we suffer, we have seen the England of our dreams—the Black Prince . . . and all the company of the High Order of Knighthood." Those who died would ascend to Heaven, said Edmund John in a poem written in November 1914, where "kings and knights of the old chivalry / Now hail thee at the last." Through the latter months of 1914 rumors persisted that at the pivotal Battle of Mons, where the British stopped the German advance, "St. George had brought his Agincourt Bowmen to help the English." Arthur Machen, who helped to stimulate this legend through his chivalric tales of war, thought that it reflected a need for spiritual affirmation: "It is precisely because our whole atmosphere is materialist that we are ready to credit anything."[24]

The hope that the war would revalidate the chivalric outlook was misguided: it could not turn back the clock. Rifle power, not ghostly arrows, decimated the German division at Mons. In fact, the chivalric motif propelled men forward into a conflict based on mass production, deeper into the clutches of war machines and bureaucratic regimentation of society, not toward the simpler world romantics craved.

The chivalric code made it impossible to see the absurdity in the mass hatreds of 1914. In his story "The Bowmen," Machen drew an invidious comparison between sturdy British yeoman soldiers and the Germans, from "a country ruled by scientific principles" that used poison gas and other technological atrocities. The British public accepted the propaganda picture of Germany as a big bully bashing plucky little Belgium because it fit the public school teaching that life is black and white, a struggle between the school bully and the clean-cut lads from the rowing team. In this light, the Kaiser was a sort of Germanic Flashman, whose cads could easily be guilty of bayonetting babies, raping nuns, crucifying priests.[25]

The stories of four young men illustrate how easily some bright young people accepted the war and how well it fit their search for a purpose to living. Rupert Brooke, the most famous of them, was born in 1887 to a Rugby housemaster and his wife. A brilliant student, his education nevertheless seemed to fail in giving him a sense of a life's work. At twenty-six, on the eve of war, he confessed, "I don't seem myself to do very much with my existence. And I don't know of anything I very much want to do with it." Part of the problem was that, as an artist, Brooke was appalled by the materialism of the society he was growing into. The industrial magnates whom he saw in cities such as Birmingham were, like Adams's dynamo, "profound, terrifying, and of the essence of life: but unlovely."[26]

He could not through female companionship end the sense of alienation, though he tried several times. In July 1914 he wrote, "I have no respect for young women . . . I know *all* about them. And I hate them." When Katharine Cox, a girl he was attracted to, showed affection for another man, he wrote, "There is a feeling of staleness, ugliness, trustlessness about her. I don't know. Dirt."[27]

Like most public school boys, he was largely removed from girls in his formative years and his closest female relationship was with his mother. She "was person of strong character, though without much sense of humour, and she watched over Rupert's moral and physical welfare with an affectionate, but critical eye." She profoundly influenced his emotional life and left him ambivalent toward the female. Brooke often referred to the horrors of family life and in his poetry the mother is a special but frightening figure. In "On the Death of Smet-Smet, the Hippopotamus-Goddess," he refers to this "wrinkled and huge and hideous" earthly god figure who "was our Mother," a mother who extracted terrible things from her children in the night. "We shuddered and gave Her Her will in the darkness; we were afraid." Brooke fears being robbed of his sexuality by this dominating female figure.[28]

Brooke experimented with homosexuality. In 1906 he flirted with a younger boy who "is very Greek to see, and quite intelligent—a thing so rare in the beautiful!" Then in 1909 he seduced Denham Russell-Smith, another junior boy. But Brooke did not become a confirmed homosexual. Rather, he lived a strained asexuality. He tried to find innocence in the south sea islands but failed. On the way back to Britain he visited the United States where he was appalled by the power of money and the forwardness of women.[29]

In the early summer of 1914 Brooke arrived in England. Privileged, handsome, brilliant, he was also sexually repressed and without firm purpose. He might have whiled life away as a wittily disengaged, disenchanted professor of literature. But then the war came to make Brooke whole. He rejoiced in the call from self to sacrifice:

Now, God be thanked Who has matched us with His hour,
   And caught our youth, and wakened us from sleeping,
With hand made sure, clear eye, and sharpened power,
   To turn, as swimmers into cleanness leaping,
Glad from a world grown old and cold and weary,
   Leave the sick hearts that honour could not move,
And half-men, and their dirty songs and dreary,
   And all the little emptiness of love![30]

For a young man who had been given everything, here was a chance to return the debt. In "The Soldier" Brooke spoke of all he had received from his native land and how, should he die, he would repay the obligation:

If I should die, think only this of me:
   That there's some corner of a foreign field
That is forever England.[31]

Born in 1886, the son of a retiring solicitor and his wife, Frederick Keeling attended Cambridge University, where he knew Brooke and Lytton Strachey. A product of the educational system which was uncomfortable with the industrial wealth that helped to sustain it, Keeling had trouble enjoying work after graduation. In 1910 he became manager of the Leeds Labour Exchange, which put him in the heart of the industrial Midlands. He disliked the captains of industry, saying, "These miserable employers are poor creatures in many ways. They eat too much; they drink too much; they want their women too much." The carnal appetite offended a young man educated to loathe overt sexuality. "I am more of a puritan than ever," he confessed. He dreamed of becoming a latter-day Cromwell, reforming the industrial sector, but shrank from the realities of labor politics. Frustrated, he had a sense that "I have done nothing to justify the huge debt I owe to society."[32]

Keeling too failed to find satisfaction with the opposite sex. This he blamed on his mother, who had been delegated the dominant role early in his life. He felt that she had not socialized him properly. His inability to share with women became acute after he married and his wife became pregnant. He stayed away from her for two months, explaining in his journal: "it is because R. [his wife, not blessed with a full name] does not share my intellectual interests that I allow myself to be separated from her now." After the birth of the child, he did not again make a common home with his nuclear family. He confessed in April 1912, "I simply cannot work most of my moods into the necessary conditions of existence with a wife and children. You can't ignore them when you feel inclined, and I, at any rate, have never been able to accept them as part of my normal self."[33]

Here is an intelligent, educated man, standing inadequate and wretched on the periphery of his own life. The war came as something of a blessing. On December 5, 1914, Keeling wrote, "Assuming this war had to come, I feel nothing but gratitude to the gods for sending it in my time. Whatever war itself may be like, preparing to fight in time of war is the greatest game and the finest work in the world." And then in May of 1915, a telling comment: "I wonder if I could ever find a family an adequate substitute for a regiment."[34]

Donald Hankey, born 1884, like Brooke was a graduate of Rugby, and he came from the same tier of middle-class professionals and lesser gentry. Before the war he drifted from project to project. He went from Rugby to the army technical school at Woolwich and then into the artillery. Here he had a religious experience and determined to enter the ministry. But first he went to Oxford, matriculating in the spring of 1907. After university he wandered in warmer and, he hoped, simpler climes, visiting east Africa, Mauritius, and Madagascar. From here he went to clergy school in 1911 and then to run a boys' club at the Bermondsey mission. But he could not get close to the ordinary people there and so in 1913 he went out to south Australia as a plain farmer, rubbing shoulders with the common people. The experience was only marginally successful.[35]

Hankey was critical of much contemporary life. He disliked "society" because "the whole thing is so artificial and complicated," with elaborate rules for visits, dress, etc. He thought that much of the world of the theatre, "night clubs and a good bit of the world of art, is simply disgusting and devilish." The business class "fails to be heroic. They are lacking in intrinsic nobility, have no sense of eternal *noblesse oblige*." They had produced a materialistic world in which "very few people are not worshippers at *some* shrine of Mammon, though there are many."[36]

Like the others, Hankey was not sexually attracted to women. According to his sister Hilda, Hankey's lack of interest in girls made him feel "dubious" about himself. But it is doubtful that he was homosexual. He was more likely asexual. Probably this was due in part to school training and a father who was distant, withdrawn into his own philosophical musings, so that the moral tutoring of the boy fell to the mother. Hankey adored her. "'Ma' was everything, the only woman who has ever had my whole love, my whole trust, and has made my heart ache with the desire to show my love." As a result of her moral precepts and his great regard for her, he could not think of a woman sexually. He was horrified by sexual jokes at school, saying that a boy often "talks about things that I won't even *think*!"[37]

It is in the context of Hankey's distaste for the carnal that we must put a friend's comment, "His life was a Romance [adventure] of the most noble and beautiful kind." For he was a knight sworn to chaste pursuit of the grail and quite uncomfortable in the twentieth century. He spoke of needing "the zest of a quest," which would allow him to transcend the flesh. Such a crusade was the war against wicked Germany, whose Uhlans, he believed, raped virgins in the very act of praying to the Mother Mary. In the war Hankey found himself and unity with his kind. "Over and above the individuality of each man, there is the corporate personality of the soldier which knows no fear and only one ambition—to defeat the enemy and so further the righteous cause for which he is fighting."[38]

Julian Grenfell was born in 1888 and was among the brightest young men of his generation. But he was born into a family where alienation and aloneness were systemic. Julian's father Willy was disappointed by life and marriage. He took refuge in aloofness and being away on frequent hunting trips, squeezing something of life out of taking it. Here his appetite was voracious. On one shoot he bagged three hundred partridges, on another day he killed four stags. Julian's mother was the more influential parent. But she too was disappointed in marriage and filled the void by endless innocuous flirtations with gentlemen who routinely pledged platonic love to her.[39]

Julian felt stifled. In 1909 he wrote that "conventionality envelops him [the youth] like a pall, thrown over him by his parents and his relations." He saw himself as one "who every year has an increasing desire to live in a blanket under a bush, and will soon get tired of the bush and the blanket." Frustration led to wildness. At Oxford he toilet-papered trees, stripped a colleague in the street, was rowdy and insolent to the dons, beat a cab man almost senseless over a question of the wrong change. He boxed with fury: "I beat my first man to death in 1 3/4 rounds, and they had to stop the fight or I would have killed him outright."[40]

His father ignored all this but it outraged his mother, who could not see why Julian did not just enjoy his privileged life in a seemly way. Their parental rejection was painful to him. He could become withdrawn, saying that "he could feel absolutely no interest nor take any pleasure in the society of any living soul but himself." His relations with girls were clumsy, sophomoric. He would either propose marriage on a casual acquaintance or retreat into cloddish masculinity, treating girls heavy-handedly as "good chaps." Overall there hung his inability to please his mother, a failure made more painful by his father's neglect. L. E. Jones, who knew him well during the Oxford days, said he was often depressed by this. A grovelling, apologetic letter to his mother, sent after one of his juvenile stunts, was illustrated with a female angel (of mercy or death) hovering over a frightened boy, cowering in a corner with his head in hands.[41]

The war turned a misfit into a hero. Julian always enjoyed killing and so there was little doubt, as Jones put it, "but that he would become a distinguished soldier and leader of men." He recalled that "Julian went to war with high zest, thirsting for combat." Grenfell revelled in campaign life. On October 11, 1914, from near Ypres, he wrote, "It's all the best fun ever dreamed of." On the 17th he added, "It's a great war whatever. Isn't it luck for me to have been born so as to be just the right age and just in the right place?"[42]

He could reach out to others through a rifle. He loved sniping, using a fine weapon, equipped with telescopic sights, which his father sent him. He exulted: "The fighting excitement revitalizes everything—every sight and word and action. One loves one's fellow man so much more when one is bent on killing him." He entered his kills in his game book, along with his record of birds and animals shot. His relations with his mother improved, as she admired his courage. "I *adore* war," he wrote. "It is like a big picnic without the objectlessness of a picnic. I've never been so well or so happy." With rifle in hand and living in a tent, he thought he had "Plato's idea of happiness realized—no personal property or ties, just as ready to move or to stay."[43]

These were Peter Pan's lost boys and they each came face to face with the "awfully big adventure." Grenfell was killed in action early in the fighting. Brooke succumbed to food poisoning on his way to the eastern front during 1915. Keeling was killed by a bullet while bombing Germans out of a trench during August 1916. Hankey, the last to go, fell to a machine gunner while trying to rally his men under fire in an attack on the Somme, October 12, 1916.

EIGHT | # The Best Place to Be

By 1915, or 1916 at the latest, the horrific nature of mass warfare, dominated by efficient killing machines, should have registered in the British public mind, dissipating the old affirmative view of battle, and leaving a more realistic attitude. This was not entirely the case. There was shock at the beastlier aspects of modern war but many old ideas carried on, sometimes in modified form. The same was true of the United States, which did not enter the war until 1917 and had to wait until 1918 to have large numbers of troops on the firing line. America was not in the war long enough for a radical transformation of ideas to take place.

Vivian Gilbert's memoir is again interesting, as illustrating the continuing affirmation of war. We left Gilbert happily departing for war, leaving the stage to women and old men. He wanted to believe that "we were all knights dedicating our lives to a great cause, training ourselves to aid France, to free Belgium, to crush Prussianism, and make the whole world a better place to live in." After these heady expectations, the trenches were a letdown. "The mud, the flies and the stench, and death forever waiting around the next traverse! Worst of all, it was dull, unromantic."[1]

To make matters worse, Gilbert lost a brother at Gallipoli; another was crippled for life, and the youngest was killed after that. But then came glorious news. Gilbert was transferred to General Allenby's army in Egypt for the assault on Palestine. He was now a crusading knight again, fighting for the holy places. "What ghostly figures of dead and gone Crusaders should we not meet out there to encourage and guide us to our goal?"[2]

He loved the sights, sounds, and smells of fighting men on the march. The more he soldiered, the more he found that "the outer layers of supersensitive insincerity and decadent refinement were wearing thin, allowing some of my truer nature within to assert itself." Altogether, "I knew my life had become fuller and more vital in every way." At the end of the war he was satisfied, despite the loss of his brothers: "We had finished our crusade, peace and freedom were in the Holy Land for the first time in five hundred years—and it all seemed worth while."[3]

Gilbert's experience is atypical in that he served in the east. On the desert floor, cavalry had the opportunity "of proving to the world that they were as much needed in modern warfare to-day as they had been in wars of the past." In France this was not true. But even before his posting to Egypt, Gilbert had found massive compensation for grim war in the fellowship of men in uniform and the power over them conferred by officer status. Early in the war he wrote: "For weal or woe they were *my* men, I was their commanding officer, their master! Any orders I might give they would have to obey." Males have sometimes sacrificed a great deal for control.[4]

For the first time, Gilbert got to know working-class men intimately. He saw blue-collar heroism. His batman, Sale, had started a small, struggling business, which he left his wife to run when he volunteered. She encouraged him to go. This fortitude inspired Gilbert. He admired the tutor role of angelic women, even working-class ones: "It made me proud to think that there were so many English wives like that; for are not we men what our women make us?" One bitter night Sale got both legs blown off and Gilbert knelt weeping, with the lad's head in his lap. But even here were compensations. Gilbert had been moved to cry, a massive emotional freeing for a respectable Englishman. And he now felt that he and Sale were equals. It is odd that it took war to suggest their common humanity to many British people.[5]

Though war continued to be affirmed, there was revulsion at front-line conditions. "A modern battlefield," wrote Coningsby Dawson from the front, "is the abomination of abominations." The countryside is "pitted with shell-holes as though it had been mutilated with small-pox. There's not a leaf or a blade of grass in sight." In the trenches, "from the sides feet stick out, and arms and faces—the dead of previous encounters." "Nothing stirs. The only live sound is at night—the scurry of rats." The landscape was a lunar wasteland, a surreal nightmare.[6]

The effect of the machine gun was shocking to people who had only read about its impact on natives in far-away places. T. S. Hope, a front-line soldier, observed that an expert gunner "should be able to cut daisies," because when the gun was aimed "to hit below the waist," "no living object could pass such a deadline." The few who survived would be like the wounded tommy with "five perforations at the foot of the abdomen, a nasty wound; but then, the machine-gun is a nasty weapon."[7]

The heavy artillery shell was even more exasperating. Captain Thomas Michael Kettle wrote, "I have seen war and faced modern artillery, and know what an outrage it is against simple men." Shelling was particularly horrible because men had to shelter underground in enforced inactivity; they could take no positive action to alleviate their misery. This violates a basic animal instinct to react. Lieutenant Clement Aubrey

Syncons said that "it's not human nature to stand still and do nothing while being bombarded day after day and go on doing nothing." Eddie Rickenbacker, watching from the air a creeping barrage, "wondered why men in the trenches did not go utterly mad with terror."[8]

Machines and machine-made equipment so dominated the war that the conflict itself sometimes appeared as a great machine, a sausage-maker. Philip Gibbs, a civilian, was sickened by "the abomination of a war between civilized peoples whose scientists had invented a machinery of slaughter unknown before in its annhilating power."[9]

War was often not as sporting as many had anticipated. The shooting of prisoners was common and the behavior of the armies was anything but that of Christian knights. After some troops fraternized on Christmas Day 1914, the generals next year laid down a barrage on Christ's birthday. Women, who had to bear the loss of men and live on, were sometimes quicker to see the point than their menfolk. Ruth Comfort Mitchell wrote of war that man should have "done with knightly joke of it," for "dying men wait for maggots & crows to peck at them."[10]

Yet overt opposition to war was a minor key in the society. For most people the cause remained pure and the value of war clear. The most abused figure during the war years was the pacifist. It is perhaps a law of human existence that our physical circumstances change faster than our ability to adapt our philosophies and shed our outworn intellectual garments for ones more appropriate to the times. This was particularly true of men raised in the English public school tradition which, as T. C. Worsley put it, "could not provide England with educated gentlemen enough to lead Europe out of war, or even with clever enough gentlemen to be good soldiers . . . it provided instead the solid games-trained plodders who had learned to obey and to stick to it." The correspondent Philip Gibbs said that all the generals he had met were of the same type. They were clean cut, honorable, and courageous. "But with few exceptions, they did not reveal any spark of genius, or any imagination, or any touch of spirituality, or any eccentricity of mind."[11]

At the front, playing the game and sticking up for the school side remained dominant concerns. Geoffrey Thurlow wrote before the "stunt" in which he was killed, May 1, 1917, that "he would like to do well, for the School's sake." Harry Sackville Lawson, the headmaster of Buxton College, who volunteered in 1915 and was killed in 1918, wrote in 1917 to his pupils from the trenches: "I've got one thing in particular to say to you all—just the main thing we've talked about together in its different bearings in the past—just the one important thing which keeps life sweet and clean and gives us peace of mind." It was: "Playing the game for the game's sake," which meant doing one's duty and obeying orders. It was this, he said in another letter, "which distinguishes the Englishman from the Hun. The Hun is a dirty fighter, that's the first and last word out here; and a dirty fighter is an abomination unto the Lord." The war must go on, said Lawson, until the German "sees the error of his ways and understands the meaning of the word Gentleman."[12]

Playing the game meant that the obsession with sports continued. One officer, going behind the lines for a bath, was startled to see "a group of officers coursing a haré, following a big black hound on horseback." General Julian Byng kept his eye out for excellent shooting ground whenever his command was marching and would cry out, "Wouldn't the partridges come out here nicely?" During the Battle of the Somme, hussar L. E. Jones was called to his colonel's tent. Anticipating orders to charge through "the Gap" which the British always expected to make in the German lines, he was told instead that the regiment would in the future accept no officer worth less than £400 a year. This would ensure that newcomers could field a proper polo stable.[13]

War remained a sort of game for many. Lieutenant Christian Creswell Carver, a Rugby graduate killed in July 1917, wrote in February of that year "that the grand obstacle Hun Hunt is now open." One could "take a nasty toss" at a fence, i.e., be killed, but "one couldn't do it in a better cause." Charles Carrington said some treated the Somme as a sporting event, advancing officers "dribbling a football or blowing a hunting-horn." "Major Townshend, a sporting type in the 8th, went over the top with a shot-gun—no bad weapon for trench-fighting—and a terrier to flush the game. He survived and told me afterwards that he had bagged two or three brace . . ." Paul Jones said in 1917 about a big attack: "The excitement of the last half-hour or so before it is like nothing on earth. The only thing that compares with it are the few minutes before the start of a big school match."[14]

Americans also frequently used sporting language. Troops going into battle "went under fire as at a football game, in shirtsleeves, with the sleeves rolled up over nervous biceps." Sporting metaphors helped to humanize the war and keep at bay its mechanistic nature. David D. Lee, the latest biographer of Sergeant York, says that York represented what Americans wanted to believe they were and not what they had actually become: he was rural in an urban age, he rejected riches at a time of crass materialism, as a mountaineer he represented a simpler age. Most importantly, "York's victory over what was the most deadly emblem of the machine age, the machine gun, represented for many the final supremacy of man over the instruments of destruction he had created." That York's actions, however remarkable, were not typical, and that he had triumphed over machine-gunners from an exhausted, demoralized army, was forgotten.[15]

In the attempt to show that man retained superiority over the machine, it was important to demonstrate that the war was still an arena for chivalry. Lord Northcliffe, writing in September 1916, thought the British soldiers were "knights in the Great Crusade," deserving of the highest degree in the ranks of chivalry. F. S. Oliver, a government bureaucrat, said of the junior officers he met at the front in October 1917: "The young school of to-day are the stuff of which knights have been made ever since the world began." Arthur Machen, the man partly responsible for the Bowmen of Mons rumors, turned out many tales depicting the tommies as medieval soldiers. In "The Dazzling Light" a man has a vision of long lines of helmeted infantry with maces and crossbows, crossing a medieval countryside. However, the scene turns out to be modern France, the helmets are those of *poilus*, the maces are really bomb-throwers and the crossbows are grenade launchers.[16]

The fullest expression of the chivalric myth as a framework for the war was given by the popular English writer Henry Newbolt in his 1917 offering, *The Book of the Happy Warrior*. "Chivalry," said Newbolt, "was a plan of life, a conscious ideal, an ardent attempt to save Europe from barbarism," and "it still survives, and still gives the answer to both barbarians and pacifists." For chivalry was as much needed in 1917 as in the Middle Ages. There were still weak peoples like the Belgians to be defended and their women protected against brutality. Knights "set women in their right place, as the stars and counsellors of men," superior beings to whom the knights tendered "a readiness to serve, based upon a real feeling of reverence." The value of chivalry to the present world was shown in the magnificent military performance of the public school men: "that class has not only made possible the winning of this war, it has proved to be almost the only trustworthy source of leadership."[17]

The birthright of the English lad is soldiering: "Nearly all English boys arc born to the love of fighting and of service." This inheritance comes directly to the public schools from the real-life school of knighthood and not from the monastic schools which produced "sneaks or book-worms." English boys do not like books, Newbolt says proudly. The public school "has derived the housemaster from the knight to whose castle boys were sent as pages; fagging from the services of all kinds which they there performed; prefects from the senior squires or 'masters of the hench-men'; athletics, from the habit of out-door life; and the love of games, the 'sporting' or 'amateur' view of them, from tournaments and the chival-ric rules of war."[18]

In addition to sports, there should be war games at school. "If our games are to be a thorough training for war, they must include throwing the bomb as well as the cricket ball, and racing not only in boats, but in aeroplanes and armoured cars." So the purpose of education is not intellectual development but to fit boys for killing. Note with what eager-ness Newbolt proposes youth as a time to prepare for war and death—he positively shoves youth into the cauldron.[19]

The problem is that chivalry is difficult to square with the modern battle landscape, a morbid wasteland where men live amid slime, excreta, and the rot of bodies, and where prisoners are shot or bayonetted. Yet somehow chivalry was to be found in all this. In September 1916 Newbolt talked to a wounded corporal who had killed a surrendered German machine gun squad. Instead of being appalled, Newbolt saw the love of man for man, for the corporal was driven by the death of pals, "chaps you love like your own brother—you know, sir, you do love 'em like that out there." There was a whiff of chivalry too, for hadn't the Black Prince, a paragon of soldierly virtue, ordered the execution of French prisoners at Crécy to secure the safety of his English army?"[20]

If the ground war did prove too mucky and real ultimately, there was the air to look to. Chivalry lived on through the dogfight fought among cleansing mists. Air war, said Professor Walter Raleigh in 1918, "demands all the old gallantry and initiative." Lieutenant Leslie Y. Sanders, Royal Engineers, watching a dogfight from the ground on March 4, 1917 (shortly before his death), wrote that "there's one thing air fighting has done—it has brought back something of the old delight of battle to war." "There, in the swift battle that flashed by us this afternoon, two men staked their lives upon their own skill and judgement; creatures of glorious power, freed from the trammels of earth, whirlwind-charioted in the eyes of death. And in that there is nothing mean."[21]

Failing to beat the machine, it was coopted into the scenario so that the love affair with war could continue. Missing from the romantic picture was the fact that a flyer's life expectancy at the front was measured in weeks; the beautiful machines burned quickly, entombing the parachuteless pilot in an agonizing coffin. Yet the flyers themselves believed that theirs was a nobler pursuit than the foot soldier's. Victor H. Strahm, an American in the 91st Aero Squadron, thought "there is always more of the sport & game side of war in flying than in any other branch." Eddie V. Rickenbacker became absorbed in the gallantry of the skies, writing that "with American flyers, the war has always been more or less of a sporting proposition and the desire for fair play prevents a sportsman from looking at the matter in any other light, even though it be a case of life or death."[22]

In understanding why soldiers retained enthusiasm for war, the sense of power involved in killing and the animal adrenalin flow of battle cannot be ignored. "In the small space of the dug-out the air is electrified," wrote veteran T. S. Hope. "It seems as if the excitement created in one body could transfer to another, the process involving the whole atmosphere." Combat was a "grand and glorious feeling," said American lieutenant James Norman Hall. "It comes in richer glow, if hazardous work has been done, after moments of strain, uncertainty, when the result of a combat sways back and forth . . ."[23]

But it was not only the nervous thrill that kept men convinced the front was the place to be. It was also being away from "them," the others: stuffy older civilians and women. The trenches were a young-male club and, just as adolescents haunt quick-mart parking lots today, many soldiers breathed a sigh of relief when they returned to France. Thus some of the soldiers' grumbling about the inadequacies of the civilians is youth's perennial disdain for those who have had the bad taste to age. Between Blighty and the trenches was a generation gap.

To the soldiers, older civilians had not earned the right to praise so fulsomely war's virtues. The civilian attributed to the soldier an unending joy in combat. The joy might be there but the soldier also wanted the layman to be sensitive to the discomfort, fear of mutilation, and depression. Most civilians had no real concept of trench war and this made it hard to discuss the experience with them. With their boys' book tone, reports by noncombatants could seem insensitive. An American correspondent described tank crews as "adventurers" "with the zest of boys on holiday." "With infinite humor they described how the enemy sometimes surrounded them when they were struck, and tried in vain to crack their shell, while they themselves sat inside laughing." Actually, crews of machines hit by fire could die hideously as bolts and rivets careened through the hull. The soldier wishes to be seen as a gay blade but not as a moron.[24]

The soldiers expected much civilian gratitude and deference to their

CADET: "Really, from the way these College Authorities make themselves at home you'd think the place belonged to them."

Soldier schoolboys, training for France, lord it over their erstwhile masters. (*Mr. Punch's History of the Great War.* New York: Frederick A. Stokes, 1920.)

warrior status, inverting the junior to senior standing of the prewar days. In the poem "Master and Pupil," a public school housemaster muses on the boy he used to coach who is now his and England's defender: the child is now "my pupil and my master." Where parents expected a continuation of old roles, there could be great resentment. At a British base hospital, Siegfried Sassoon saw a father trying to tend to his wounded son, and noted that "more than once I had seen the son look at his father as though he disliked him." "Time for some more beef-tea," cried a nurse, and "nourishment is administered under approving parental eyes." Back to the nursery. Robert Graves, home on leave, had to attend three-hour church services with his parents.[25]

Soldiers were shocked to find much business as usual at home. Captain Charles Greenwell spoke to a colleague back from leave: "Like most of us, he seems rather disgusted with the general public at home, who don't seem to take any interest in anything much and are frankly bored by the war." Basil Liddell Hart concluded that "whilst the men at the front have proved that the best elements of the nation are more virile than ever, the public and press at home have demonstrated their degeneracy. . . ." The soldiers, Guy Chapman said, thought the men at home were "profiteering, drinking, debauching the women." Charles Carrington agreed: "Only in the trenches (on both sides of No Man's Land) were chivalry and sweet reasonableness to be found."[26]

The flaw in the theory that bloodletting is good for society was that military service fell on youth, the least flabby. If war is a good thing, why doesn't everybody go to the ball? When Conan Doyle said that "the front firing trench" was "the most wonderful spot in the world," why didn't he stay there instead of taking advantage of his age to go home? Yet the gap between younger and older men can be exaggerated; the bickering took place within a well-defined framework of agreement about the war's value. The most distancing was from women.[27]

Some men saw the chance for sexual escapades in overseas service but others were repulsed by the kinds of foreign women they could easily "make"—lower-class widows, prostitutes, factory girls. These unfortunates were often badly treated. James McConnell, an American soldier, decided that "a little rough play was about the best system" of handling his French maid-mistress. Sidney Rogerson said that most British soldiers rejected the "shapeless cart-horse peasant women" and instead would "build up each his own idea of a dream woman, a 'woman of the horizon,' some one who should be soft, and silken, and scented." T. S. Hope rebuffed an enthusiastic French girl, saying, "Girls to me are a sacred sex composing all that's good and clean." Woman fades into the horizon, still angelic, still untouchable.[28]

Rogerson also noted a deep mother love among the men: "We saw in his letters home which came to us for censoring, the filial devotion of the 'toughest,' drunkenest private for his aged mother. . . ." Mother remains the ideal of unthreatening femininity. Henry Williamson thought French women ugly and painted but pictured his mother praying before he went over the top. He associated other women with danger. Under shell-fire one night he "imagined a girl smiling in the darkness." He paused, exposed, "to be alone with the light-blasts giving him the soft glances for his desire." But if the female is alluring she is also deadly; the shells change to gas and he must escape: "The white luring of the celestial-satanic female merging into his body fled away in the fear of green-cross gas shells. . . ."[29]

The dislocation of war did not necessarily shake the moral standards of young men in uniform. Lieutenant Eric Lubbock, Royal Flying Corps, wrote from the front to his younger brother in March 1917, urging him to "keep yourself unspotted from the world," "for a thousand virtues do not atone for one vice." According to Enid Bagnold, young nurses too were "conformists" who pretended that "in spite of our tasks, our often immodest tasks, our minds were as white as snow." Not that much had changed, including the female role of reforming men. Monica Dickens, a volunteer nurse, said that ward sisters often denied pain killers to men in agony because they needed a "purge of suffering" and "must stick it out."[30]

In the trenches an intense male companionship replaced the company of women. Though not believing in the romance of war, Captain Theodore Wilson saw "a new sort of comradeship" arising from the battlefield. Guy Chapman felt the sense of a battalion marching in the sun together "a draught more heady than doctored *vin blanc*, than the forgotten kisses of the girl in the billet." If the soldiers had a mistress, it was war. Adjutant Gilbert Frankau, poring over a headquarters map, plotting the dispositions for battle, wrote: "We have decked the map for our masters as a bride / is decked for the groom."[31]

The compensations of the front line were bought at terrific risk of injury or death. Yet many soldiers did not question the worth of the slaughter or the justice of the cause. "The empire has a great work to perform," General Smith-Dorrien told his wife from the trenches. "Those who go to eternity before the task is completed are heroes, and must be thought of as such and not mourned." The religious context of the western nations prepared them for the sacrifice of life, because at the center of Christianity is the image of the son, killed to atone for human sin. Now many sons were called to the cross. The Rev. W. J. Dawson saw "an England purged of all weakness, stripped of flabbiness, regenerated by sacrifice." His son, at the front, wrote that with "the first Prussian gun the cry came to the civilized world, 'Follow thou me,' just as truly as it did in Palestine. Men went to their Calvary singing Tipperary. . . ."[32]

The atonement was for materialism and democracy's corrupt peace. Lieutenant Jack Donaldson wrote on August 6, 1917, that a fellow officer "has died the death he would have chosen and in a good cause. Many a time he said to me that he was sure he would never survive the war, and that he did not, for himself, greatly care, for he was not built for a mercenary age."[33]

Death released young men from the grip of materialism. Field Marshal Lord Grenfell wrote after the deaths of his wards, Francis and Riversdale, that they were "freed from the feverish anxieties they suffered ere they went to war," that is, released from the painful attempt to live in the modern world. John Buchan, their friend, said that they "who had once lived cheerfully in the sun, but for months had been among the fogs and shadows, went back to the sunlight." Their deaths were better than struggling with adjustment to twentieth-century complexities. He found a similar moral in the end of Auberon Thomas Herbert, a Balliol man who lost a leg in the Boer War and became a cabinet minister in 1914. Apparently, for Herbert, "the long round of conferences, deputations, unmeaning speeches, idle debates was wholly distasteful." In London, "he seemed to find the world rather tarnished and dusty, and to be longing for a clearer air." So he joined the Royal Flying Corps; "up in the clouds he had come to his own and discovered the secret of life."[34]

Buchan's writing continually suggests that death in war is the purpose for which these men lived; it leads them to a better life. Dying makes wooden-legged Herbert young again and he soars off into springtime. Buchan was not unusual. John Masefield wrote exuberantly of early death in his account of the Gallipoli campaign. All Masefield's soldiers are happy warriors. Australians desperately strengthening emplacements were "working like schoolboys," "they liked the fun, and when praised for it looked away with a grin." As attacking boats row for the beaches, "all the life in the harbour was giving thanks that it could go to death rejoicing. All was beautiful in that gladness of men about to die. . . ." Masefield's sincere cheerfulness is chilling. The death of young men is a transcendental experience. In an action where wounded men caught on Turkish wire drowned by the hundreds, Masefield believes "they went like kings in a pageant to the imminent death."[35]

Central to this praise of death is the concentration on being young that characterized the period. Youth was associated with vigor and beauty, a firm body. Youth was also virginal, sexually clean. Maturity meant flabbiness and loss of innocence. Age might almost be a personal failure. Perhaps better then to die young, as the experience which accompanies age is not worth having. "Not a bad place and time to die, Belgium, 1915," wrote Rupert Brooke. "Better than coughing out a civilian soul amid bedclothes and disinfectant and gulping medicines in 1950."[36]

Earlier, in his poems, Brooke had shown horror at aging. In a vivid piece, "Menelaus and Helen," the Greek king destroys Troy to regain his "lovely and serene queen." But, over the years, she becomes a "gummy-eyed" hag and Menelaus, an old blowhard, loathes her. "So Mene-

laus nagged; and Helen cried; / And Paris slept on by Scamander side."
Note that Paris, dying young, does not decay like the others but "sleeps."
Benjamin Apthorp Gould, in an epitaph for a soldier friend, echoes the
point:

> For him no blight of searing age;
>   Eternal youth is his and joy—
>   The cheerful gladness of the boy
> Shall be his constant heritage.[37]

There is mental sleight of hand here. Old people corrupt even before
they die and they will sour in the grave. But young dead don't decay;
they sleep by streams or fly into spring. Sydney Herbert made the idea
literal: "I feel as if all of us were dead and only they were alive." This
reflects a conundrum in Christian thinking: in Heaven, how will people
look? Will they be different? Or will they be forever as on the day they
died? Apparently this was a popular belief. Paul Jones's father said of
their last meeting: "He looked the incarnation of young manly vigour,
courage and hope, and there was about him a fresh and fragrant air
like the atmosphere of that delicious Spring morning." The father seemed
actively pleased that his son was "like an athlete in the pink of condition,"
as though this meant he would be in top form always.[38]

These are deep waters and not easily fathomed. Does the parent regret the child growing up and thus feel that, when the boy is killed,
he is captured in time forever? Or is it simply too painful to face the
fact that a young life has been blighted? Do the aging parents live vicari-
ously through their children and are they redeemed through their bloodletting? Frances Balfour wrote to Ettie Grenfell, after the death of her
son, "There is something very wonderful in motherhood today; we were
given our children at a time when they would be ready to fight the good
fight . . . and it is given to us to know that what we have given of ourselves
has done its duty." "None of us who give our sons in this war are so
much to be pitied as those who have no sons to give," said Lord Grey.
Is it possible too that death might satisfy some envy of youth? And was
the icon of innocence so important that older people could take pride
in virgin deaths of children? In "The Dead Soldier," Sydney Oswald, a
British major, wrote of a younger man whose eyes "but yesterday / Shone
with the fire of thy so guileless youth" and whose "sweet red lips" "never
knew the stain / Of angry words or harsh, or thoughts unclean."[39]

Some soldiers recognized that death would keep upon them the spotlight which they had enjoyed as the lean boy-heroes. Lieutenant Eric
Lever Townsend said, "But for this war I and all the others would have
passed into oblivion like the countless myriads before us. We should have
gone about our trifling business, eating, drinking, sleeping, hoping, marrying, giving in marriage, and finally dying with no more achieved than

when we were born, with the world no different for our lives." But now "we shall live for ever in the results of our efforts. We shall live as those who by their sacrifice won the Great War." There are two points here. First, the generational smugness is clear: Townsend thinks those who have gone before, living peaceful lives, left no worthwhile legacy. Second, there is a deadly conclusion to his thinking: to be remembered you must die; otherwise you will grow old, fat, and forgotten in the postwar world. "Though life be lost, immortal is the praise!" wrote H. H. Bliss. Therefore, the dead were to be envied:

> Would I were with you crowned with victory's bays
> O Happy Warrior 'midst our English dead.[40]

There was a fallacy in this. Young men were prepared to die to be remembered for their sacrifice. Through their sacrifice, society would be purged and a brighter world would emerge. But what would this world look like? It would be a world without war, for this was "the war to end all wars." But a world at peace, full of prosperity, was precisely the kind that bred the rot of materialism. So one bequeathed ultimately a world as boring and unattractive as that from which one had fled into the trenches. The Great War sacrifice would be in vain because everyone would become flabby and unheroic again.

The flabbiness came. But this, rather than making men feel that death in the trenches had been wasted, made them more envious of the killed who had gone west before the crusade could sour. Charles Carrington, twelve years after the war had ended, said that "as we survivors of the war pass into a sordid unheroic middle age, it is not pity that we feel for those who died on the field of honour. God grant that we may be as lucky on the occasion of our death, and may meet it with a soldier's gay courage."[41]

NINE | # Good-Bye to All That?

The term Lost Generation conjures an image of sad-eyed veterans denouncing war and urging peace upon future generations. The reality is more complex. Much feeling in Britain and America remained as positive about the value of war after 1914-1918 as it had been before. Some thorough antiwar material was produced but many attitudes were essentially unchanged. The twenties saw more pro than antiwar books. Writers who, on one level, appear to condemn war wholeheartedly can be saying something more ambiguous, less pacific, when viewed from another angle.

In part, the less obvious message is this: "Yes, it was hell, but it made men of us, and you who didn't serve should be filled with awe and envy. For there is no experience quite like battle." War still separates the lean Spartans from flabby civilian men and women. To a greater degree than we have acknowledged, the beastliness of No Man's Land did not stop men from enjoying it or endorsing war as a worthwhile endeavor. How else could our society be saturated still with ideas glorifying collective violence? If there had been a true hiatus in love of fighting between the world wars, then the second conflict would have been nothing more than an odious but necessary chore, like taking out the garbage, and we should have put away all our drums and guns and bugles in 1945, as dangerous toys to be locked in the closet. But our endless involvement with violence on film and in print connects us back through the decades of this century to the Victorians. The links in the chain of communication may have bent between the wars, but they did not break.

The point was made explicitly at the end of one of the great Lost Generation books, the memoirs of Robert Graves. He entitled his work *Good-Bye to All That*, as though the war had swept away an era with all its values and left a changed, also chastened, world. Had it? Graves asks himself a crucial question: if he had to relive it all, would he act differently? The obvious Lost Generation response is that he would refuse to fight. Actually, Graves says the opposite. He concedes that, although something of a social outsider, he is so ingrained with the conventional morality of the British respectable classes that he would repeat his steps:

"If condemned to relive those lost years I should probably behave again in very much the same way; a conditioning in the Protestant morality of the English governing classes, though qualified by mixed blood, a rebellious nature and an over-riding poetic obsession, is not easily outgrown."[1]

A well-known American painting of 1919 typifies the idea that the end of the war was hailed with universal relief by an exhausted, peace-craving world. The picture, by Charles LeRoy Baldridge, himself a soldier, shows two weary doughboys, hollow-eyed and arms dragging, staggering up out of the mud on Armistice Day, November 11, 1918. The mood of exhausted relief was deepened by the verse of Hilmar R. Baukhage which accompanied the sketch. It ran in part:

> If you had listened then I guess you'd heard
> A sort of sigh from everybody there,
> But all we did was stand and stare,
> Just stand and stand and never say a word.[2]

The image is of a shaken, contrite mankind awaking from a nightmare of war-lust to a recognition of shared, vulnerable humanity. The problem is that not all soldiers felt this way, particularly Americans, who had been in the war only for a relatively short time. Eddie V. Rickenbacker said that there was no mood of "live and let live" in his squadron during the last week of the war. Requests for missions increased. "Not content with the collapse of the enemy forces the pilots wanted to humiliate them further with flights deep within their country where they might strafe airplane hangars and retreating troops for the last time."[3]

On Armistice Day, Rickenbacker wondered how he would keep up the adrenalin flow. "How can one enjoy life without this highly spiced sauce of danger? What else is left to living now that the zest and excitement of fighting airplanes is gone?" Male comradeship would be lost: Armistice Day saw "the end of that intimate relationship that since the beginning of the war had cemented together brothers-in-arms into a closer fraternity than is known to any other friendship in the world."[4]

These words are ominous for the future. The war has been fought supposedly to end wars, but a survivor writes for coming generations of young men that war provides unsurpassed excitement and intimacy otherwise unattainable. Bert Hall wrote that the war had "a fascination about it that ruins a man for anything else. I know that I will never be much good at work again." James Norman Hall, hearing his comrades discuss their adventures, wondered what "will seem interesting to them after the war, after such a life as this."[5]

William Alexander Percy, a volunteer from Louisiana, wrote of his feelings on Armistice Day: "It's over, the only great thing you were ever part of. It's over, the only heroic thing we all did together. What can you do now? Nothing, nothing." Could he go back to being a country lawyer in a sleepy southern town? "You can't go back to the old petty things without purpose, direction, or unity—defending the railroad for killing a cow, drawing deeds of trust ... You can't go with that kind of thing till you die." So the claustrophobia of civilian life still makes violence appealing. Percy said of those too young to fight, "We feel sorry for them, knowing they missed a lot of fun and a lot of grief that was better than fun." Even war's grief is now an enviably intense sensation.[6]

The soldier continued to deride the unheroic qualities of civilian life. Coningsby Dawson was more afraid of the approaching dullness of peace than he was of enemy bullets. "There's something splendid and exhilarating about going forward among bursting shells—we, who have done all that, know that when the guns have ceased to roar our blood will grow more sluggish and we'll never be such men again." The message to the future remained that war may be ghastly but you're not a full man without it. "There'll be a sense of dissatisfaction when the old lost comforts are regained. There'll be a sense of lowered manhood." He saw his postwar role as gloomy: "You'll work from breakfast to dinner and earn your daily bread. And you'll do it to-morrow and to-morrow world without end."[7]

Basil Liddell Hart felt the war "was the most valuable experience of our lives," giving "lessons in life that no substitute could have provided to the same extent, tending to the development of sympathy and understanding, correcting the 'cash nexus' of modern civilization ..." Part of the moral inversion of war talk is that killing men breeds human sympathy. Liddell Hart's friend, Sidney Rogerson, said, "The pacifist may inveigh against war's hideousness," but "the war years will stand out in the memories of vast numbers of those who fought as the happiest years of their lives." This is because "we were privileged to see in each other that inner, ennobled self which in the grim, commercial struggle of peace-time is all too frequently atrophied for lack of opportunity of expression." Killing brings out compassion: "We were privileged, in short, to see a reign of goodwill among men, which the piping times of peace, with all their organized charity, their free meals, free hospitals, and Sunday sermons have never equalled." Why not keep war when it does more good than a social welfare system?[8]

Some went on killing if they couldn't see a good path into peace. Michael O'Suilleabhain, of the Irish Republican Army, said that his adversaries in the notorious Auxiliaries were ex-officers who still wanted "the prospect of adventure." He described their dress as resembling that of pirates and cowboys, suggesting that Peter Pan had survived the war. Men sought the continuation of killing because a large part of the pleasure of war is in the sense of power derived from depriving others of life. We should not be misled on this score by the soldiers' claims that they loved their enemies. Often such comments were made in a context of comparing the opponent favorably to the flabby civilians at home. The enemy soldier was often maltreated in practice. Captain F. C. Hitchcock, with the British occupation forces in Germany, took cynical advantage of German soldiers, buying as souvenirs their hard-won medals sold for food. When several German veterans refused to salute his men, he had them savagely beaten.[9]

Soldiers waiting for demobilization often felt, with Guy Chapman, that "the whole of our world was crumbling. Presently we could not find a rugger fifteen; not even a soccer eleven." The number of servants, part of the officers' good life, decreased. "Our civilization," said Chapman, using a singularly inappropriate word to describe the milieu of the trenches, "was being torn to pieces before our eyes. England was said to be a country fit only for profiteers to live in." A prowar future is being set up because this war has apparently failed in its bloodletting mission to cure materialism. "We had no longer a desire to go back. It was an island we did not know."[10]

When the soldiers did return home, it was often to a society which had gone on without them. In May 1919 Douglas MacArthur wrote that "there was no welcome for fighting men; no one even seemed to have heard of the war. And profiteers! Ye gods, the profiteers!" Later, E. L. Woodward further crystallized the resentment, saying, "There was . . . no sense of sin among the older generation, no urgency of remorse, no desire to make reparation." Indeed, he concluded, "The men who came back from the war have counted for less, perhaps, in the political life of their country than any generation during the last two or three centuries." This alienation would color Lost Generation writing, which is not only about combat but resentment of the civilians who do not appreciate the soldier.[11]

The veterans' feelings would take a long time to process and it would be the late twenties before much of their work came to fruition. In the meantime, imaginative attempts to deal with the war, often by older civilian writers, tended to carry on earlier themes of war's wholesome effects and the need to believe the suffering worthwhile. Representative pieces were *The Soul of Susan Yellam* by Horace Annesley Vachell and *A Well-Remembered Voice* by J. M. Barrie, both produced in 1918. These authors had contributed before the war to filling boys with the notion of fighting as the great adventure.

Vachell's play depicts the triumphant response of a British village to the crisis. At first, the insular rurals begrudge England's commitment to the continent, but they are rallied by the local elite and the village gives more than its share of sons to the cause. The local squire, Sir Geoffrey Pomfret, is relieved by the patriotic upsurge. "He—and thousands like him—had been tormented by the fear that a nation stigmatized as shopkeepers would place self-interest before honour." The vicar, who like Pomfret sends a son to war, also finds the times inspiring. Looking at the young men departing, he sees that it was "good to be young and valiant, at such a good time, good even to die, if the supreme sacrifice were demanded, clean of limb and mind, leaping joyously upward, unfettered by disease or vice, *fit*." Vachell still believes it is better to be machine-gunned than masturbate.[12]

The boys are all happy warriors. Young Lionel Pomfret, home with a wound, "admitted with a laugh—with a laugh!!!—that the enemy was 'hot stuff,'" and he told "stories of France bubbling over with humour and high spirits." Wounded tommies billeted in the village share the same frolicking schoolboy attitude and Vachell states carefully "that the high spirits of these gallant fellows came *from* the trenches. . . ."[13]

The English social system and values are vindicated through war. The seemingly shallow public school education is proved sound. The vicar ruminates that he had thought Lionel Pomfret a light fellow, "cradled in ease and luxury, popped on a pony to ride through life as soon as he was short-coated, sent to a great public-school, not to acquire learning, but manners and skill at games. . . ." Yet the system must work because Lionel has become a courageous soldier. "The fact bristled in front of him that Lionel, and thousands like him, had 'made good' against all odds, vindicating an education which consistently disdained efficiency except at games and sports." Anti-intellectualism proves the best approach in the end.[14]

The conservative role of women is also vindicated. When war comes, "violent suffragists" are rejected and the women revert to being angels, "the mightiest lever to raise and regenerate a nation." Women would be "a beacon steadily shining. The women would have their opportunity. One could adumbrate triumph or disaster by the effort, sustained or otherwise, made by them. The men would play their part, if the inspiration of the women lay behind them." The war gets women out of politics and back into the role of providing moral support.[15]

Most important, the war had lessened materialism. Again, using the inversion of sense by which the culture cloaks the inhumanity of war, it is the vicar, servant of a pacific Christ, who sees that killing is a great good. He "decided that the time for peace might be far distant, if the designs of Omnipotence were rightly apprehended by him. Armageddon would continue till the pain had purged the whole world, till materialism in its hydraheaded forms was slain by spirituality. . . ."[16]

The war has been wholesome. But Vachell has a problem. Many of his audience have suffered losses, either through the war or the influenza epidemic of 1918. Can this really be for the best? To answer this question is the role of the lead female character, Susan Yellam. She loses both her son in the war and his wife in childbirth. Susan doubts the existence of God and any meaning in human suffering. But her dead son comes to assure her that all is well; there is a higher purpose. Susan is happy again and Vachell concludes with the message: put your trust in blind faith and the reiteration of clichés.[17]

Barrie makes a similar plea for blind optimism. In his play *The New Word* (1918) a mother of several soldiers says to one son, "It is the noble war they all say it is. I'm not clever, Rogie, I have to take it on trust. Surely they wouldn't deceive mothers." Of course they wouldn't, for motherhood was sacred. Therefore the war had to be right.[18]

In *A Well-Remembered Voice* Barrie falls back on the device used by Vachell: the dead soldier son returns to assure the parent that boys remain happy even after violent death. In this case, Dick Don informs his father that dead troops have plenty of laughs beyond the veil: "We are all pretty young, you know, and we can't help having our fun still." The father is relieved and sees that "there is such a serenity about you now." "It's a ripping good thing to have," replies dead Dick. "I should be awfully bucked if you would have it, too." Britain's dead youth will be happy if their parents don't question the bloodbath. When father tries to talk about the trenches, Dick stops him: "We have a fine for speaking about the war."[19]

Barrie has another, covert, message for men, about war bringing males together. The play suggests that the son's death unites him with the father, safe from the interference of women and the tension which previously marked their relationship. Before the war, Dick had been closer to Mrs. Don. "His mother was his chum. All the lovely things which happened in that house in the days when Dick was alive were between him and her; those two shut the door softly on old Don . . . and ran into each other's arms." Mrs. Don dominated her husband, "a man of no great account in a household where the bigger personality of his wife swallows him like an Aaron's rod."[20]

Mother uses her closeness to the boy to hurt her husband. After Dick's death, she tries to contact him through a medium. Dick's failure to communicate is blamed on Mr. Don's skepticism about the séance. This is cruel, and it is to Mr. Don that Dick later appears. They are united after years of Dick's connivance in his mother's schemes. The father can accept Dick because, being dead, he is no longer a threat. All ends happily in the male embrace. A propellant toward war, escape from the endearing-damaging mother-female, which had pushed on boys like Julian Grenfell, continues in the drama of another driven boy, J. M. Barrie. It also appears that older men might find some relief from generational conflict in the death of younger males.[21]

A more critical postwar view was advanced by H. G. Wells. In 1922 he published *Men like Gods*, a futuristic novel in which a party of humans trespass into Utopia. The Utopians reverse human patterns. They are unashamedly naked, they enjoy "fearless and spiteless love-making." The human approach to sex is furtive and hypocritical. Lady Stella owns "a particularly charming and diaphanous sleeping suit" but she is shocked when the Utopians ask her to wear it: "It's almost—*sacred*! It's for nobody to see—*ever*." The vicar abhors Utopian nakedness but "is disgustingly excited by the common human body." As the Utopians make love freely and naturally, sex does not produce anxiety or hatred. Even teenagers may indulge. Mr. Barnstaple compares this to his own adolescence when girls were off limits and he was taken homosexually at his public school; he remembers "the stuffy, secret room, the hot and ugly fact."[22]

The Utopians have abolished war along with the gender hatreds which help to breed aggression. They tell Mr. Catskill, British Minister for War, that "there are thoughts and ideas like yours in our ancient literature of two or three thousand years ago, the same preaching of self-ish violence as though it was a virtue." It is recognized that humans make war because their lives are unfulfilled and to avoid monotonous work, "toil so disagreeable that it makes everyone of spirit anxious to thrust away as much of it as possible and to claim exemption from it on account of nobility, gallantry or good fortune."[23]

The more sensitive humans grasp the superiority of Utopian philosophy. When Catskill plots violence against the Utopians, Barnstaple stops him, saying, "You are be-Kiplinged. Empire and Anglo-Saxon and boy-scout and sleuth are the stuff in your mind." Humans cannot stay in Utopia because they infect it with their aggression. As Barnstaple leaves, he comments regretfully that the world war had given earth a chance to be Utopian: "The black clouds and smoke of these dark years had been shot with the light of strange hopes, with the promise of a world reborn. But the nationalists, financiers, priests and patriots had brought all these hopes to nothing." War, said Wells, did not produce a better world.[24]

Douglas Goldring also questioned the war's value, in two pieces published during 1919 and 1920. *The Fortune* is the story of Harold Firbank, who has a typical public school education. Goldring criticizes "the process of forcing all the boys into the same mould," a system in which "any sign of intelligence, any interest displayed in 'work' . . . was treated as a crime, only to be excused by athletic prowess." A boy who does not fit in is beaten up by OTC cadets "for going off with a book, instead of watching the great cricket match of the season against Radsted." Upon graduation, Harold becomes the tutor to the children of a Belgian baroness. But the woman's overt sensuality repulses him, for his education avoided female sexuality. "He began to think more of the cold, clean English girls he knew," and he enters a passionless marriage with one of them.[25]

Goldring makes a connection between torpid sexuality and violence. When war comes, the thought of impending killing makes Harold's wife more attractive to him. "The emotional turmoil of the war had suddenly increased his appreciation of her." But his real engagement is with men. As a soldier he will have chums again in an all-male world like school. "He would recapture his boyhood, and the thought of having, once more, a brief spell of life among a crowd of men was not without its charm."

Because he is an artist, he feels he has been missing real life. "All that was trumpery and soft in his existence and in his character would be burnt away in the furnace of war, and he would emerge with the iron strength to which he had always aspired."[26]

This was a telling criticism: English education was so anti-intellectual that the social elite prized violent action over ideas. Ivor Spencer, another artist, cuts his flowing hair and joins the tough Black Watch regiment: "He had shed his Cubism and his decadence with characteristic ease. . . . It was as an artist that he had been a masquerader. In uniform he was himself." Only the fellow who was beaten up by cadets sees the point: the elite have not enough introspection to analyze their predicament. "There's no kick in the poor sons—the public schools while making them 'manly' have turned them into moral eunuchs."[27]

Harold is happy enough at first. He feels a hero, like the best athletes at school. His mother and sister, who disapproved of his artistic phase, now accept him. The sister "did not refrain from telling him that the Army had 'made a man of him.'" He is even treated better by his in-laws, who had distrusted him as "one of these fellows with *ideas*, don't you know." He is at one with his community.[28]

War quickly disenchants Harold. ". . . his ideas of war had been romantic, glamorous, now he saw it in all its actual brutal, beastiality. Every evil passion raged in the men around him: the evil which the glucose school ascribe only to one's enemies." War degrades, not ennobles. Goldring elaborates the point in *The Fight for Freedom*. A British officer, Captain Michael Henderson, is crazed by the war and, while on leave, rapes a woman who had refused to marry him. "Women, all women, love a master," he screams. Goldring sees that the anger generated between the sexes is ignoble and not a spur to valor.[29]

Meanwhile, society bumbles on, spouting clichés, oblivious to the pain produced by the war. A sanctimonious cavalry officer turned vicar, failing to see that Michael is mad, tells him, "What an ennobling and purifying effect this war is having on the nation! I envy you your privilege, Michael." The problem, to Goldring, is that the British, because of their acculturation, are incapable of thinking in unconventional ways to meet the crisis. The epitome of their values is the trim-moustached professional officer, so perfect in manners and courage "that the average Englishman dared not even suggest to himself that there could be such a thing as a reverse to the medal." Good form lies blanket-like on the mind. Trapped, Michael cracks, and Harold is killed by his platoon for showing generosity to Irish rebels in the 1916 rising.[30]

Goldring's powerful criticisms were blunted by several weaknesses. The first is stylistic. Goldring uses the best drawing-room manner, and this softens his punch. When Harold has his epiphany, rejecting the establishment view of the Irish rebels, he can only state his case with limp good form: "As far as I have observed them they appear to be rather a sporting lot." Hardly the line to knock an audience out of conventional thought patterns.[31]

Goldring is also ambivalent. He claims that war degrades man, but he also asserts that "in the darkest places a Christ-like self-sacrifice and devotion would be revealed again and again, a love of comrade for comrade 'passing the love of woman.'" A writer wanting to turn young men away from war must stop extolling its unexcelled powers of male bonding.[32]

Finally, although he attacks the public schools for stunting original thinking, he also is a victim. He offers no coherent alternative to the current system, no radical redefinition of British social values. In *The Fight for Freedom* he suggests only a dimly perceived parlor socialism championed by a young gentleman, Oliver Beeching, who, like Harold, is incapable of ringing statements. When Michael goes mad, Harold observes vaguely, "You know, I can't help thinking this blasted war had something to do with it all! But then I'm a crank." Goldring concludes with a regressive suggestion. Oliver pairs off with Miss Lambert, an older woman who will mold his youthful idealism. Goldring, the public school critic, asks us to believe that change will come from bright-eyed youth inspired by a mother figure. It might be a scene from *Tom Brown's Schooldays*.[33]

As the artists struggled to give literary interpretation to the war, society settled back into conformity. Robert Graves noted that any hope of an antigovernment uprising by ex-servicemen quickly faded. "Once back in England, they were content with a roof over their heads, civilian food, beer that was at least better than French beer, and enough blankets at night." The Versailles Treaty had less impact on the public than "the marriage of England's reigning beauty, Lady Diana Manners; and a marvellous horse called Panther—the Derby favourite, which came in nowhere."[34]

Most did not question Germany's war guilt or their own national patriotism. Millicent Garrett Fawcett, a leading suffragist, in 1924 reiterated her support of Britain's war aims and her pride in the active part women had taken. Henry Newbolt, whose poems had instilled the sacrificial spirit in schoolboys, was gratified to find that, when he toured Canada in 1923, his most famous piece, "Play Up and Play the Game" (about boy officers defending the flag and the old school), was still popular. He said that "they roar for 'Play up': they put it on their flags and on their war memorials and their tombstones: it's their National Anthem."[35]

Although the war had been dominated by technology, it did not quash belief in sports as the best qualification for life. Douglas MacArthur, as superintendent of West Point, emphasized sports in the curriculum. "He had been greatly impressed during the war with how much better athletes among the officer corps performed than did non-athletes and with how much enlisted men admired athletes." Valerie Pakenham believes that the British "public schools urged their pupils on harder than ever to play the game," and that "in the Colonial Office, the belief that cricket and soundness in colonial administration went together was stronger than ever."[36]

A young subaltern on active service between the wars, like M. C. A. Henniker, found that senior officers assumed the *arme blanche*, chivalry, polo, and hunting would go on for ever. To pass an examination conducted by a veteran cavalry officer, Henniker had to say that he would attack machine guns and barbed wire with cavalry, as the instructor considered tanks "new-fangled nonsense."[37]

Traditional male values were championed in the twenties by Christopher Percival Wren, a highly successful author who had been in the French Foreign Legion. His first novel, *Beau Geste*, was published in June 1924, and by December 1925, it had gone through eighteen printings, suggesting the postwar mood. In Wren's books it is hard to tell that the Great War has happened; we might be with Kitchener in the Sudan or Roosevelt in Cuba. He admired Newbolt's line "to love the game beyond the prize," and felt that life remains a game, with war being the grandest sport. The highest complement is to be a "soldier of the finest type, keen as mustard, hard as nails, a thorough sportsman, and a gentleman according to the exacting English standard."[38]

Wholesome fellows don't think too much. "'Well, logic isn't everything,' said the Englishman. Most of our best impulses and ideas are illogical.'" Thinkers are despicable creatures, "the brittle intellectuals who crack beneath the strain." True men don't show emotion. "As became good Anglo-Saxons, we were ashamed to express our feelings, and were, for the most part, gruffly inarticulate where they were concerned," says John Geste. Heavy-handed humor, wrestling, and back-slapping are major means of communication. Misfits are debagged or thrashed. They meet sad ends, like Augustus, a sneak killed by a horse.[39]

Normal peacetime pursuits have no place here. The right chap is a modern knight who strives "for the world's salvation from materialism" through adventures. Wren idolizes the British empire but he also has a warm spot for Americans. They share English attitudes and escapades. They are not from urban-industrial America, building skyscrapers and Model T Fords, but are cowboys or gentlemen daredevils from the Ivy League. The English and Americans are tied together by a common language and a shared love of violence: Hank and Buddy become comrades of John and Digby Geste because "our deeds of homocide and arson had raised us higher in the estimation of these good men than any number of pious acts and gentle words could ever have done."[40]

Wren can put cowboys in the desert because in his books the horse still reigns; the tank and machine gun have not arrived. "I am a cavalry man and the *arme blanche* is my weapon. Cold steel and cut and thrust, for me, if I had to go down fighting," says dashing Major de Beaujolais of the Spahis. Cavalry still rides over the artillery; Moorish horsemen easily take "almost defenseless little mountain-guns."[41]

Women are slighted in this masculine world. Good women have an "instinctive love of mothering and succouring the injured." They are angels in the house: "A woman needs a home more than a man does," certifies an American. Woman may have the vote but her role is to be a handmaiden: she is "the faithful hound," as Beau labels his doting cousin Isabel. Women who challenge this dog's life come to no good: "I was bad . . . Rotten . . . I loved money and myself," confesses Claudia, who dies painfully in a car crash.[42]

Even on her pedestal, woman is not to be trusted. Beau dies because of the dishonesty of his aunt and Claudia in the matter of the Blue Water gem. Women distract men from their duty or play them false. "Woman punishes man, or we punish ourselves—through Woman," says a Frenchman. One legionnaire recounts how he was tortured by Amazon women. "Do you know, it was for all the world like a lot of nice little girls sitting on the lawn under the trees with their kitten, joyously discussing how they should dress him up, and which ribbons they should put round his neck."[43]

Females are shallow ("Women are so attracted by externals"), they are stupid ("Women always know better than men—until they find they know nothing about the matter at all"), and like to be raped ("All women are cave-women at heart, and would like to be swept off their feet once in their lives" "by a Strong, Silent He-Cave-Man"). Worst of all, "Women always come between men an' their friends." The solution is to retreat from women into the company of men. This is done by acknowledging woman from afar, riding away from her to do good deeds in her name. "There are men who regard a woman as something to live with." These fellows have no finer feelings. "There are others who regard her as someone to live for." These are the right sort.[44]

The real love of men is for the company of other men. John Geste confides that Michael's "little grip of my arm, and squeeze, has been one of my greatest rewards and pleasures, all my life." Major Beaujolais says about another officer, "I know that one man can really love another with the love that is described as existing between David and Jonathan. I do not believe in love 'at first sight,' but tremendous attraction, and the strongest liking 'at first sight,' soon came to be a case of love at second sight." Such attraction is not consummated physically. That would not be cricket. Men share the excitement of battle.[45]

Beaujolais is "wildly happy" in battle. "I wave my saber and shout for joy." The English, more restrained, admit to "a strong sensation of pleasurable excitement" with "that undercurrent of slight nervous anxiety which one experiences before going in to bat, or when seated in a corner of the ring, awaiting the word '*Time*' at the beginning of a boxing

Manly camaraderie continues unsullied by the blood and muck of the recent trenches. John and Digby Geste face the desert. (P. C. Wren, *Beau Geste*. New York: Grosset & Dunlap, 1926.)

contest." If one has the bad luck to be killed, there is the compensation that "It's a privilege to die in your society, *mes amis.* . . . To die with men of one's own sort." The killed do not get shot to pieces or die in agony but become happy warriors beyond the veil: Michael's face, after he is killed by Arabs, is "peaceful, strong, dignified, and etherealized beyond its usual fineness and beauty."[46]

Wren carried on the male formulae of the prewar period. He was able to do this partly by avoiding entirely the specter of the western front. His setting was the desert which, like the Old West, has a never-never quality. Others, more boldly, attempted to apply directly to the western front the "good clean fun" approach to war. In *A Helluva War* (1927), an American veteran, Arthur Guy Empey, has his Irish-American cavalry hero punch, drink, and fool his way through a series of supposedly light-hearted episodes on the western front. The war is lowered to the level of a jock prank.[47]

However, one year later, in 1928, a work appeared which tried to deal starkly with the lasting damage done by the war. A central figure in D. H. Lawrence's *Lady Chatterley's Lover* is a sexually emasculated war hero. He is of almost no use to anyone, including his wife, who finds fulfillment with the gamekeeper. Lawrence attacked frontally the idea that war makes men stronger and more valuable to society. Almost inevitably, his work was seen as pornographic, somehow defiling the community with its message of the centrality of love, not violence. The book was not allowed to be published in Britain without expurgations until the 1960s, an ironic victim of a war supposedly fought for democracy and freedom of thought.[48]

Another provocative piece, one which tried to get at the malaise underlying the gender differences which propelled men toward war, was *To the Lighthouse* by Virginia Woolf. In this, a brother and sister both die, she in childbirth, he in uniform. Unlike Vachell, who used the same theme to support convention, Woolf suggests they have been sacrificed to their societally enforced roles. By implication, change is needed in gender roles and child-raising methods to produce an androgynous society. War was the result of inculcating extreme masculine, anti-female values in boys. World War I, says Carolyn G. Heilbrun, recurred in Woolf's writing as "perhaps her most pointed and damning condemnation of the 'masculine' world." She concludes, "To the androgynous view, war is indefensible."[49]

As civilians with radical social views, neither Woolf nor Lawrence was taken seriously as a war writer. But in the late 1920s and after, powerful works that spoke directly about the experience of the trenches were produced in a steady stream. They dealt in detail with every facet of the front-line experience. Often they said no more than earlier writers such as Goldring, but they took the analysis out of the drawing room and into the muck, where men stank, spat, blasphemed, and hung their

water bottles on feet protruding from trench walls. They insisted on view-
ing the war experience starkly. Henry Williamson's *The Patriot's Progress*
is an almost unrelieved story of mutilation and suffering, culminating
in the sardonic comment, "It hadn't been such a bad time, taken all round:
he wouldn't have missed it really. They said you could do a lot on an
artificial leg."[50]

In America, Dalton Trumbo grimly described the total impact of war
on the human body in his 1939 story, *Johnny Got His Gun*, about a young
soldier who is condemned by wounds to live without ears, eyes, nose,
mouth, or limbs. The popular inversion of logic held that war produced
bodily vigor among males. Trumbo suggested instead that it left a car-
cass incapable of turning over in bed.[51]

These, the true Lost Generation writers, seemed to attack every cherished conventional belief. Ford Madox Ford waded into the games-playing
mentality, charging that it had produced an intellectual blight in which
it was "suspected that brilliance was synonymous with reprehensible tendencies." Thoughtlessness had produced the war, and the sports creed
meant that England didn't care how many individuals got killed because
the game was worth more than the players. Richard Aldington also attacked the system represented in the professional officer, "an adult Boy
Scout, a Public School fag in shining armour—the armour of obtuseness.
He met every situation in life with a formula, and no situation in life
ever reached him except in the shape imposed upon it by the appropriate
and predetermined formula."[52]

Part of this formula was that a little bloodletting was good for the
soul. "It is *so* important to know how to kill," says a headmaster. Indeed,
"unless you know how to kill you cannot possibly be a Man, still less
a Gentleman." This idea, that killing ennobles, Aldington saw as the
great lie. "'Our splendid troops' were to come home—ah, very soon—
purged and ennobled by slaughter and lice, and were to beget a race
of even nobler fellows to go and do likewise." Aldington's protagonist in
Death of a Hero commits suicide to end the misery of real war.[53]

These pungent denunciations attracted enthusiastic and angry comment. Charles Carrington, a veteran, was typical of those offended.
Rather than seeing the war as an error, he called his service years "the
happiest of my life." Technology had not made war unbearable. For: "most
men like adventures. Anyone who has ever been through a street accident,
anyone who has climbed a mountain, knows that. It is one of the strange
attributes of the mind that we enjoy what makes our flesh creep . . ."
Carrington claimed to "have seen a man go to spend the afternoon in
a trench under heavy shellfire because he was bored with sitting in a
safe dugout." The Lost Generation writers exaggerated war's evils because they were self-pitying misfits, writing "sensational fiction chiefly
notable for graphic descriptions of those bodily functions that most of

us prefer to perform in private." As with Lawrence, naked honesty is considered pornographic.[54]

If Carrington had been less angry, he might have seen that his literary antagonists had much in common with him. Despite their critical stance, they in many ways validated traditional views, especially with regard to war as a special male experience. They show ambivalence about 1914-1918 and in some sense are basically proud of having served. This message they gifted to the future along with their more obviously caustic attitudes.

Siegfried Sassoon is a good example. His erstwhile friend Robert Graves recognized that Sassoon was divided about the war. A letter would begin by saying the war was purposeless. "Yet he wrote the next paragraph in his happy-warrior vein, saying that his men were the best he'd ever served with." Graves felt that "I had never been such a fire-eater as he," for Sassoon killed with relish. But he was also more outspoken against the war. The ambivalence can be seen in Sassoon's memoirs of his war service. After he publicly denounced the war, he was placed under psychiatric care. To escape this, he returned to the front. Once there, he slipped into being the happy warrior. "I was lapsing into my rather feckless 1916 self," he confessed. "It was, in fact, what I called 'playing my natural game.'"He recalled after one attack, "It had been great fun, I felt."[55]

Other symptoms of failure to resolve conflicts in thinking occur. Sassoon remained impressed by the type of officer who could make his "men finger their bayonets and pull themselves together when his cigarette end glows in the dusk, a little planet of unquenchable duty" in a war Sassoon didn't believe in. He had contempt for draftees, yet these men simply preferred not to be shot until forced to it. He described them as "undersized, dull-witted, and barely capable of carrying the heavy weight of their equipment." Even in a bad war the better fellow steps right up to be killed, rather than pausing to think things through.[56]

The pride in being a good soldier in a rotten war infects much Lost Generation thinking. Wilfred Owen was killed before the war ended but afterwards he became a cult figure to the disillusioned who relished his bitter assaults on patriotic rhetoric. He catalogued the terrible wounds soldiers received and then advised his reader not to tell,

> To children ardent for some desperate glory,
> The old Lie: Dulce et decorum est
> Pro patria mori.

He confessed it had been vain and foolish to wish to die young and at the peak:

> We used to say we'd hate to live dead-old,
> Yet now . . . I'd willingly be puffy, bald, and patriotic.

But despite the challenging tone, Owen is as ambivalent as Sassoon, whom he met in hospital and idolized. Long after he lost faith in the war, he won the military cross for gallantry in an action where, he said, "I lost all my earthly faculties, and fought like an angel." He was killed one week before the armistice, recklessly exposing himself to urge his men across a defended canal.[57]

Graves was also paradoxical. He came to think the war futile yet despised pacifists or other noncombatants and draftees, describing a typical inductee as a "nasty-looking little man, who closely resembled a rabbit." When asked by Bertrand Russell, a pacifist, if his men would fire on striking munitions-workers, Graves said yes. Asked why, he said that all the troops "loathe munitions-workers, and would be only too glad of a chance to shoot a few. They think that they're all skrimshankers." In other words, the war is wrong but men fortunate to have job-related deferments should be shot. Russell asked if the soldiers "realize that the war's wicked nonsense?" "Yes, as well as I do!" returned Graves.[58]

Much Lost Generation literature came after a decade of peace in which the materialism supposedly cured by war ran more rampant than before and veterans felt neglected by a public that wanted to forget bad lungs and war neuroses. Consequently, some writing is not only about war but a continuation of the sense of civilian betrayal some soldiers had felt during the fighting. The war, which laid bare the structure of society in crisis, formed a useful setting for the airing of soldiers' disgruntlements about civilian attitudes.

In Aldington's *Death of a Hero*, the protagonist, George Winterbourne, is made bitterly unhappy by philistine British society, which does not recognize the validity of his artistic vision. Once in the war, he is betrayed by those he leaves behind, particularly his wife, who believes in free love and is flagrantly unfaithful to him. It is largely because of her that Winterbourne deliberately climbs out of a trench to be killed. Aldington loathes and distrusts women, believing that they enjoy the men's suffering. When George dies, the effect on his mother is "almost wholly erotic. The war did that to lots of women. All the dying and wounds and mud and bloodiness—at a safe distance—gave them a great kick, and excited them to an almost unbearable pitch of amorousness."[59]

Aldington's savage portrait reminds us that, rather then ending hatred between the sexes in mutual bonds of suffering, the war often exacerbated it. Soldiers who thought they had been fighting for moral rejuvenation and traditional values, including modesty and chastity, found that the girls they left behind had taken to short skirts, smoking in public, and uninhibited dances the veterans didn't know. British veteran Basil Liddell Hart developed a formula for analyzing periods of history, in which looseness in women's fashions was equated with social decadence and the decline of empires.[60]

William Faulkner attacked the postwar woman. Like some other Lost Generation authors, Faulkner felt self-pity. This was not brought on by suffering in the war, for he saw no front-line service, but by rejection in love, which drove him into the British Royal Air Force. Faulkner liked to cast himself as a battle-scarred and troubled veteran but this was only the stage persona through which he expressed his real hurt and anger at women and American society. The central figure in his novel *Soldier's Pay* is the character Faulkner fantasized he might have been, a badly wounded pilot, Donald Mahon. He returns to his hometown to die in a rebuke to all those who had mistreated him, as if to say, "Now aren't you sorry that you didn't love me enough when you had the chance?" In particular, he is rejected by his fiancée, who finds the almost-dead soldier boring. Women are treacherous. So are noncombatant males like Januarius Jones. "The feminine predominated so in him, and the rest of him was feline: a woman with a man's body and a cat's nature." Jones is also a classics teacher. In 1926, the bright academic is still suspect in a male world of action.[61]

The self-pity is obvious at a dance where the veterans are wallflowers, unfamiliar with the new dances. "Puzzled and lost, poor devils. Once society drank war, brought them into manhood with a cultivated taste for war; but now society seemed to have found something else for a beverage ..." The soldiers are too traditional for this world. When Gilligan, a veteran, proposes to a soldier's widow, she offers to live with him instead. Despairingly, he must reject this new woman's violation of his standards.[62]

Female unreliability is a major theme of Ernest Hemingway's *A Farewell to Arms*. As Judith Fetterley pointed out, Lieutenant Henry survives all that the war throws at him; steel cannot break him. But finally a woman lets him down by dying in childbirth, leaving Henry alone to face the bleak postwar world. Kenneth S. Lynn notes that Hemingway had little exposure to combat, and the bit he saw he enjoyed. But he used his self-made image as a wounded, haunted veteran to pursue his real hurts and concerns, which often were not in the trenches.[63]

In John Doss Passos's *Three Soldiers* woman is again dangerous and untrustworthy. There is great hatred between the genders. American troops watching a propaganda film about alleged German atrocities want sexual revenge. "I'd give a lot to rape some of those goddam German women," says Chrisfield. In a nightmare, he is pursued by a brutal sergeant "who turned into a woman with huge flabby breasts." Andrews meets a working-class French girl, Jeanne, with whom there is a chance of happiness. But she doesn't have his intellect (he is a music writer) and so, after seducing her, he leaves. An upper-class woman also falls short by failing to see why he must desert the army. Andrews comments that "people were always alone, really; however much they loved each other, there could be no real union."[64]

Cynicism about relationships pervades the book, and throughout we see the self-pity of the unappreciated male. There is a "despair so helpless as to be almost sweet." The only woman Andrews has ever known who did not disappoint him is his mother, "the only person who has ever really had any importance in my life." Her function has been totally subsidiary and supportive: "She used to spend hours making beautiful copies of tunes I made up." But Andrews is finally betrayed by an older woman, his landlady, who tells the military police he is a deserter.[65]

As a woman betrays Andrews, so does the larger society which, in a democratic, mass culture, ignores his unique value as a creative being. From this perspective, the horror of army life lies not in killing but in the weight of uncaring bureaucracy. Andrews joins the army because he is tired of being an artist in intellectual rebellion against his society. "He was sick of revolt, of thought, of carrying his individuality like a banner above the turmoil. This was much better, to let everything go, to stamp out his maddening desire for music, to humble himself into the mud of common slavery." It doesn't work. From his first humiliating exposure to the army when he is stripped naked at the recruiting station until his desertion, Andrews finds that the army, reflecting the culture, is indifferent to him as an individual and insists on reducing him to a number in a file.[66]

At U. S. army headquarters in Paris, Andrews finds room after room of filing cabinets full of index cards. Each card is the bureaucratic distillation of an individual life. The artist who had enlisted to find life's basics is further than ever from real meaning. Always there was "the feeling he had of being lost in the machine, of being as helpless as a sheep in a flock," of being on "this vast treadmill." Confronted with full exposure to modern regimentation, Andrews can see no purpose to existence. "Was there any sense to it all? Had his life led in any particular direction, since he had been caught haphazard in the treadmill, or was it all chance? A toad hopping across the road in front of a steam roller."[67]

These are good questions for anyone living in the twentieth century. They are central to the nature of life in the developed countries. However, they can lead Lost Generation writers totally away from the real horror of war, the butchery of destruction, which at times can appear in their works as a refreshing interlude from the ruination of public and private relationships. Even Dos Passos's protagonist, Andrews, deserts largely because the army demeans him rather than because he finds slaughter morally repugnant. But he does walk away; most do not. In assaulting the uniformity of modernity, some writers are caught in a paradox. Though they denounce conformity, they are quick to shelter in the crowd when it comes to taking personal responsibility for pulling the trigger.

Their ultimate tragedy is that in crucial issues they failed to become the individualists they wanted to be.

Lost Generation speakers insinuate over and over that they, as combatants, cannot be held responsible for what they have done. It is someone else, usually older people, who made them do it. Siegfried Sassoon said that "the War was a dirty trick which had been played on me and my generation." The implication is that he went to war wet behind the ears. Yet he was in his late twenties when the war came. At what age does one become personally accountable for one's actions? The Victorians extended childhood, and the more adolescence is prolonged, the more will the adult cling to the morally irresponsible role of the child. The best and brightest of the war generation went off to kill with unthinking enthusiasm. Graves wanted a war and "I hoped that it might last long enough to delay my going to Oxford in October, which I dreaded." Even after losing faith in the cause, with few exceptions they carried on being good soldiers in the conventional sense of the term. They stayed with the herd.[68]

The sense of idealistic youth sacrificed on the altar of older people's stupidity permeates Vera Brittain's moving memoir, *Testament of Youth*. Brittain's generation appears doomed from birth by vast external forces:

> . . . imminent and fierce outside the door,
>   Watching a generation grow to flower,
> The fate that held our youth within its power
>   Waited its hour.

Youth is not responsible for what it is to do because there is some ulterior power, specifically the older adult world. There are two problems here. First, you cannot demand individuality and also posit vast predetermined forces which hold you in their grasp. Second, in the case of the Brittain family, blaming the older adult won't do. For Vera's father opposed the war and begged his son Edward not to volunteer.[69]

In *Chronicle of Youth*, the more candid war journals kept by Vera and published long after *Testament*, Mr. Brittain's innocence is clear. During one breakfast argument in August 1914, "Daddy worked himself into a thorough temper, raved away at us, & said he would not allow Edward to go abroad whatever happened." Edward replied, with the assurance of youth, "that no one could prevent him serving his country in any way he wanted to." Far from agreeing with his father, Vera accused him of cowardice, of "not possessing the requisite courage," and of lack of refined feeling, "showing how utterly incomprehensible everything spiritual & nobel & selfless is to him." She thought that his going to a state rather than a public school might be to blame.[70]

Because of father's embarrassing failure of patriotism, "It is left to

Edward & I to live up to our name of 'Brittain.'" This Vera did, telling young men that they had no chance with her unless they volunteered. Maurice Ellinger, a suitor, was told "to come back 'covert de gloire' & that then I would show him off with great pride to all the community in general."[71]

Vera was happy when Edward was commissioned and left as the happy warrior: "He has departed, leaving home laughing, with a delighted sense that he is not to be one of those men who will be branded for life because they have not taken part in the greatest struggle of modern times." She thought, "He has never looked so well as he does in his military clothes," for "he seems so tall & absolutely grown up." This is revealing, for part of the reason young people vehemently supported the war was that it made them look adult and turned the tables on their seniors, who were dependent now on their care and protection.[72]

Vera, too, wanted a part in the great adventure, writing in 1916, "Oh I am so *sick* of this everlasting Latin & Mathematics—if only I could do some interesting work. I really am weary & bored with everything . . . life is short of something & I am miserable." She became a nurse. Only later, when dull peace had returned and the drama was over, did she question the war. In the twenties, Oxford undergraduates of the next generation openly mocked her war service and she began to doubt the crusade. But she was still proud to wear her active service ribbons when the Queen and Princess Mary visited Oxford. "I reflected with a slightly bitter satisfaction that, for the first time since returning to Oxford, I hadn't had to feel ashamed of the war."[73]

The final betrayal of the Lost Generation was that they aged and, in peacetime, the spotlight passed from them to the more youthful and to other issues. Faulkner made the point in a short story, "All the Dead Pilots." He said that all the heroes had died on Armistice Day, 1918. Their snapshots revealed them to be "lean, hard, in their brass and leather martial harness, posed standing beside or leaning upon the esoteric shapes of wire and wood and canvas in which they flew without parachutes, they too have an esoteric look; a look not exactly human, like that of some dim and threatful apotheosis of the race seen for an instant in the glare of a thunderclap and then forever gone." Of course, not all the pilots were dead literally by Armistice Day. Some became the living dead, killing their youthful heroism by becoming flabby, soft-jawed, middle-aged civilians. Technically they live. "But they are all dead now. They are thick men now, a little thick about the waist from sitting behind desks, and maybe not so good at it, with wives and children in suburban homes almost paid out, with gardens in which they putter in the long evenings after the 5:15 is in, and perhaps not so good at that either: the hard, lean men who swaggered hard and drank hard because they had found that being dead was not as quiet as they had heard it would be."[74]

Given that scenario, many people would rather have gone west on a dawn patrol. And this is the point: the Lost Generation, as much as their detractors, continued the allure of war by romanticizing the role of Great War warrior. By removing responsibility from youth for doing the killing, they denied the individual's moral responsibility for decisions, making the conscience irrelevant and acquiescing in the power of the state which they claimed to oppose. They embellished the portrait of the tragic war hero as having achieved fulfillment and comradeship amidst the muck of the trenches. Hence our involvement with war as an alternative to the humdrum of daily living carried on apace.

Philip Oakes grew up in England between the wars and attended a public school on the eve of the second great war. Yet his memoirs could have been written as easily in the years preceding World War I, so little has changed. Killing for sport was still a national pastime. Philip's father was religious and on Sunday nights the family sang hymns. The boy's attention would wander to "the picture rail where there hung a display of tiles depicting hunting scenes so vivid and bloody that I could never understand how they qualified as decoration. There were hounds tearing out the throat of a stag; a hawk pecking the eyes of a heron; a hare bounding across an undulating heath while all around it small white clouds blossomed from the muzzles of shotguns aimed by top-hatted hunters."[75]

On Remembrance Day, the headmaster wore his Great War uniform and urged the boys to "follow the rules and play the game" as his generation had done in France. Then they would sing "Fight the good fight with all thy might." When Mr. Granger, a master, said that "human life was sacred and announced that if war was declared he would not fight," "an hour later someone had pinned a white feather to the door of his study." By contrast, Mr. Smith, a professional cricketer but mediocre teacher, viewed peace "like a prisoner yearning for freedom." When war became certain, he volunteered for the Royal Air Force. "I won't pretend I'm sorry," he said about the impending conflict. "You'll be like Biggles, sir," said one of the boys. "Very likely," said Mr. Smith, flattered by the comparison. Biggles was the clean-cut hero of boys' adventure books; we are still with Baden-Powell on the veldt, Custer in the west.[76]

When war was officially announced, Oakes's mother broke down, weeping. Oakes, like Vivian Gilbert before him, found this an important moment for showing his masculine strength. "Don't cry," he said, "I'll look after you. We'll be all right." While his mother wept, Philip "spread my arms and zoomed around the lawn spitting imaginary bullets at the lupins and antirrhinums. No one stopped me. No one reminded me that it was Sunday and I should be quiet. I flew on wings of my own making into the first quiet morning of the war." In 1939 a boy still knew that war meant freedom, especially from the female, and the prospect of a great adventure.[77]

Retrospect

Some crucial ideas cherished by Victorian and Edwardian people still influence our world. In particular, we still wrestle with the gender-based social roles that became so central a pillar of nineteenth-century culture. They failed to produce the wholesome state of society for which they were intended. This is not to say they were entirely inadequate to their purpose. Nor is it to endorse the view of some feminist scholars that women were kept out of the market place deliberately to prevent them from enjoying the pleasure and fulfillment found there by males.

The angel in the house model was a sincere attempt to reform society through the influence of sanctified womanhood. Many women took the role seriously. The females of my grandparents' generation were forces to be reckoned with in the private sphere of morals and home management. So I am not arguing that the roles didn't work at all or that the majority of people objected to them. But I do believe that, by dividing roles along gender lines and by arbitrarily assigning human qualities as either exclusively male or female, the Victorians increased the potential for disturbed relations, even estrangement, between the sexes.

Upon woman was placed the enormous burden of responsibility for the moral welfare of society, expressed through her role as the nurturer of children and caretaker of private values. It is a role that has continued in large measure into our era, and it places too much emphasis on the relation between women and their children. As authors like Nancy Chodorow and Dorothy Dinnerstein have pointed out, infants still spend the vast majority of their time with women, so that women are the primary recipients of the children's love but also of their hatred, because they are the first crucial authority figures in the youngsters' lives. On the mother falls the main weight of the supercharged emotional bond between parent and child. Such intensity cannot be healthy.[1]

We have seen how a significant number of soldiers came from homes where the mother was a dominant figure, the father being an aloof, even shadowy presence. For the male in particular, overidentification with the female parent can lead to damaging consequences. Love of the mother can be so intense as to preclude finding another woman as partner who can live up to the idealized model. Concern over the extent of identification with the mother can lead to rejection of the female entirely. It can eventuate in overtly aggressive masculinity as a way of denying the felt attraction to the female.

Women who feel that they must live through their children as visible evidence of their skill in nurturing can demand too much from their progeny. Betty Friedan makes the point clearly in *The Second Stage*:

> The costs are spelled out in the case histories of all the children smothered by the love-hate of the mothers who had to live through them, and of all the men exhorted to impossible, insatiable, never satisfied demands for status, glory and power by the women who had to meet their own needs for power and glory through them. As mothers, then as wives, women had only one powerful weapon over men: to give, or deny, that loving touch; to foster by denying, that insatiable need for love in them, which became their need for power and glory—violent deeds, for Nielsen or Dow Jones ratings. And was sometimes transmuted into man's insatiable cruelty, in revenge, rape and even murder of women, children and the weak.[2]

A society divided on gender lines encourages male violence. In the division of human characteristics, women are allowed to be soft, caring, weeping; men must be tough, aggressive, unflinching. We still give children gender-specific toys which deliberately inculcate old roles: girls get dolls and tea sets, boys get guns, trucks, and laser blasters. Children's commercial television, dominated by a male perspective, is saturated with egocentric male struggles for power through violence. This carries into adult programming. Much prime-time television emphasizes white male physical power and aggression, often aimed at the female. It is not surprising that adolescent male crime in the United States has reached epidemic proportions. We are talking not simply about the unfortunate products of the slum environment. Just as British males, who were the best and brightest that the public schools could offer, revelled in killing fellow creatures, so do many middle class adolescents and even adult males harbor violent fantasies about their perceived enemies, especially women and minorities.

We make sporadic and largely ineffectual attempts to slow the international arms race. But if we ever want to end war we shall have to dig much deeper. Among other things, we shall have to create an androgynous society in which being male does not mean a preoccupation with toughness and staying in control but includes the full range of openly expressed human feelings, including nurturing and caring. Men have much to gain from such change. It is discriminatory that only male youths have to register for the military draft in the United States. But this is compatible with gender-specific social roles.

A second major point is that the schools of the Victorian-Edwardian period, particularly in Britain, failed in a central mission of education: to awaken the child to the endless possibilities for matching individual creativity to fulfilling work for the betterment of the human condition. The schools emphasized adherence to learned rules of behavior, good form, which lauded past ways of doing things and crimped individual development. To suggest change was to be an outsider, a bounder.

Yet at the same time that youth was being boxed in and stunted, it was told how much was expected of it. This was a deadly contradiction which was finally to cripple a generation. The Victorians stressed adolescence. They emphasized the joy and innocence of youth. They said how crucial the young were to the future of society. The young believed them. They were ready for mighty endeavors. With youth's vanity, they saw themselves in mighty roles. Yet, as change was frowned upon, they were given no avenue for channeling their youthful energy into a beneficial mission. Boys were told to heed a call, but a call to what? It should have been a beckoning to social reform, of which there was great need. For the schools were correct in pointing out how an excessive concern with profit, with selling and consuming, warps a community's values. But the schools didn't dare exhort their pupils to undertake major social reformation, for the change would have impacted Eton as well as Manchester, Groton along with New York. So boys were spotlighted, inspired, and given no place to go. Until the battlefield provided a great crusade. In war, young men could repay society's attentions and justify the expectations placed on them.

Education should have challenged youth to question; to change what was not working in society so that the community might have a better tomorrow. Instead, an acceptance of what was, a veneration of accepted conduct, an unthinking love of country amounting to the proportions of a civic religion, were substituted for intellectual stimulation of the student. Our educational system still purveys a civic religion. It says that all is well; there are no problems here. Our society has no poverty, racism, or other gross inequities. Many of our students no longer even know that there was ever slavery in the United States, and even fewer have any idea of what the peculiar institution was like.

The schools still insist all too often that students must not probe or question. When my son was twelve, he was asked to write an essay for the bicentennial of the United States Constitution. He pointed out the great strengths of the document as the basis for a republican form of government, but he also noted that women, blacks, and Indians had been excluded originally. The essay made the teacher uncomfortable. The next day, my eleven-year-old daughter's class was told to say only "happy things" about the Constitution in their essays. So my daughter wrote of the political benefits she had been given in 1787, even though she knew that women were denied the vote and the Equal Rights Amendment had failed to pass. My children's involvement in any immediate personal way with the Constitution's history and development has ended. It is a holy relic of the civic religion, not to be questioned but also of no relevance to one's real life.

In denying our children's legitimate questions and insisting that we live in the best of all possible societies, we have set up something like the equation which decimated a generation of Edwardian youth: we stress youth's role but then reduce its significance to trivia. Even more emphasis is now placed on the importance of youth. We insist that being young is special, pivotal. Pepsi Cola extols youth as the Now, the Pepsi, generation. Coca Cola had a television commercial not long ago in which children told us that they were our better future, our hope. But hope for what? If, as we say, our world is just as it should be, then all the young can aspire to is more of the same. The future can be only a material one. We offer the possibility of more technical amusements like VCRs, color televisions, computer games. No wonder that some of our young people dope up and bottom out.

We allow our children little room for curiosity in many vital areas of life. In sexual relations, for example, many parents still believe that the proper stance for their progeny to take until, and if, they marry is abstinence (and ignorance). Many adolescents still come of age with only crude perceptions of human sexuality and vague but potent images of sex as sinful, dirty, funny, or as a game, often a violent one, played against the opposite sex. The attempt to provide intelligent advice to adolescents on how to have safe sex and thereby avoid AIDS along with other sex-related diseases led to an outcry against immorality by church leaders, parents, politicians, even educators. Placing prophylactic machines in college dormitories was denounced as an invitation to debauchery, as though our undergraduates didn't know sex existed until we tried to recognize it on an open and serious level. Some youth grows up as far from a healthy knowledge of sexuality as when H. G. Wells attacked our sexual malaise in *Men like Gods*. And many males and females are about as far apart in sympathetic understanding as they were in 1922.

The approach to sexuality in our society is unimaginative. So is much else; many of our citizens are acutely bored much of the time. But it could not be otherwise when we downplay the role of intellect, deny the right to philosophical change, and stress only material growth. Victorian and Edwardian critics were right in arguing that sheer materialism produces a spiritual wasteland. We have proved it in ways they could not yet imagine. Their error was in prescribing violence as the antidote. We have traced where that led them. Today our answers remain largely inadequate. Our tools for evading boredom rely on material consumption and many of them are merely improved means to unimproved ends, as Thoreau would say. Most television programming does not intellectually stimulate and a large percentage of it is frenetic and/or violent, because the passive viewer needs increasingly exciting images to have the illusion of activity, of life.

We still laud sports as a temporary release from the pressures and tedium of modern life; high prizes go to athletes. But as many participants in sport are merely spectators, and the games they watch showcase male aggression, there is more of disease than cure in this therapy. The stress on athleticism as a philosophy of life is as questionable as it was in Theodore Roosevelt's day. We drag out the cliché about a healthy mind and a healthy body but only the body gets real respect and attention. Intellects are left to atrophy. We still pretend that sports breeds sportsmanship, even though in games, as in the larger society, it is only winning that counts finally. The United States unleashing its terrifying arsenal on a poorly equipped opponent in Vietnam was no more sporting or fair play than the British massacring natives at Omdurman. And some Americans have not forgiven the underdog for taking the outside chance and winning with it. But the ultimate point about sports is this: they are recreational only and we show our philosophical shallowness when we elevate them to be the most significant events in our lives. Sports have never yet solved a major social problem.

Confronted with vast change, the people in this book failed to respond successfully. Though alienated by gross materialism and sensing real faults in their culture, they flinched from basic reform and denied the need for individual spiritual growth that might have made that reform possible. People were molded into categories in the hope that this would provide the stability to neutralize the trauma of change. Women were sent to child bearing, men to lives of rigid duty, and finally to killing as an antidote for collective malaise. And in so doing they squandered their talents and blighted their civilization. Those who took part in the Great Adventure bequeathed to us a century of fear and hate because they were too conventional for unconventional times. Perhaps we are too.

Each year I teach ROTC cadets in my military studies courses. Most of them are bright, eager, idealistic. I hope that none will be killed in squalid little wars and I am in awe of how much good work could be done if we applied their energies to the defeat of our pressing enemies, poverty, bigotry, ignorance. Sometimes, my topic brings me to the story of Roland Leighton. I cannot tell it without a tightening of the throat. The tightening is for him, for them, for me.

Roland Leighton was among the best young men of his generation in Britain. Sensitive, artistic, gentle by nature, he should have been destined for a life fulfilling to himself and beneficial to his society. He attended public school at Uppingham, where he took seven of eight school prizes in his final year. He had a scholarship and was slated to go to Oxford, where great things were expected of him. But the Great War intervened and Roland applied for a commission.[3]

On Roland's last speech day at Uppingham, the British equivalent of commencement, the headmaster stated in his year-end remarks "that if a man could not be useful to his country he was better off dead." This was July 11, 1914. By 1918 the school's war memorial listed 449 alumni killed in the war. This was from a school with a total enrollment of 400 in 1914. Vera Brittain said that the head "was widely regarded as a woman-hater" and that this helped to explain his belligerent masculinity. It is from Vera that we know what happened that Speech Day at Uppingham; she was there, as her brother Edward was a student in the school. It was then that she began to love Roland Leighton.[4]

Roland got his commission and he was proud to be a British soldier. As his departure for France neared, he grew a little apprehensive. But he braced up and carried through like a proper Englishman in command of his feelings. Though he and Vera were deeply in love by this time, they had not shared a single kiss when he left, keeping their affection pure and unworldly.[5]

Roland was often anguished in the trenches by the deaths of those he cared about. He felt it dimmed the glory of war. Yet he retained a conceit about being a fighting man, announcing that he doubted now he could settle to college and "ever waste my time on Demosthenes again." He lost patience with the contemplative life, saying that war's "reality raises it above the reach of all cold theorizing." He considered staying in the army after the war, because "a literary life would give no scope for the adventurous & administrative facet of my temperament." In Vera's view, "he almost delights in danger—in the vigour and exuberance of it."[6]

Home on leave, Roland revelled in the dramatic role of battle-hardened veteran. Because he was less than twenty, the posturing verged on the sophomoric. He stalked about London stores looking for a stabbing dagger to give Vera's brother for use on night patrols. He would handle each weapon knowingly, while ostentatiously displaying the active-service wear on his uniform and talking loudly about his five months at the front. "He was rather fond of proclaiming this at all the shops he went into & was proud of the extra attention this distinction gained him."[7]

While at home, Roland often spoke of his desire to get a wound, a red badge of courage. He said, too, that should he fall, he wanted a romantic death. He thought that "he could wish for no better end than to be found dead in a trench at dawn." Because he was young and immature, he said he would like a Viking funeral on a burning boat (Beau Geste gets such a ceremony in the book of that name). But then Leighton returned to France and reality. He was killed just before Christmas 1915.[8]

Vera at first pictured Roland dying serenely in a hospital as the cold blue dawn light steadily illuminated his handsome face. It was the death of a knight. The actuality was different. Leighton's squad had taken over a section of unfamiliar front-line trench. The officer he relieved forgot to tell him that the Germans kept a rifle trained on a particular break in a hedge through which the British crawled at night to mend their wire. Roland went out that evening with a section to check wire. When the Germans heard him, they pulled the trigger of the fixed rifle, and he went down in the mud, his arms flailing wildly and his threshing head crushing his cap into the earth. He was shot through the base of the spine and had lost all motor control. Roland Leighton had ceased to exist as a human being. He was filled with morphine to kill the awful agony and he died the next day, oblivious to his circumstances.[9]

When the package of his personal belongings returned home, Vera went down to the Leightons for the ceremony of opening the parcel. It was not the sacred moment they had expected. His cap, which he had worn rakishly, was bent out of shape and the badge caked with mud. His tunic was torn savagely back and front by the passage of the bullet. His khaki undershirt was stiff with dried blood and his officer's riding breeches were ripped open where the surgeon had searched for the wound. There was a pervasive putrescent odor; it was "not a pure smell of earth." The reality of Roland's death was so horrible that his mother told her husband to take the clothing away and bury it.[10]

In 1980, Clare Leighton could still recall vividly the horror of that bleak morning when all that they had left of her bright, promising brother was put under ground. "It is a cold morning in January and I am in the garden of our cottage in Sussex. My father is with me. I carry two heavy kettles. They are filled with boiling water, for we are about to bury the tunic—blood-stained and bullet-riddled—in which Roland has been killed." The water was to thaw the frozen soil enough for a hole to be dug for the package. Then "I am to throw the frozen earth so that it may be buried out of sight."[11]

Life is an adventure and we should all be adventurers, pursuing our unique quests toward more fulfilled existences. Roland Leighton wanted to take part in a great adventure. But the one he found led to death, not growth, and his life was cut short. His story is one of disaster for himself and grievous loss for his culture. Perhaps ultimately this is the lesson to be learned from all the bronze and stone soldiers who still stand in towns and villages, silent sentinels of the Great War. They serve to remind us that a culture in which young people end this way has bankrupted morally and philosophically as well as diplomatically. It can leave for posterity no more fitting symbol of itself than its war memorials.

NOTES

PREFACE

1. Fitzgerald, *Tender Is the Night* (New York, 1933), p. 57.
2. Gilbert and Gubar, *No Man's Land: The Place of the Woman Writer in the Twentieth Century*, Vol. II: *Sexchanges* (New Haven, 1989), pp. 258–307.

INTRODUCTION: RESPONSES TO CHANGE

1. Henry David Thoreau, *Walden* (Boston, 1957), pp. 36, 80–81.
2. William Makepeace Thackeray, *The Roundabout Papers*, reprinted in Gerald B. Kauvar and Gerald C. Sorenson, eds., *The Victorian Mind* (New York, 1969), pp. 118–119.
3. Edmund Burke, *Reflections on the Revolution in France* (1790). Baroness Orczy, *The Scarlet Pimpernel* (Garden City, N.Y., n.d.), pp. 60–61.
4. *Scarlet Pimpernel*, p. 25. Angela Carter, *The Sadeian Woman* (New York, 1980), p. 18.
5. Louis B. Wright and Marion Tinling, *The Great American Gentleman: William Byrd of Westover* (New York, 1963), e.g., pp. 6, 42, 210. Buchan, *Pilgrim's Way* (Cambridge, Mass., 1940), p. 149. The question of Victorian sexuality has been a matter of intense debate in our century, and the literature is vast. The traditional view, following post-Victorians such as Lytton Strachey (in *Eminent Victorians*, 1918), is that the Victorians were sexually restrictive, even repressive. One of the most comprehensive statements by this school is Ronald Pearsall's *The Worm in the Bud* (1969). A further dimension was added by studies examining the role of the medical profession in the articulation and imposition of sexual norms. G. J. Barker-Benfield in *The Horrors of the Half-Known Life* (1976) and John S. Haller, Jr., and Robin M. Haller in *The Physician and Sexuality in Victorian America* (1974) suggested that Victorian sexuality was more complex and varied than previously thought. Such had been implied earlier by Steven Marcus who, in *The Other Victorians* (1966), explored the seething world of prostitution and pornography underlying the surface of Victorian respectability. A more comprehensive assault on the traditional view was launched by Peter Gay in *The Bourgeois Experience* (1984). Gay maintained that the Victorian sexual world was rich in variety and possibility. He is a provocative writer but, like Marcus, his case rests on a limited variety of sources. The focus of the debate was changed by the French scholar Michel Foucault who argued (most notably in *The History of Sexuality*, Vol. I: *An Introduction*, 1976) that Victorians did not repress sex, they got it into the open and talked about it in order to control it. The extent of difference between Foucault and the traditional school can be exaggerated: control is not incompatible with restriction. Foucault is not proposing that the Victorian dialogue on sexuality was to encourage permissive practices. The discussion has been further widened by feminist scholars like Carroll Smith-Rosenberg who have viewed physical sexuality correctly as part of a more complex interaction between the genders. I have tried to synthesize the viewpoints where possible, while retaining my conviction that the Victorians were restrictive sexu-

ally as part of a broader distancing between the genders.

6. Wiliam Cory, *Extracts from the Letters and Journals of William Cory* (Oxford, 1907), pp. 550–551. Lytton Strachey, *Eminent Victorians* (New York, 1963), p. 213. Niels Henry Sonne, *Liberal Kentucky 1780-1828* (Lexington, 1968).

7. Leonard L. Richards, *"Gentlemen of Property and Standing": Anti-Abolition Mobs in Jacksonian America* (New York, 1970), and Michael Feldberg, *The Turbulent Era: Riot and Disorder in Jacksonian America* (New York, 1980). Alexis de Tocqueville, *Democracy in America* (New York, 1981), p. 150. John MacGregor, *Our Brothers and Cousins* (London, 1859), pp. 122–124, 139.

8. Frances Trollope, *Domestic Manners of the Americans* (New York, 1949), pp. viii, lxxvii.

9. Joseph G. Baldwin, *The Flush Times of Alabama and Mississippi* (New York, 1957), pp. 59–64.

10. Thoreau, *Walden*, p. 25. Anna Cora Mowatt, *Fashion*, Act V, printed in Myron Matlaw, ed., *The Black Crook and Other Nineteenth-Century American Plays* (New York, 1967). Charles Dickens, *A Christmas Carol* (London, 1970), p. 29.

11. Harvey Wish, ed., *Ante-Bellum: Writings of George Fitzhugh and Hinton Rowan Helper* (New York, 1960), p. 85. Harvey Green, *The Light of the Home* (New York, 1983), p. 56.

12. James Fenimore Cooper, *Notions of the Americans*, quoted in G. J. Barker-Benfield, *The Horrors of the Half-Known Life: Male Attitudes toward Women and Sexuality in Nineteenth-Century America* (New York, 1977), p. 40.

13. Catherine Clinton, *The Plantation Mistress* (New York, 1982), p. 105.

14. Ellen K. Rothman, *Hands and Hearts: A History of Courtship in America* (New York, 1984), p. 187. Clinton, *Mistress*, p. 104.

15. John S. Haller, Jr., and Robin M. Haller, *The Physician and Sexuality in Victorian America* (New York, 1977), p. 98, for Acton. Barker-Benfield, *Horrors* p. 56, on Jarvis, and pp. 120–121, on female castration. The amount of upper-class male sexual involvement with working women is questioned by Janice Burke Steinberg in "The Development of a Social Policy Towards Illegitimacy in England, 1870-1918," Ph. D. dissertation, University of Cincinnati, 1980, pp. 137–138.

16. Theodore Roosevelt, "Address to the 1st International Congress in America on the Welfare of the Child," 1908, quoted in Barbara Ehrenreich and Deidre English, *For Her Own Good: 150 Years of the Experts' Advice to Women* (New York, 1978), p. 171. Also, Roosevelt, *The Strenuous Life* (New York, 1902), p. 4. Cecil Woodham-Smith, *Florence Nightingale* (London, 1950), p. 193.

PART I: SEPARATION OF THE SEXES

1. Thomas Hughes, *Tom Brown's School-Days* (New York, n.d.), pp. 5, 275.
2. Hughes, *School-Days*, pp. 292, 71.
3. Hughes, *School-Days*, p. 89.
4. Hughes, *School-Days*, pp. 102, 101, 107.
5. Hughes, *School-Days*, pp. 297.
6. Hughes, *School-Days*, pp. 355, 354.
7. Hughes, *School-Days*, pp. 140, 220, 178.
8. Hughes, *School-Days*, pp. 312–313.

CHAPTER ONE: MEN AND WOMEN

1. Peter Gay, *The Bourgeois Experience: Education of the Senses* (New York,

1984), pp. 295–297, 309–310.

2. Jeffrey Weeks, *Sex, Politics and Society: The Regulation of Sexuality Since 1800*, 2nd. ed. (New York, 1989), p. 27. John Chandos, *Boys Together: English Public Schools 1800–1864* (New Haven, 1984), p. 242, on caning.

3. Ronald Pearsall, *The Worm in the Bud: The World of Victorian Sexuality* (New York, 1969), p. 214. Vern L. Bullough and Bonnie Bullough, *Sin, Sickness, and Sanity: A History of Sexual Attitudes* (New York, 1977), p. 103.

4. Ellen K. Rothman discusses the indignity felt to be inherent in the sex act in *Hands and Hearts: A History of Courtship in America* (New York, 1984), p. 255. Ronald G. Walters, "The Erotic South: Sensuality in American Abolitionism," in Randy Roberts and James S. Olson, eds., *American Experiences*, Vol. I: *1607–1877* (Glenview, Ill., 1986), pp. 270–274.

5. Frederic Hamilton, *My Yesterdays: The Days before Yesterday* (London, n.d.), p. 39. L. E. Jones, *An Edwardian Youth* (London, 1956), p. 163.

6. Alexis de Tocqueville, *Democracy in America* (New York, 1981), pp. 486–488. William S. McFeely, *Grant: A Biography* (New York, 1981), p. 27. Henry Adams, *The Education of Henry Adams* (Boston, 1974), pp. 85, 122, 353. David R. Contosta, *Henry Adams and the American Experiment* (Boston, 1980), pp. 112–116.

7. Hundley, *Social Relations in Our Southern States* (New York, 1973), pp. 73–74.

8. Sandra M. Gilbert and Susan Gubar, *No Man's Land: The Place of the Woman Writer in the Twentieth Century*, Vol. I: *The War of the Words* (New Haven, 1988), pp. 28, 35. Reay Tannahill, *Sex in History* (New York, 1980), p. 408. Charlotte Perkins Gilman, *Herland* (New York, 1979), pp. 58–59, 66, 138–141.

9. Eleanor Hallowell Abbott, *Being Little in Cambridge When Everyone Else Was Big* (New York, 1936), pp. 151–153. Trollope, *Manners*, pp. 112–113.

10. Jones, *Youth*, pp. 94, 121. Frank M. Richardson, *Mars without Venus: A Study of Some Homosexual Generals* (Edinburgh, 1981), pp. 7, 13. Pearsall, *Worm*, p. 323, on Baker. Colonel Repington was forced to resign from the army when he had an affair with a married woman; see W. Michael Ryan, *Lieutenant-Colonel Charles à Court Repington* (New York, 1987), pp. 35–46.

11. Arthur Ponsonby, *The Decline of Aristocracy* (London, 1912), pp. 179–181. Abbott, *Being Little*, pp. 104, 194–196. Vera Brittain, *Testament of Youth* (London, 1933), pp. 45, 48.

12. Leon Edel, ed., *The Diary of Alice James* (New York, 1982), p. 206. Byron Farwell, *Eminent Victorian Soldiers* (New York, 1985), p. 240. Gay, *Bourgeois*, p. 285.

13. Pearsall, *Worm*, pp. 40, 512–514, 103. Gay, *Bourgeois*, p. 284.

14. Pearsall, *Worm*, p. 106. On Victorian child prostitution, see Michael Pearson, *The Five Pound Virgins* (New York, 1972).

15. Phyllis Rose, *Parallel Lives: Five Victorian Marriages* (New York, 1984), p. 57. Pearsall, *Worm*, pp. 75, 514.

16. Hamilton, *Boy*, pp. 167, 242. Nicholas Mosley, *Julian Grenfell: His Life and the Times of His Death* (New York, 1976), pp. 30–31, 45–46.

17. Bell Irvin Wiley, *Confederate Women* (Westport, Conn., 1975), pp. 35–36. Stephen W. Sears, *Landscape Turned Red: The Battle of Antietam* (New Haven, 1983), pp. 222–223.

18. Mary S. Hartman and Lois Banner, eds., *Clio's Consciousness Raised* (New York, 1974), pp. 16–17. Harvey Green, *The Light of the Home* (New York, 1983), p. 57. Margaret Fountaine, *Love among the Butterflies* (New York, 1982), pp. 67, 125. Edel, *James*, pp. 5–6, 149. Contosta, *Adams*, p. 91.

19. Byron Farwell, *Mr. Kipling's Army* (New York, 1981), pp. 235–236. Bram

Dijkstra, *Idols of Perversity* (New York, 1986), esp. ch. 4.

20. Pearsall, *Worm*, p. 500.

21. Blease, *The Emancipation of English Women* (New York, 1977), p. 254.

22. Benson, *As We Were: A Victorian Peep Show* (London, 1930), p. 147. Millicent Garrett Fawcett, *What I Remember* (London, 1924), pp. 34–36. Fountaine, *Love*, p. 165.

23. Barbara Kaye Greenleaf, *Children through the Ages: A History of Childhood* (New York, 1979), pp. 123, 78–79, 82. Rothman, *Hands*, pp. 54, 115–116. Chandos, *Boys*, pp. 290–291.

24. James McLachlan, *American Boarding Schools: A Historical Study* (New York, 1970), p. 269. Thorstein Veblen was among the first to analyze the changed role of children, in *The Theory of the Leisure Class*.

25. McLachlan, *Schools*, pp. 116–117.

26. Louisa May Alcott, *Little Women* (New York, 1983), pp. 14, 48–49, 65, 245–246.

27. William Cory, *Extracts from the Letters and Journals of William Cory* (Oxford, 1907), p. 565. T. J. Jackson Lears, *No Place of Grace: Antimodernism and the Transformation of American Culture 1880-1920* (New York, 1981), pp. 248–249.

28. Hamilton, *Boy*, pp. 13, 15.

29. Dorothy Dinnerstein, *The Mermaid and the Minotaur: Sexual Arrangements and Human Malaise* (New York, 1977). Judith Fetterley, *The Resisting Reader: A Feminist Approach to American Fiction* (Bloomington, 1978), p. 3.

30. Noel B. Gerson, *Sad Swashbuckler: The Life of William Walker* (New York, 1976), pp. 14, 20, 24-25, 9, 75, 77, 54, 16, 18.

CHAPTER TWO: MEN TOGETHER

1. Carroll Smith-Rosenberg, "The Female World of Love and Ritual: Relations between Women in Nineteenth-Century America," *Signs*, I (Autumn 1975), pp. 1–25.

2. Ellen K. Rothman, *Hands and Hearts: A History of Courtship in America* (New York, 1984), p. 193. L. E. Jones, *An Edwardian Youth* (London, 1956), pp. 37, 162–163. F. G. Loring, "The Tomb of Sarah," is reprinted in *The Dracula Book of Great Vampire Stories* (Secaucus, N.J., 1977), p. 163. Ronald Pearsall, *The Worm in the Bud: The World of Victorian Sexuality* (New York, 1969), p. 416.

3. Archibald Forbes, *Chinese Gordon* (New York, 1884), p. 124. J. F. C. Fuller Papers in the Liddell Hart Centre for Military Archives, University of London's King's College, September 17, 1899.

4. James O. Patti, *The Personal Narrative of James O. Patti of Kentucky* (Cincinnati, 1831), p. 27. Horace Porter, "The Philosophy of Courage," *Century Illustrated Monthly Magazine*, XXXVI (May-October 1888), p. 253.

5. Lew Wallace, *An Autobiography* (New York, 1906), I. p. 219. Dorothy Hammond and Alta Jablow, *The Myth of Africa* (New York, 1977), pp. 166–167, 191.

6. Henry David Thoreau, *Walden and Civil Disobedience* (Boston, 1957), pp. 150–151.

7. Michael Barton, *Goodmen: The Character of Civil War Soldiers* (London, 1981), pp. 2–4, 71, 73. James Fowler Rusling, "The Yankee as a Fighter," *United States Service Magazine*, IV (1865), pp. 27–43.

8. Walter H. Taylor, *Four Years with General Lee* (New York, 1962), p. 77, and John Esten Cooke, *Wearing of the Grey* (Bloomington, 1959), p. 358. George M. Fredrickson, *The Inner Civil War: Northern Intellectuals and the Crisis of*

the Union (New York, 1965), pp. 86–87. Oliver Wendell Holmes, "My Hunt after the Captain," *Atlantic Monthly*, X (December 1862), pp. 738–764.

9. John Stuart Mill, *The Subjection of Women* (Arlington Heights, Ill., 1980), p. 66.

10. Sara Jeannette Duncan, *An American Girl in London* (New York, 1891), pp. 187–188, 244. Herman Melville, *Moby Dick* (New York, 1964), pp. 557–565, 590.

11. Duncan, *Girl*, p. 97.

12. Younghusband, *A Soldier's Memories in Peace and War* (London, 1917), pp. 244, 268–269, 276–277.

13. Paul Fussell, *The Great War and Modern Memory* (London, 1975), p. 305. L. E. Jones, *A Victorian Boyhood* (London, 1955), pp. 139, 156.

14. Tilden G. Edelstein, *Strange Enthusiasm: A Life of Thomas Wentworth Higginson* (New York, 1970), pp. 26, 313, 254, 282. Thomas Wentworth Higginson, *Army Life in a Black Regiment* (New York, 1962), pp. 72, 161–162. Vera Brittain, *Testament of Youth* (London, 1933), p. 157.

15. Ian Hamilton, *When I Was a Boy* (London, 1939), p. 89. John Chandos, *Boys Together: English Public Schools 1800–1864* (New Haven, 1984), p. 338.

16. James McLachlan, *American Boarding Schools: A Historical Study* (New York, 1970), pp. 11, 15, 290.

17. Alec Waugh, *The Loom of Youth* (London, 1947), pp. 140–141. Hammond and Jablow, *Myth*, p. 185.

18. Rupert Wilkinson, *Gentlemanly Power: British Leadership and the Public School Tradition* (London, 1964), p. 45.

19. McLachlan, *Schools*, p. 167. Frederic Hamilton, *My Yesterdays: The Days before Yesterday* (London, n.d.), p. 120.

20. George F.-H. Berkeley, *My Recollections of Wellington College* (Newport, Wales, 1945), p. 24. Percival Marling, *Rifleman and Hussar* (London, 1931), p. 33.

21. On military schools, Marcus Cunliffe, *Soldiers and Civilians: The Martial Spirit in America* (London, 1969), pp. 75–80. G. J. Barker-Benfield, *The Horrors of the Half-Known Life: Male Attitudes toward Women and Sexuality in Nineteenth Century America* (New York, 1976), p. 246. Dixon Wecter, *The Hero in America* (Ann Arbor, 1963), p. 377.

22. Patrick Howarth, *Play Up and Play the Game: The Heroes of Popular Fiction* (London, 1973), pp. 117, 134, 136, 123.

23. Howarth, *Play Up*, pp. 43–44. G. Manville Fenn, *George Alfred Henty: The Story of an Active Life* (London, 1907), pp. 314, 319–321.

24. J. A. Mangan, *Athleticism in the Victorian and Edwardian Public School* (Cambridge, 1981), p. 186.

25. Harvey Green, *The Light of the Home* (New York, 1983), pp. 54–55. Berkeley, *Recollections*, p. 94. Mark Girouard, *The Return to Camelot: Chivalry and the English Gentleman* (New Haven, 1981), p. 258.

26. Pearsall, *Worm*, p. 417, on mutilation. McLachlan, *Schools*, p. 178. Barbara Kaye Greenleaf, *Children through the Ages: A History of Childhood* (New York, 1979), p. 83, on suicides. Hamilton, *Boy*, p. 101.

27. Frances Trollope, *Uncle Walter* (London, 1852), pp. 51–52. Herman Melville, *White Jacket* (New York, 1967), pp. 217–218.

28. Douglas MacArthur, *Reminiscences* (New York, 1964), pp. 80–81.

29. Byron Farwell, *Mr. Kipling's Army* (New York, 1981), pp. 26–27. James Arthur Lyon Fremantle, *The Fremantle Diary* (Boston, 1954), p. 120.

30. Farwell, *Kipling's Army*, p. 233. John Y. Simon, ed., *The Papers of Ulysses S. Grant*, Vol. X: *January 1–May 31, 1864* (Carbondale, 1982), p. 394. Peter

Burchard, *One Gallant Rush: Robert Gould Shaw and His Brave Black Regiment* (New York, 1965), pp. 81–82.

31. Horace Smith-Dorrien, *Memories of Forty-Eight Years' Service* (London, 1925), pp. 1–2. Byron Farwell, *Eminent Victorian Soldiers* (New York, 1985), pp. 239–240. Evelyn Wood, *From Midshipman to Field Marshal* (London, 1906), I, p. 2. Basil Liddell Hart Papers in the Basil Liddell Hart Centre for Military Archives, University of London's King's College, "Modern Woman. By a Modern Man," p. 8. Winston Churchill, *My Early Life* (London, 1947), p. 4. Stephen E. Ambrose, *Duty, Honor, Country: A History of West Point* (Baltimore, 1966), p. 207.

32. MacArthur, *Reminiscences*, p. 25. Arthur Conan Doyle, *Memories and Adventures* (Boston, 1924), p. 343.

33. Jones, *Boyhood*, pp. 34–37, 116–117, and *Youth*, pp. 117, 129.

34. C. Day Lewis, *The Collected Poems of Wilfred Owen* (New York, 1965), pp. 13, 18. E. E. Reynolds, *Baden-Powell* (London, 1943), pp. 14, 172–173. R. S. S. Baden–Powell, *The Matabele Campaign 1896* (Westport, Conn., 1970), preface.

35. T. J. Jackson Lears, *No Place of Grace: Antimodernism and the Transformation of American Culture* (New York, 1981), pp. 238–240.

36. Philip Magnus, *Kitchener: Portrait of an Imperialist* (New York, 1968), pp. 5–7, 10, 68, 117, 235, 263. Frank M. Richardson, *Mars without Venus: A Study of Some Homosexual Generals* (Edinburgh, 1981), pp. 119–120. Conan Doyle, *Memories*, pp. 131, 179.

37. Christopher Hibbert, *The Great Mutiny: India 1857* (New York, 1980), esp. pp. 292–293, 295, 424. Richardson, *Mars*, p. 131. Patrick Brantlinger has an excellent section on mutiny literature in *Rule of Darkness: British Literature and Imperialism, 1830-1914* (Ithaca, 1988), pp. 199–224. He comments that the mutineers were gunned down partly because, to the British, they embodied disallowed sexual urges (p. 212).

38. My view of Pearse is based on Max Caulfield, *The Easter Rebellion* (London, 1965), pp. 41, 79, 310, 314, and William Irwin Thompson, *The Imagination of an Insurrection: Dublin, Easter 1916* (New York, 1972), p. 121.

39. Thompson, *Imagination*, pp. 75–77, 212, 123–124. Caulfield, *Rebellion*, p. 43, on the death wish.

40. Thompson, *Imagination*, pp. 58, 148, 148–149. Caulfield, *Rebellion*, p. 236.

41. Caulfield, *Rebellion*, p. 359. Thompson, *Imagination*, p. 25.

CHAPTER THREE: MALE GAMES

1. Stephen Crane, "The Bride Comes to Yellow Sky," in Ellen C. Wynn, ed., *The Short Story: 50 Masterpieces* (New York, 1983), pp. 248, 251.

2. "Yellow Sky," pp. 253–255.

3. "Yellow Sky," pp. 257–258.

4. Jules Henry, *Culture against Man* (New York, 1963), p. 30.

5. Leon Edel, ed., *The Diary of Alice James* (New York, 1982), p. 187. David Newsome, *Godliness & Good Learning* (London, 1961), p. 81. L. E. Jones, *A Victorian Boyhood* (London 1955), p. 199. George F.-H. Berkeley, *My Recollections of Wellington College* (Newport, Wales, 1945), pp. 34, 45.

6. James McLachlan, *American Boarding Schools: A Historical Study* (New York, 1970), p. 283. Francis A. Walker, "College Athletics: An Address Before the Phi Beta Kappa Society, Alpha, of Massachusetts," *Technology Quarterly*, VI (July 1893), pp. 2–3, 6, 13. H. H. Arnold, *Global Mission* (New York, 1949), pp. 6–7.

7. Berkeley, *Wellington*, p. 63. Douglass A. Naverr and Lawrence E. Ziewacz, *The Games They Played: Sports in American History* (Chicago, 1983), p. 29.

8. McLachlan, *Schools*, p. 283. Mark Girouard, *The Return to Camelot: Chivalry and the English Gentleman* (New Haven, 1981), p. 233.

9. J. A. Mangan, *Athleticism in the Victorian and Edwardian Public School* (Cambridge, 1981), p. 186. Donald J. Mrozek, *Sport and American Mentality, 1880-1910* (Knoxville, 1983), pp. 24–25. McLachlan, *Schools*, pp. 284–285.

10. Mrozek, *Sport*, p. 38. Dixon Wecter, *The Hero in America* (Ann Arbor, 1963), p. 308. Harold Begbie, *The Story of Baden-Powell: The Wolf That Never Sleeps* (London, 1900), pp. 65, 209, 193, 212–213.

11. John Raymond, ed., *The Remniniscences and Recollections of Captain Gronow* (New York, 1964), pp. 253–254. Mangan, *Athleticism*, p. 57. Stephen E. Ambrose, *Duty, Honor, Country: A History of West Point* (Baltimore, 1966), p. 312. See also, Joseph Bocklin Bishop, ed., *Theodore Roosevelt's Letters to His Children* (New York, 1964), p. 46.

12. E. A. H. Alderson, *With the Mounted Infantry and the Mashonaland Field Force 1896* (Buldwayo, 1971), p. 248. Neville Lyttelton, *Eighty Years: Soldiering, Politics, Games* (London, n.d.), p. 267.

13. Alexis de Tocqueville, *Democracy in America* (New York, 1981), p. 229. Quentin Reynolds, *They Fought for the Sky* (London, 1960), p. 40.

14. Garnet Wolseley Papers, Hove Public Library, January 4, 1883. Percival Marling, *Rifleman and Hussar* (London, 1931), p. 225. Lawrence R. Borne, *Dude Ranching: A Complete History* (Albuquerque, 1983), p. 11.

15. George Richards Greaves, *Memoirs of General Sir George Richards Greaves* (London, 1924), pp. 20, 36–37. Francis Howard, *Reminiscences 1848–1890* (London, 1924), pp. 211, 213. W. R. Birdwood, *Khaki and Gown: An Autobiography* (New York, 1957), pp. 60, 40.

16. Borne, *Dude*, p. 10.

17. Douglas MacArthur, *Reminiscences* (New York, 1964), p. 16. Elliot Whitney, *The Rogue Elephant* (Chicago, 1913), p. 32.

18. E. E. Reynolds, *Baden-Powell* (London, 1943), p. 200. L. E. Jones, *An Edwardian Youth* (London, 1956), p. 46. John Higham, *Writing American History* (Bloomington, 1970), p. 86.

19. J. F. C. Fuller Papers in the Liddell Hart Centre for Military Archives, University of London's King's College, May 7, 1901. See also "Pigsticking and the Purgation of Lusts," in Philip Woodruff, *The Men Who Ruled India*, Vol. II: *The Guardians* (London, 1953). Mangan, *Athleticism*, p. 138. Anthony Hope, *Memoirs and Notes* (Garden City, N.Y., 1928), p. 215. Mrozek, *Sport*, p. 66.

20. Alderson, *Lessons from 100 Notes Made in Peace and War* (London, 1908), p. 26. E. A. H. Alderson, *Pink and Scarlet: Or Hunting as a School for Soldiering* (London, 1900), pp. 209–210, 3, 86–87, 145.

21. Alderson, *Pink*, pp. 159–160.

22. Alderson, *Pink*, pp. 150–151. Valerie Pakenham, *Out in the Noonday Sun: Edwardians in the Tropics* (New York, 1985), pp. 175–176.

23. G. Manville Fenn, *George Alfred Henty: The Story of an Active Life* (London, 1907), p. 13. Bishop, *Letters*, p. 33. Wecter, *Hero*, p. 378. Elizabeth B. Custer, *Following the Guidon* (Norman, Ok., 1966), p. 15. Howard, *Reminiscences*, p. 219.

24. Howard, *Reminiscences*, pp. 14–15. Baden-Powell, *Matabele*, p. 60. George H. Hodson, ed., *Twelve Years of a Soldier's Life in India* (Boston, 1860), p. 356.

25. David Hunter Strother, *A Virginia Yankee in the Civil War* (Chapel Hill, 1961), p. 166.

26. Stephen Z. Starr, *The Union Cavalry in the Civil War*, Vol. III: *The War*

in the West 1861-1865 (Baton Rouge, 1985), p. 177. Emory M. Thomas, *Bold Dragoon: The Life of J. E. B. Stuart* (New York, 1986), p. 116. See also, Custer, *Guidon*, p. 7. Donald R. Morris, *The Washing of the Spears* (New York, 1965), pp. 563–564. Thomas Pakenham, *The Boer War* (New York, 1979), pp. 143, 395, 522, 574. Marling, *Hussar*, pp. 105–106. Erskine Childers, *In the Ranks of the C.I.V.* (London, 1900), pp. 94, 152, 150.

27. Custer, *Guidon*, pp. 274-275. Peter Singleton-Gates, *General Lord Freyberg* (London, 1963), pp. 65–66.

28. George John Younghusband, *A Soldier's Memories in Peace and War* (London, 1917), p. 64. David Nevin, *The Old West: The Soldiers* (Alexandria, Va., 1974), p. 181.

29. Ernest W. Bennett, *The Downfall of the Dervishes*, 3rd. ed. (London, 1899), p. 161. Byron Farwell, *Eminent Victorian Soldiers* (New York, 1985), p. 197. Garnet Wolseley, *The Story of a Soldier's Life* (London, 1903), I, p. 229; II, p. 25. Jones, *Boyhood*, pp. 87, 83–84.

30. Jones, *Boyhood*, p. 150. Greaves, *Memoirs*, pp. 44–45.

31. Ernest Crosby, *Captain Jinks: Hero* (Upper Saddle River, N.J., 1968), pp. 269, 275.

32. Richard Slotkin, *Regeneration through Violence: The Mythology of the American Frontier, 1600-1860* (Middletown, Conn., 1973), p. 551. Thomas Wentworth Higginson, *Army Life in a Black Regiment* (New York, 1962), pp. 151–152.

PART II: WAR AND MALE FULFILLMENT

1. Stephen Crane, *The Red Badge of Courage* (New York, 1976), pp. 50, 41. On romantic battle art see W. Fletcher Thompson, Jr., *The Image of War: The Pictorial Reporting of the American Civil War* (New York, 1960), esp. pp. 15–24.

2. Crane, *Red Badge*, p. 100.

3. R. W. Stallman, "Stephen Crane: A Revaluation," in John W. Aldridge, ed., *Critiques and Essays on Modern Fiction, 1920-1951* (New York, 1952), pp. 251–269. Harold R. Hungerford, "'That Was at Chancellorsville': The Factual Framework of *The Red Badge of Courage*," *American Literature*, XXXIV (January 1963), pp. 520–531.

4. Crane, *Red Badge*, p. 94.

5. George Wyndham, *New Review*, XIV (January 1896), pp. 32–40.

6. Crane, *Red Badge*, pp. 8–10.

7. Crane, *Red Badge*, pp. 10, 21, 61.

8. Crane, *Red Badge*, pp. 81, 87, 109.

9. Bibliographical detail on Crane's life is taken primarily from Frederick C. Crews's introduction to *The Red Badge of Courage* (Indianapolis, 1954), pp. vii-xiv. Crane's involvement with outcast women led to "Maggie: A Girl of the Streets" (1893). He dramatized his shipwreck in "The Open Boat" (1897).

10. Gerald F. Linderman, *The Mirror of War: American Society and the Spanish-American War* (Ann Arbor, 1974), p. 106.

CHAPTER FOUR: A LITTLE BLOODLETTING

1. Lester J. Cappon, ed., *The Adams-Jefferson Letters* (Chapel Hill, 1959), II, p. 549.

2. Samuel Putnam Waldo, *Memoirs of Andrew Jackson* (Hartford, Conn., 1818), p. 16. John William Ward, *Andrew Jackson: Symbol for an Age* (London,

1955), p. 25.

3. Alexis de Tocqueville, *Democracy in America* (New York, 1981), pp. 514, 541. J. Frost, *The Mexican War and Its Warriors* (New Haven, Conn., 1849), pp. 331–332.

4. Charles Dickens, *Hard Times for These Times* (New York, 1958), Book I, ch. 2, pp. 6–7; Book III, ch. 8, p. 264.

5. Justin McCarthy, *A History of Our Times* (Chicago, 1881), II, p. 225. See also, Alexander William Kinglake, *The Invasion of the Crimea* (New York, 1887), I, pp. 263–264.

6. Christopher Ricks, ed., *The Poems of Tennyson* (New York, 1972), pp. 1034–1036.

7. James D. Kissane, *Alfred Tennyson* (New York, 1970), p. 144. Stopford A. Brook, *Tennyson: His Art and His Relation to Modern Life* (New York, 1970), pp. 235-236, 238. Danzig is quoted in Ward Hellstrom, *On the Poems of Tennyson* (Gainesville, Fl, 1972), p. 87. See also, E. D. H. Johnson, *The Alien Vision of Victorian Poetry* (Hamden, Conn., 1963), p. 31.

8. Tennyson, "The Third of February, 1852," stanza VIII, lines 43, 45, p. 1002; stanza VI, lines 29–35, p. 1001; "Suggested by Reading an Article in a Newspaper," stanza VIII, lines 45–48, 50, pp. 1005–1006; stanza XIV, lines 79-92, p. 1006; stanza IV, lines 32–35, p. 996; "Rifle Clubs!!!" stanza I, lines 3–4, p. 997, in Ricks, ed., *Poems*. See also my "Tennyson's Crimean War Poetry: A Cross-Cultural Approach," *Journal of the History of Ideas*, XL (July–Sept. 1979), pp. 405–422.

9. *Maud*, Part I, lines 23–24, 43–45, 34–35, pp. 1042–1043; Part III, lines 39–42, p. 1092, in Ricks, ed., *Poems*.

10. London *Times*, November 9, 1854.

11. Henry David Thoreau, *Walden and Civil Disobedience* (Boston, 1957), pp. 4, 10, 48; *Walden and Other Writings*, ed. Brooks Atkinson (New York, 1950), pp. 635-659.

12. George Templeton Strong, *Diary of the Civil War, 1860-1865* (New York, 1962), April 5, 1861, p. 114. I deal with northeastern self-doubt in *Our Masters the Rebels: A Speculation on Union Military Failure in the East, 1861-1865* (Cambridge, Mass., 1978).

13. Francis J. Grund, *Aristocracy in America* (New York, 1959), pp. 13–16. Tilden G. Edelstein, *Strange Enthusiasm: A Life of Thomas Wentworth Higginson* (New York, 1970), pp. 118, 158.

14. Thoreau, "A Plea for Captain John Brown," in Atkinson, ed., *Walden*, p. 695. George Ticknor, *Life, Letters, and Journals*, 5th ed. (New York, 1968), II, p. 433. William Howard Russell, *My Diary North and South* (New York, 1965), p. 46; see also pp. 37–38 for southern views that trade had emasculated English manhood.

15. Wendell Phillips, *Speeches, Lectures and Letters*, First Series (Boston, 1892), pp. 274-275, 396–397. W. W. Howe in Frank Moore, ed., *The Rebellion Record* (New York, 1861), I, "Poetry & Incidents," p. 31. New York *Tribune*, April 17, 1861.

16. George M. Fredrickson, *The Inner Civil War: Northern Intellectuals and the Crisis of the Union* (New York, 1965), pp. 153-154.

17. Wilbur R. Jacobs, ed., *Letters of Francis Parkman* (Norman, 1960), I, p. 141.

18. Theodore Lyman, *Meade's Headquarters 1863-1865: Letters of Colonel Theodore Lyman* (Boston, 1922), pp. 186–187.

19. Bruce Catton, *The Centennial History of the Civil War* (New York, 1967), III, pp. 284–285. Charles S. Wainwright, *A Diary of Battle* (New York, 1962),

p. 338. Francis Withrop Palfrey, *Campaigns of the Civil War*, Vol. V: *The Antietam and Fredericksburg* (New York, 1882), p. 135.

20. Henry Adams, *The Education of Henry Adams* (Boston, 1974), pp. 247, 328, 264–266, 334–335, 272, 280; *Democracy: An American Novel* (Leipzig, 1882), p. 20.

21. New York *Herald*, July 12, 1876. Bruce A. Rosenburg, *Custer and the Epic of Defeat* (University Park, Pa., 1974), p. 106.

22. I have not concentrated on Social Darwinism because I agree with Richard Hofstadter that "It would nevertheless be easy to exaggerate the significance of Darwin for race theory of militarism either in the United States or in western Europe. Neither the philosophy of force nor doctrines of *Machtpolitik* had to wait upon Darwin to make their appearance," *Social Darwinism in American Thought* (Boston, 1955), p. 171. Charles Darwin, *The Origin of Species* (New York, 1979), p. 116.

23. Hofstadter, *Darwinism*, p. 192. S. B. Luce, "The Benefits of War," *North American Review*, CLIII (1891), pp. 672–673. John P. Mallan, "Roosevelt, Brooks Adams, and Lea: The Warrior Critique of the Business Civilization," *American Quarterly*, VIII (Fall 1956), p. 219.

24. Gerald F. Linderman, *The Mirror of War: American Society and the Spanish-American War* (Ann Arbor, 1974), p. 97. See also T. J. Jackson Lears, *No Place of Grace: Antimodernism and the Transformation of American Culture 1880-1920* (New York, 1981), pp. 112, 115. Mallan, "Warrior Critique," pp. 218-219. See also Theodore Roosevelt, *The Strenuous Life* (New York, 1902), pp. 1–2, 8.

25. Homer Lea, *The Valor of Ignorance* (New York, 1909), pp. 58–59, 11.

26. W. F. Butler, *Sir William Butler: An Autobiography* (London, 1911), pp. 16, 135. William F. Butler, *Charles George Gordon* (London, 1889), pp. 17, 25–26, 87.

27. Byron Farwell, *Eminent Victorian Soldiers* (New York, 1985), p. 80. J. F. C. Fuller Papers in the Basil Liddell Hart Centre for Military Archives, University of London's King's College, October 1897 [no day given]; May 22, 1901.

28. Fuller Papers, February 18, 1906. Evelyn Wood, *Winnowed Memories* (London, 1918), p. 235.

29. Wood, *Memories*, p. 305.

30. Garnet Wolseley Papers, Hove Public Library, March 18, 1902; March 31, 1887; July 3, 1902; June 22, 1875.

31. Wolseley Papers, September 2, 1881; September 27, 1873; April 11, 1880; July 1893 [no day given]; July 7, 1893.

32. Garnet Wolseley, *The Story of a Soldier's Life* (London, 1903), I, p. 20; II, pp. 368–369. Wolseley Papers, W/W 1/11, pp. 25, 26, 28–29.

33. Butler, *Autobiography*, pp. 218–219; see also 349, 372.

34. Butler, *Autobiography*, p. 425. Frederick Maurice Papers in the Liddell Hart Centre for Military Archives, University of London's King's College, July 7, 1900.

35. Arthur Conan Doyle, *The Complete Sherlock Homes* (New York, n.d.), II, p. 980.

CHAPTER FIVE: KNIGHTS AND THEIR DRAGONS

1. Stephen W. Sears, *Landscape Turned Red: The Battle of Antietam* (New Haven, 1983), p. 63. C. Vann Woodward, ed., *Mary Chesnut's Civil War* (New Haven, 1981), p. 441. Varina Howell Davis, *Jefferson Davis: A Memoir* (New York, 1890), II, p. 648.

2. Bruce Catton, *Mr. Lincoln's Army* (New York, 1964), p. 17. George Hughes Hepworth, *The Whip, Hoe, and Sword* (Boston, 1864), pp. 9–10. George Freeman Noyes, *The Bivouac and the Battle-Field* (New York, 1863), p. 66.

3. John Y. Simon, ed., *The Personal Memoirs of Julia Dent Grant* (New York, 1975), pp. 45–46, 68. T. J. Jackson Lears, *No Place of Grace: Antimodernism and the Transformation of American Culture 1880-1920* (New York, 1981), p. 78.

4. Philip Gibbs, *The Pageant of the Years: An Autobiography* (London, 1946), p. 123. L. E. Jones, *A Victorian Boyhood* (London, 1955), pp. 16–18. Frederic Hamilton, *My Yesterdays: The Days before Yesterday* (London, n.d.), pp. 18, 89.

5. Nicholas Mosley, *Julian Grenfell: His Life and the Times of His Death* (New York, 1976), p. 105. Dorothy Hammond and Alta Jablow, *The Myth of Africa* (New York, 1977), pp. 53, 61. Horace Smith-Dorrien, *Memories of Forty-Eight Years' Service* (London, 1925), p. 31.

6. W. R. Birdwood, *Khaki and Gown: An Autobiography* (New York, 1957), p. 134. Byron Farwell, *Eminent Victorian Soldiers* (New York, 1985), p. 84. Garnet Wolseley, *The Story of a Soldier's Life* (London, 1903), II, pp. 323-324. Arthur Conan Doyle, *Memories and Adventures* (Boston, 1924), p. 161.

7. John Dickson Carr, *The Life of Sir Arthur Conan Doyle* (New York, 1975), pp. 91, 260–261.

8. Dixon Wecter, *The Hero in America* (Ann Arbor, 1963), p. 319. William H. Townsend, *Lincoln and the Bluegrass* (Lexington, 1955), p. 215. Henry Adams, *The Education of Henry Adams* (Boston, 1974), p. 39. Siegfried Sassoon, *Memoirs of a Fox-Hunting Man* (New York, 1937), p. 19. Henry Nash Smith, *Virgin Land: The American West as Symbol and Myth* (Cambridge, Mass., 1970), p. 158. Mark Twain, *Life on the Mississippi* (New York, 1929), p. 376.

9. Sara Jeannette Duncan, *An American Girl in London* (New York, 1891), pp. 102, 104.

10. Duncan, *Girl*, pp. 105–115.

11. Frances Trollope, *Domestic Manners of the Americans* (Oxford, 1984), p. 220.

12. John P. Mallan, "Roosevelt, Brooks Adams, and Lea: The Warrior Critique of the Business Civilization," *American Quarterly*, VIII (Fall 1956), p. 222. William Butler, *Charles George Gordon* (London, 1889), pp. 88–89.

13. Adams, *Education*, pp. 72, 207, 342–343, 457–459. David R. Contosta, *Henry Adams and the American Experiment* (Boston, 1980), pp. 121, 129.

14. Adams, *Education*, p. 53. Rupert Wilkinson, *Gentlemanly Power: British Leadership and the Public School Tradition* (London, 1964), p. 65. Douglas Goldring, *Reputations: Essays in Criticism* (Port Washington, N.Y., 1968), p. 103.

15. E. E. Reynolds, *Baden-Powell* (London, 1943), pp. 126–127, 198, 135. Mark Girouard, *The Return to Camelot: Chivalry and the English Gentleman* (New Haven, 1981), p. 254. Lears, *No Place*, p. 109.

16. Ellen K. Rothman, *Hands and Hearts: A History of Courtship in America* (New York, 1984), p. 198.

17. Elizabeth B. Custer, *"Boots and Saddles": or Life in Dakota with General Custer* (Williamstown, Mass., 1969), p. 130. Elizabeth B. Custer, *Following the Guidon* (Norman, 1966), pp. 2, 67.

18. Peter Gay, *The Bourgeois Experience*, Vol I: *Education of the Senses* (New York, 1984), p. 434. Ronald Pearsall, *The Worm in the Bud: The World of Victorian Sexuality* (New York, 1969), p. 129.

19. Emory M. Thomas, *Bold Dragoon: The Life of J. E. B. Stuart* (New York, 1986), pp. 279–280. Thomas Cooper DeLeon, *Belles, Beaux and Brains of the 60's* (New York, 1907), pp. 221–222.

20. Anthony Hope, *The Prisoner of Zenda* (Garden City, N.Y., n.d.), p. 181; *Rupert of Hentzau* (New York, 1938), p. 105.

21. Hope, *Hentzau*, pp. 384, 66. Louisa M. Alcott, *Little Women* (New York, 1983), p. 522.

22. John Chandos, *Boys Together: English Public Schools 1800-1864* (New Haven, 1984), p. 299. Also Girouard, *Camelot*, pp. 217–218.

23. David Axeen, "'Heroes of the Engine Room': American 'Civilization' and the War with Spain," *American Quarterly*, XXXVI (Fall 1984), p. 481.

24. Frederic Remington, "Wigwags from the Blockade," *Harper's Weekly*, May 14, 1898, p. 462.

25. George H. Hodson, ed., *Twelve Years of a Soldier's Life in India* (Boston, 1860), pp. 50–51. John Ellis, *The Social History of the Machine Gun* (New York, 1975), p. 84. Butler, *Gordon*, p. 255. See also Archibald Forbes, *Chinese Gordon* (New York, 1884), p. 7.

26. Liddell Hart Papers in the Liddell Hart Centre for Military Archives, University of London's King's College, entry for 1913.

27. Conan Doyle, *Memories*, pp. 207–208. Carr, *Doyle*, pp. 200, 213–214. Thoeodore Roosevelt, *The Rough Riders* (New York, 1961), pp. 31–32. Neville Lyttelton, *Eighty Years: Soldiering, Politics, Games* (London, n.d.), pp. 64–65.

28. Rollin G. Osterweis, *Romanticism and Nationalism in the Old South* (Gloucester, Mass., 1964), pp. 48, 79. Winson S. Churchill, *My Early Life* (London, 1947), pp. 64–66.

29. Sir John French, *1914* (Boston, 1919), pp. 11–12.

30. Bernard Shaw, *Arms and the Man* (Baltimore, 1952), pp. 7, 17.

31. Shaw, *Arms*, pp. 34, 66, 37, 64.

32. Christopher Hibbert, *The Great Mutiny: India 1857* (New York, 1980), pp. 209–210. Garnet Wolseley Papers in the Hove Public Library, November 9, 1879. Churchill, *Life*, p. 19.

33. J. F. C. Fuller Papers in the Liddell Hart Centre for Military Archives, University of London's King's College, May 21, 1902.

34. George John Younghusband, *A Soldier's Memories in Peace and War* (London, 1917), pp. 44, 50–51.

35. Richard G. Stone, Jr., *A Brittle Sword: The Kentucky Militia 1776-1912* (Lexington, 1977), p. 82.

36. George Griffith, "The World of the War God," reprinted in Kingsley Russell, ed., *Science Fiction by the Rivals of H. G. Wells* (Secaucus, N.J., 1979), pp. 131, 133–134, 138–139, 141–144.

37. Ernest N. Bennett, *The Downfall of the Dervishes*, 3rd ed. (London, 1899), pp. 69, 227–230.

38. Mark Twain, *A Connecticut Yankee in King Arthur's Court* (Berkeley, 1979), esp. pp. 426–440.

CHAPTER SIX: CIVIC CLAUSTROPHOBIA

1. *The History of Mr. Polly*, in H. G. Wells, *A Quartette of Comedies* (London, 1928), pp. 394, 400, 429.

2. *Polly*, pp. 403, 475, 479-481.

3. *Polly*, pp. 389–399, 434.

4. *Polly*, pp. 495, 518–520, 546.

5. *Polly*, pp. 566ff., 520–523.

6. "First and Last Things" (1908), quoted by William James, "The Moral Equivalent of War," in John J. McDermott, ed., *The Writings of William James* (New York, 1968), p. 670.

7. Wells, *Little Wars* (Boston, 1913), pp. 152–158.

8. Donald Mitchell, *Reveries of a Bachelor* (New York, 1859), p. vii. E. E. Kelletts, "The Lady Automaton," *Pearson's Magazine*, June 1901, reprinted in Kingsley Russell, ed., *Science Fiction by the Rivals of H. G. Wells* (Secaucus, N.J., 1979), pp. 349–363.

9. Herman Melville, *Moby-Dick* (Indianapolis, 1964), p. 593. John Y. Simon, ed., *The Personal Memoirs of Julia Dent Grant* (New York, 1975), p. 43.

10. Frederic Hamilton, *My Yesterdays: The Days before Yesterday* (London, n.d.), p. 298.

11. Henry Adams, *The Education of Henry Adams* (Boston, 1974), pp. 297–298, 307. Henry David Thoreau, *Walden and Civil Disobedience* (Boston, 1957), pp. 4, 220. Alec Waugh, *The Loom of Youth* (London, 1947), esp. final pp.

12. One of the best depictions of the constrictions placed on women is "The Yellow Wallpaper" by Charlotte Perkins Gilman, first published in the *New England Magazine*, January 1892. John S. Haller and Robin M. Haller, *The Physician and Sexuality in Victorian America* (New York, 1977), pp. 275, 279–280. Also, for instance, Virginia Berridge, "Opium in the Fens in Nineteenth-Century England," *Journal of the History of Medicine*, XXXIV (July 1979), pp. 293–313.

13. G. J. Barker-Benfield, *The Horrors of the Half-Known Life: Male Attitudes toward Women and Sexuality in Nineteenth-Century America* (New York, 1976), pp. 297–298. James I. Robertson, Jr., *General A. P. Hill: The Story of a Confederate Warrior* (New York, 1987), pp. 11–12. W. A. Swanberg, *Sickles the Incredible* (New York, 1956), pp. 53, 63–64.

14. Bram Stoker, *Dracula* (Garden City, N.Y., n.d.), p. 33. Philip Gibbs, *The Pageant of the Years: An Autobiography* (London, 1946), p. 136. Melville, *Moby-Dick*, pp. 24, 213.

15. David S. Stanley, *Personal Memoirs of Major-General D. S. Stanley* (Cambridge, Mass., 1917), p. 243. Owen Wister, *The Virginian* (New York, 1945; first published 1902), pp. 374, 264, 4.

16. Dorothy Hammond and Alta Jablow, *The Myth of Africa* (New York, 1977), pp. 78, 108.

17. Elizabeth B. Custer, *Following the Guidon* (Norman, 1966), pp. 256, 250–251.

18. Margery Perham, *Lugard*, Vol. I: *The Years of Adventure* (London, 1956), p. 35. Emory M. Thomas, *Bold Dragoon: The Life of J. E. B. Stuart* (New York, 1986), p. 31. Ian Hamilton, *When I Was a Boy* (London, 1939), p. 302. J. F. C. Fuller Papers in the Basil Liddell Hart Centre for Military Archives, University of London's King's College, April 23, 1901. Philip Magnus, *Kitchener: Portrait of an Imperialist* (New York, 1968), pp. 17, 68, 77, 83.

19. Edward G. Longacre, "Sir Percy Wyndham," *Civil War Times Illustrated*, VII (December 1968), pp. 12–17. William F. Butler, *Charles George Gordon* (London, 1889), p. 101; see also 33, 105.

20. Stephen Z. Starr, *Colonel Grenfell's Wars: The Life of a Soldier of Fortune* (Baton Rouge, 1971), pp. 18–21, 33, 15. Mabel Clare Weaks, ed., "Colonel George St. Ledger Grenfell," *Filson Club Quarterly*, XXXIV (1960), p. 8.

21. Frances Trollope, *Domestic Manners of the Americans* (Oxford, 1984), p. 14. Also Thomas D. Clark, *The Rampaging Frontier: Manners and Humors of Pioneer Days in the South and the Middle West* (Bloomington, 1964), p. 183. Stanley, *Memoirs*, pp. 12–14.

22. James Arthur Lyon Fremantle, *The Fremantle Diary* (Boston, 1954), p. 105. William C. Davis, *The Imperilled Union 1861-1865*, Vol. I: *The Deep Waters of the Proud* (Garden City, N.Y., 1982), p. 63. Charles Bracelen Flood, *Lee: The Last Years* (Boston, 1981), pp. 233, 238–239. William S. McFeely, *Grant: A Biog-*

raphy (New York, 1981), pp. 68, 513.

23. George H. Hodson, ed., *Twelve Years of a Soldier's Life in India* (Boston, 1860), p. 176. Garnet Wolseley, *The Story of a Soldier's Life* (London, 1903), I, pp. 158–159. Also p. 7 and II, p. 68. Wolseley Papers in the Hove Public Library, November 3, 1873 and November 7, 1873.

24. G. Manville Fenn, *George Alfred Henty: The Story of an Active Life* (London, 1907), p. 15. Ernest Bennett, *The Downfall of the Dervishes*, 3rd ed. (London, 1899), pp. 3–4. Erskine Childers, *In the Ranks of the C. I. V.* (London, 1900), pp. 102, 296–297.

25. Mason Wade, ed., *The Journals of Francis Parkman* (London, n.d.), I, p. 125. Hawthorne, letter to Commodore Horatio Bridges, May 26, 1861, in *Harper's Weekly*, February 17, 1883, p. 99.

26. Tilden G. Edelstein, *Strange Enthusiasm: A Life of Thomas Wentworth Higginson* (New York, 1970), pp. 10–12, 17, 29–32, 152, 316, 25–26, 205. Ronald G. Walters, "The Erotic South: Sensuality in American Abolitionism," in Randy Roberts and James S. Olson, eds., *American Experiences* (Glenview, Ill., 1986), p. 275.

27. Edelstein, *Higginson*, pp. 316, 195, 185, 332, 252. Robert Gould Shaw, who, like Higginson, commanded a black regiment, went from Harvard in 1858 to his uncle's New York mercantile firm. His spirits wilted and he said, "I am a slave now." Peter Burchard, *One Gallant Rush: Robert Gould Shaw and His Brave Black Regiment* (New York, 1965), p. 23.

28. Edelstein, *Higginson*, pp. 214, 242, 380. Thomas Wentworth Higginson, *Army Life in a Black Regiment* (New York, 1962), pp. 94–95, 104, 152, 154.

29. John William DeForest, *Miss Ravenel's Conversion from Secession to Loyalty* (Columbus, Ohio, 1969), pp. 22–24, 276–277.

30. George M. Fredrickson, *The Inner Civil War: Northern Intellectuals and the Crisis of the Union* (New York, 1965), pp. 219–220. Theodore Roosevelt, *The Rough Riders* (New York, 1961), pp. 21, 32.

31. Roosevelt, *Rough Riders*, pp. 71, 82, 97. Gerald F. Linderman, *The Mirror of War: American Society and the Spanish-American War* (Ann Arbor, 1974), pp. 111-112.

32. James, "Moral," p. 664.

33. James, "Moral," pp. 668–669.

34. Sandra M. Gilbert and Susan Gubar, *No Man's Land: The Place of the Woman Writer in the Twentieth Century*, Vol. I: *The War of the Words* (New Haven, 1988), p. 78. Also George Dangerfield, *The Strange Death of Liberal England 1910-1914* (New York, 1961), p. 369.

35. David Newsome, *Godliness and Good Learning: Four Studies on a Victorian Ideal* (London, 1961), pp. 225–226.

36. G. G. Coulton, *Fourscore Years: An Autobiography* (Cambridge, 1943), p. 73. James McLachlan, *American Boarding Schools: A Historical Study* (New York, 1970), p. 290. Also poem, p. 246.

37. Dixon Wecter, *The Hero in America* (Ann Arbor, 1963), p. 374. R. S. S. Baden-Powell, *The Matabele Campaign 1896* (Westport, Conn., 1970), pp. 283–284. Winston S. Churchill, *My Early Life* (London, 1947), p. 77.

38. Mark Girouard, *The Return to Camelot: Chivalry and the English Gentleman* (New Haven, 1981), p. 173.

39. L. E. Jones, *A Victorian Boyhood* (London, 1955), pp. 19, 16.

40. Horace Annesley Vachell, *The Hill: A Romance of Friendship* (London, 1905), pp. 25–26, 45, 58, 196, 201, 205, 211.

41. Vachell, *Hill*, p. 242.

42. Vachell, *Hill*, p. 242.

PART III: PETER PAN'S GREAT ADVENTURE

1. John S. Goodall, *An Edwardian Summer* (London, 1976), foreword by Harold Macmillan, n.p.
2. Macmillan, in Goodall, *Edwardian Summer.*
3. Geoffrey Keynes, ed., *The Letters of Rupert Brooke* (New York, 1968), January 8, 1908, p. 121. Also March 25, 1905, pp. 19–20; December 31, 1905, p. 33; January 10, 1906, p. 38. The *Daily Telegraph* said that *Peter Pan* was "so true, so natural, so touching that it brought the audience to the writer's feet and held them captive there." Janet Dunbar, *J. M. Barrie: The Man behind the Image* (Boston, 1970), p. 170.
4. J. M. Barrie, *Peter Pan* (New York, 1911), pp. 35–36. The book was produced as a play in 1904 and as a novel in 1911.
5. Barrie, *Pan*, pp. 121, 145.
6. Dunbar, *Barrie*, pp. 34–35, 45, 53–54.
7. Dunbar, *Barrie*, pp. 45, 54, 70, 74, 107, 109, 231–233. Peter Singleton-Gates, *General Lord Freyberg* (London, 1963), p. 23.
8. Barrie, *Pan*, pp. 66, 73, 111, 128.
9. Barrie, *Pan*, pp. 85, 152.
10. Barrie, *Pan*, pp. 130.
11. Barrie, *Pan*, pp. 192, 209.
12. Barrie, *Pan*, pp. 253.
13. Dixon Wecter, *The Hero in America* (Ann Arbor, 1963), p. 390.

CHAPTER SEVEN: A PURPOSE FOR LIVING

1. Vivian Gilbert, *The Romance of the Last Crusade* (New York, 1927), pp. 1–4.
2. Gilbert, *Crusade*, p. 5.
3. Gilbert, *Crusade*, pp. 6–7.
4. Gilbert, *Crusade*, p. 9.
5. Gilbert, *Crusade*, pp. 9–10, 6.
6. Gilbert, *Crusade*, pp. 12 and preface, n.p.
7. Arthur Ponsonby, *The Decline of Aristocracy* (London, 1912), pp. 173, 201–202. T. C. Worsley, *Barbarians and Philistines: Democracy and the Public Schools* (London, 1940), p. 113.
8. Laurence Houseman, ed., *War Letters of Fallen Englishmen* (London, 1930), pp. 291–292.
9. Frederick Maurice Papers in the Liddell Hart Centre for Military Archives, University of London's King's College, August 31 and September 11, 1914.
10. John W. Cunliffe, ed., *Poems of the Great War* (Freeport, N.Y., 1971), p. 240. Basil Liddell Hart Papers in the Liddell Hart Centre for Military Archives, University of London's King's Collge, October [n.d.] 1914, November 28, 1914.
11. Stephen Gwynn, ed., *The Anvil of War: Letters between F. S. Oliver & His Brother 1914-1918* (London, 1936), pp. 65–66. Paul Jones, *War Letters of a Public-School Boy* (London, 1918), p. 253.
12. Vera Brittain, *Chronicle of Youth: The War Diary 1913-1917* (New York, 1982), p. 100. For a full analysis see Albert Marrin, *The Last Crusade: The Church of England in the First World War* (Durham, 1974). Walter Raleigh, *England and the War* (Freeport, N.Y., 1967), p. 69. Cunliffe, *Poems*, p. 264.
13. Richard Harding Davis, *The War on All Fronts*, Vol. I: *With the Allies* (New York, 1917), p. 101. Quentin Reynolds, *They Fought for the Sky* (London, 1960), pp. 87–89, 137–138. Bert Hall and John J. Niles, *One Man's War* (New

York, 1980), pp. 25 & 20.

14. On white feathers see, for example, F. P. Crozier, *A Brass Hat in No Man's Land* (New York, 1930), pp. 40–41. James Norman Hall, *High Adventure* (New York, 1980), pp. 70–71.

15. John Jay Chapman, ed., *Victor Chapman's Letters from France* (New York, 1917), p. 19.

16. Chapman, *Letters*, pp. 4–5, 7–8.

17. Horace Annesley Vachell, *Searchlights* (New York, 1915), pp. 62–63, 88.

18. Vachell, *Searchlights*, pp. 102, 122.

19. Davis, *War*, pp. 193, 198. Sir John French, *1914* (Boston, 1919), p. 301.

20. John Buchan, *Francis and Riversdale Grenfell* (London, 1920), pp. 229, 231, 189. Rudyard Kipling, *Sea Warfare* (Garden City, N.Y., 1917), pp. 135, 197, 38; also pp. 13, 165, 182.

21. Hervey de Montmorency, *Sword and Stirrup: Memories of an Adventurous Life* (London, 1936), pp. 244, 280. Also Crozier, *Brass Hat*, pp. 16–17.

22. Guy Chapman, *A Passionate Prodigality* (New York, 1966), p. 137.

23. Gilbert, *Crusade*, pp. 29–30. Ernest D. Swinton, *Eyewitness* (New York, 1972), pp. 8–9. L. E. Jones, *An Edwardian Youth* (London, 1956), p. 204.

24. Margaret Newbolt, ed., *The Later Life and Letters of Sir Henry Newbolt* (London, 1942), p. 214. Cunliffe, *Poems*, p. 139. Arthur Machen, *The Angels of Mons* (Freeport, N.Y., 1972), pp. 19–31.

25. Machen, *Angels*, p. 31.

26. Geoffrey Keynes, ed., *The Letters of Rupert Brooke* (New York, 1968), pp. 496, 600.

27. Keynes, *Brooke*, pp. 595–597, 379.

28. Keynes, *Brooke*, p. 3. George Edward Woodberry, ed., *The Collected Poems of Rupert Brooke* (New York, 1916), pp. 32–33.

29. Keynes, *Brooke*, pp. 41–42, 46, 51, 54, 59, 544, 574, 581, 592. John Lehmann, *The Strange Destiny of Rupert Brooke* (New York, 1980), p. 7.

30. Woodberry, *Brooke*, pp. 107–109.

31. Woodberry, *Brooke*, p. 111.

32. Frederick Keeling, *Letters and Recollections* (London, 1918), pp. 2, 57–58, 60, 97.

33. Keeling, *Letters*, pp. 115, 55, 57–58, 114.

34. Keeling, *Letters*, pp. 209, 225.

35. Donald Hankey, *A Student in Arms*, Second Series (New York, 1917), pp. 1–28. Hereinafter referred to as *Student* II.

36. Hankey, *Letters of "A Student in Arms"* (London, 1922), pp. 162–163, 414, 250–251, 264. See also Hankey, *A Student in Arms* (New York, 1917), p. 236. Hereinafter cited as *Student* I.

37. Hankey, *Student* II, pp. 236–237, 200–203, 222, 8–9, 22. Hankey, *Letters*, p. 434.

38. Hankey, *Student* II, pp. 1, 59, 71–72. Hankey, *Student* I, p. 231.

39. Nicholas Mosley, *Julian Grenfell: His Life and the Times of His Death* (New York, 1976), esp. pp. 50, 105, 30–31, 45–46.

40. Mosley, *Grenfell*, pp. 150, 119–120, 141. John Buchan, *Pilgrim's Way* (Cambridge, Mass., 1940), pp. 60–61.

41. Mosley, *Grenfell*, pp. 125, 140–141, 160, 163. Jones, *Edwardian Youth*, p. 55.

42. Jones, *Edwardian Youth*, pp. 54, 56, 59. Mosley, *Grenfell*, pp. 211, 107–108, 236–237.

43. Mosley, *Grenfell*, pp. 241, 243, 236, 239, 258.

CHAPTER EIGHT: THE BEST PLACE TO BE

1. Vivian Gilbert, *The Romance of the Last Crusade* (New York, 1927), pp. 36–37, 43–44.
2. Gilbert, *Crusade*, pp. 62, 63, 66.
3. Gilbert, *Crusade*, pp. 121–122, 235.
4. Gilbert, *Crusade*, pp. 222, 32.
5. Gilbert, *Crusade*, pp. 49, 135.
6. Coningsby Dawson, *Carry On: Letters in War-Time* (New York, 1918), p. 50.
7. T. S. Hope, *The Winding Road Unfolds* (London, 1965), p. 111.
8. Laurence Housman, ed., *War Letters of Fallen Englishmen* (London, 1930), pp. 168, 271. Also Charles Edmonds [Charles Carrington], *A Subaltern's War* (London, 1930), p. 161. Eddie V. Rickenbacker, *Fighting the Flying Circus* (New York, 1967), p. 275.
9. Philip Gibbs, *The Pageant of the Years: An Autobiography* (London, 1946), pp. 242–243.
10. John W. Cunliffe. ed., *Poems of the Great War* (Freeport, N.Y., 1971), pp. 187–189.
11. T. C. Worsley, *Barbarians and Philistines: Democracy and the Public Schools* (London, 1940), p. 79; also pp. 34, 84–85. Gibbs, *Pageant*, p. 191.
12. Vera Brittain, *Chronicle of Youth: The War Diary 1913-1917* (New York, 1982), p. 340. Harry Sackville Lawson, *Letters of a Headmaster Soldier* (London, 1918), pp. 36–37, 42–44.
13. Dawson, *Carry On*, p. 83. John Buchan, *Pilgrim's Way* (Cambridge, Mass., 1940), p. 173. L. E. Jones, *An Edwardian Youth* (London, 1956), p. 204.
14. Housman, *War Letters*, p. 68. Charles Carrington, *Soldier from the Wars Returning* (London, 1965), pp. 120–121. Paul Jones, *War Letters of a Public-School Boy* (London, 1918), p. 253; also 124, 146–147.
15. Douglas MacArthur, *Reminiscences* (New York, 1964), p. 58. David D. Lee, *Sergeant York: An American Hero* (Lexington, 1985), p. x.
16. Lord Northcliffe, *At the War* (London, 1916), p. 90. Stephen Gwynn, ed., *The Anvil of War: Letters between F. S. Oliver and His Brother 1914-1918* (London, 1936), p. 270. Arthur Machen, *The Angels of Mons* (New York, 1972), p. 57.
17. Henry Newbolt, *The Book of the Happy Warrior* (London, 1916), pp. vi-viii, 257, 262–263, 276.
18. Newbolt, *Warrior*, pp. 270–272, vi-viii.
19. Newbolt, *Warrior*, pp. 274–275.
20. Margaret Newbolt, ed., *The Later Life and Letters of Sir Henry Newbolt* (London, 1942), p. 231.
21. Walter Raleigh, *England and the War* (Freeport, N.Y., 1967), p. 42. Housman, *War Letters*, p. 231.
22. Richard G. Stone, Jr., *Kentucky Fighting Men 1861-1945* (Lexington, 1982), pp. 51–52. Rickenbacker, *Fighting*, p. 302; also p. 24.
23. Hope, *Road*, pp. 176–177. James Norman Hall, *High Adventure* (New York, 1980), p. 209.
24. Paul Fussell, *The Great War and Modern Memory* (London, 1975), p. 89.
25. Cunliffe, *Poems*, pp. 199–201. Siegfried Sassoon, *Memoirs of an Infantry Officer* (London, 1965), p. 93. Robert Graves, *Good-bye to All That* (New York, 1957), p. 199.
26. John Ellis, *Eye-Deep in Hall: Trench Warfare in World War I* (New York, 1976), p. 194. Basil Liddell Hart Papers in the Liddell Hart Centre for Military Archives, University of London's King's College, undated note, 1916. Guy Chap-

man, *A Passionate Prodigality* (New York, 1966), pp. 138–139. Edmonds, *Subaltern*, p. 188.

27. Arthur Conan Doyle, *Memories and Adventures* (Boston, 1924), p. 340.

28. Bert Hall and John J. Niles, *One Man's War* (New York, 1980), p. 130. Sidney Rogerson, *Twelve Days* (London, 1933), pp. 147–148. Hope, *Road*, pp. 67, 89, 92–95, 197–201.

29. Rogerson, *Twelve Days*, pp. 59–60. Henry Williamson, *The Patriot's Progress* (London, 1930), pp. 43–44, 144–146, 157–158, 108–109.

30. Housman, *War Letters*, p. 181. Enid Bagnold, *A Diary without Dates* (London, 1978), pp. 30, viii, 15.

31. Housman, *War Letters*, pp. 299–300. Chapman, *Prodigality*, p. 122. Cunliffe, *Poems*, pp. 90–91.

32. Horace Smith-Dorrien, *Memories of Forty-Eight Years' Service* (London, 1925), p. 446. Dawson, *Carry On*, pp. 102, 126–127.

33. Jones, *War Letters*, p. 259.

34. John Buchan, *Francis and Riversdale Grenfell* (London, 1920), pp. xxiv, 234–235; *Pilgrim's Way*, pp. 63, 103–104.

35. John Masefield, *Gallipoli* (New York, 1918), pp. 149, 45, 195.

36. Geoffrey Keynes, ed., *The Letters of Rupert Brooke* (New York, 1968), pp. 654–655.

37. George Edward Woodberry, ed., *The Collected Poems of Rupert Brooke* (New York, 1916), pp. 76–77. John Jay Chapman, ed., *Victor Chapman's Letters from France* (New York, 1917), p. 189.

38. Nicholas Mosley, *Julian Grenfell: His Life and the Times of His Death* (New York, 1976), p. 231. Jones, *War Letters*, pp. 180–181, 114.

39. Mosley, *Grenfell*, p. 231. Cunliffe, *Poems*, p. 204.

40. Houseman, *War Letters*, p. 278. Cunliffe, *Poems*, p. 28. Also p. 10.

41. Edmonds, *Subaltern*, pp. 200–201.

CHAPTER NINE: GOOD-BYE TO ALL THAT?

1. Robert Graves, *Good-bye to All That* (Garden City, N.Y., 1957), p. 347.

2. C. LeRoy Baldridge, *"I Was There!" With the Yanks in France* (Paris, 1919), n.p.

3. Eddie V. Rickenbacker, *Fighting the Flying Circus* (New York, 1967), p. 314.

4. Rickenbacker, *Circus*, pp. 319–321.

5. Bert Hall, *"En l'air"* (New York, 1918), pp. 96–97. James Norman Hall, *High Adventure* (New York, 1980), p. 121.

6. William Alexander Percy, *Lanterns on the Levee: Recollections of a Planter's Son* (Baton Rouge, 1973), pp. 221–223, 183.

7. Conigsby Dawson, *Carry On: Letters in War-Time* (New York, 1918), pp. 123–124.

8. Sidney Rogerson, *Twelve Days* (London, 1933), pp. xiii-xiv, 59–60.

9. Michael O' Suilleabhain, *Where Mountainy Men Have Sown* (Tralee, 1965), pp. 141–142, 171. F. C. Hitchcock, *"Stand To": A Diary of the Trenches 1915-18* (London, 1937), pp. 331, 324–326.

10. Guy Chapman, *A Passionate Prodigality* (New York, 1966), pp. 280–281.

11. Douglas MacArthur, *Reminiscences* (New York, 1964), p. 72. E. L. Woodward, *Short Journey* (New York, 1946), pp. 112, 109.

12. Horace Annesley Vachell, *The Soul of Susan Yellam* (New York, 1918), pp. 90, 124.

13. Vachell, *Yellam*, pp. 149–151, 223.

14. Vachell, *Yellam*, p. 188.

15. Vachell, *Yellam*, pp. 125–126.
16. Vachell, *Yellam*, p. 225.
17. Vachell, *Yellam*, p. 289.
18. *The New Word* in J. M. Barrie, *Echoes of the War* (New York, 1920), pp. 85–86.
19. *A Well–Remembered Voice* (1918) in Barrie, *Echoes*, pp. 170–171.
20. Barrie, *Echoes*, p. 148.
21. Barrie, *Echoes*, pp. 150–151.
22. H. G. Wells, *Men like Gods* (New York, 1923), pp. 266, 44, 106, 147, 267.
23. Wells, *Men*, p. 108.
24. Wells, *Men*, pp. 219–220, 232.
25. Douglas Goldring, *The Fortune: A Romance of Friendship* (New York, 1919), pp. 19–20, 125.
26. Goldring, *Fortune*, pp. 193, 227.
27. Goldring, *Fortune*, pp. 250, 204.
28. Goldring, *Fortune*, pp. 272–273, 260, 235–236.
29. Goldring, *Fortune*, pp. 248, 277–278; *The Fight for Freedom* (New York, 1920), pp. 38, 76.
30. Goldring, *Fight*, pp. 39–40; *Fortune*, pp. 285–287, 374.
31. Goldring, *Fortune*, p. 358.
32. Goldring, *Fortune*, p. 278.
33. Goldring, *Freedom*, pp. 96, 98, 83.
34. Graves, *Good-bye*, pp. 286, 288.
35. Millicent Garrett Fawcett, *What I Remember* (London, 1924), p. 221. Margaret Newbolt, ed., *The Later Life and Letters of Sir Henry Newbolt* (London, 1942), p. 300.
36. Stephen E. Ambrose, *Duty, Honor, Country: A History of West Point* (Baltimore, 1966), pp. 274, 330. Valerie Pakenham, *Out in the Noonday Sun: Edwardians in the Tropics* (New York, 1985), pp. 187–188.
37. M. C. A. Henniker, *Memoirs of a Junior Officer* (Edinburgh, 1951), pp. 87, 169–170; also 3, 48, 63, 223.
38. Christopher Percival Wren, *Beau Sabreur* (New York, 1926), pp. xi, 13; *Beau Geste* (New York, 1925), p. 6.
39. Wren, *Beau Ideal* (New York, 1928), pp. 40, 206, 229; *Beau Geste*, p. 106.
40. Wren, *Beau Ideal*, pp. 48, 109, 165–166, 353; *Beau Geste*, p. 368.
41. Wren, *Beau Geste*, p. 49; *Beau Sabreur*, p. 61.
42. Wren, *Beau Sabreur*, p. 197; *Beau Ideal*, pp. 170, 178, 112–113; *Beau Geste*, p. 80.
43. Wren, *Beau Ideal*, pp. 3, 11.
44. Wren, *Beau Sabreur*, pp. 162, 167, 312, 367; *Beau Ideal*, pp. 45, 38.
45. Wren, *Beau Geste*, p. 337; *Beau Sabreur*, p. 58.
46. Wren, *Beau Sabreur*, p. 61; *Beau Geste*, pp. 253, 257, 346; *Beau Ideal*, p. 33.
47. Arthur Guy Empey, *A Helluva War* (New York, 1927). Empey also wrote a memoir, *Over the Top*.
48. Penguin finally published the unexpurgated text after a prolonged legal battle.
49. Carolyn G. Heilbrun, *Toward a Recognition of Androgyny* (New York, 1973), pp. 161, 164.
50. Henry Williamson, *The Patriot's Progress* (London, 1930), p. 192.
51. Dalton Trumbo, *Johnny Got His Gun* (London, 1967), e.g., p. 55.
52. Ford Madox Ford, "Some Do Not . . ," p. 209, and "No More Parades," p. 305, in *Parade's End* (New York, 1979). Richard Aldington, *Death of a Hero* (Lon-

don, 1965), p. 18.

53. Aldington, *Hero*, pp. 74–83, 200.

54. Charles Carrington, *Soldier from the Wars Returning* (London, 1965), pp. 219, 264–265. Charles Edmonds [Charles Carrington], *A Subaltern's War* (London, 1930), pp. 26, 192–193.

55. Graves, *Good-bye*, pp. 197, 256–257, 275–276. Siegfried Sassoon, *Sherston's Progress*, pp. 211, 221, 224, 231, 237, in *The Memoirs of George Sherston* (New York, 1937).

56. Sassoon, *Progress*, pp. 175, 191; *Memoirs of an Infantry Officer*, pp. 180, 252, in *The Memoirs of George Sherston*.

57. C. Day Lewis, ed., *The Collected Poems of Wilfred Owen* (New York, 1965), pp. 55, 64, 23.

58. Graves, *Good-bye*, pp. 261, 263, 265, 249.

59. Aldington, *Hero*, pp. 60, 18–19. See also Holger Klein, *The First World War in Fiction* (New York, 1977), p. 183.

60. Liddell Hart Papers in the Liddell Hart Centre for Military Archives, University of London's King's College, "Modern Woman: By a Modern Man" (1924).

61. William Faulkner, *Soldier's Pay* (New York, 1968), pp. 227, 233, 19, 33, 37–38, 23, 54, 57–58, 84, 104, 154, 217.

62. Faulkner, *Pay*, pp. 137, 212.

63. Judith Fetterley, *The Resisting Reader: A Feminist Approach to American Fiction* (Bloomington, 1978), pp. 46–71. Kenneth S. Lynn, *Hemingway* (New York, 1987), pp. 85, 90–92, 120.

64. John Dos Passos, *Three Soldiers* (Boston, 1921), pp. 27, 182, 324, 332, 335, 413, 420, 425.

65. Dos Passos, *Soldiers*, pp. 346, 350–351.

66. Dos Passos, *Soldiers*, pp. 26, 31, 250.

67. Dos Passos, *Soldiers*, pp. 380, 63, 71, 113, 157, 228–229, 415.

68. Sassoon, *Progress*, pp. 243–244. Graves, *Good-bye*, p. 67.

69. Vera Brittain, *Testament of Youth* (London, 1933), p. 3.

70. Brittain, *Chronicle of Youth: The War Diary 1913-1917* (New York, 1982), pp. 89–90, 93, 145.

71. Brittain, *Chronicle*, pp. 101, 93. Also 84.

72. Brittain, *Chronicle*, pp. 107, 132–133.

73. Brittain, *Chronicle*, p. 73; *Testament*, pp. 493, 496–496, 510.

74. "All the Dead Pilots," in Faulkner, *Collected Stories of William Faulkner* (New York, 1934), pp. 511–512.

75. Philip Oakes, *From Middle England: A Memory of the 1930's* (New York, 1980), pp. 49–50.

76. Oakes, *England*, pp. 32, 44, 166, 65, 171.

77. Oakes, *England*, p. 185.

RETROSPECT

1. Nancy Chodorow, *The Reproduction of Mothering: Psychoanalysis and the Sociology of Gender* (Berkeley, 1978). Dorothy Dinnerstein, *The Mermaid and the Minotaur: Sexual Arrangements and Human Malaise* (New York, 1977).

2. Betty Friedan, *The Second Stage* (New York, 1981), p. 91.

3. Vera Brittain, *Testament of Youth* (London, 1933), pp. 103–104.

4. Brittain, *Chronicle of Youth: The War Diary 1913-1917* (New York, 1982), p. 78; *Testament*, pp. 87–88.

5. Brittain, *Testament*, pp. 129, 131.

6. Brittain, *Testament*, pp. 198, 197, 216; *Chronicle*, pp. 114, 270–271, 283.

7. Brittain, *Chronicle*, pp. 236, 260–261.
8. Brittain, *Testament*, pp. 116–117; *Chronicle*, p. 139.
9. Brittain, *Chronicle*, pp. 302, 315; *Testament*, p. 241.
10. Brittain, *Testament*, pp. 251–252.
11. Brittain, *Chronicle*, p. 11.

INDEX

MICHAEL C. C. ADAMS is Professor of History
at Northern Kentucky University and author of
*Our Masters the Rebels: A Speculation on Union
Military Failure in the East, 1861–1865.*